Uniform with this volume
THE WHITE DEVIL

C.R.

JOHN WEBSTER

THE DUCHESS OF MALFI

⸻⸻▬◦◦◦◦▬⸻⸻

Edited by

F. L. LUCAS

FELLOW OF KING'S COLLEGE
CAMBRIDGE
UNIVERSITY READER IN ENGLISH

The moving moon and stars from east to west
  Circle before her in the sea of air:
Shadows and gleams glide round her solemn rest.
  Her subjects often gaze up to her there:
The strong to drink new strength of iron endurance,
The weak new terrors: all, renewed assurance
  And confirmation of the old despair.

JAMES THOMSON

THE MACMILLAN COMPANY
New York
1959

PUBLISHED IN GREAT BRITAIN BY

CHATTO AND WINDUS LTD

LONDON

Reprinted, with revisions and additions,
from *The Complete Works of John Webster* (*1927*)

MADE AND PRINTED IN GREAT BRITAIN

BY PERCY LUND HUMPHRIES & CO LTD

CONTENTS

EDITOR'S NOTE

THE four-volume edition of Webster published in 1927 is exhausted. Present costs of republication in full are prohibitive. Therefore it seemed best to reissue, as separate volumes, the two plays of Webster that really matter, *The White Devil* and *The Duchess of Malfi*, so as to keep annotated editions of these available to the general reader. That, I imagine, is what Webster would have wished. And, for us, in so far as his other works have interest, it is mainly because they are by the author of these two sister tragedies.

Introduction, text, and commentary are here reprinted, with revisions and additions. (For in the last thirty years a good deal more has been written on Webster.) But, to spare the reader's pocket, I have jettisoned 32 pages of general introductory matter, and 13 of bibliography[1]; cut down the section on Webster's little-known life to a biographical note; and shortened the Textual Notes by omitting trivial or obvious corruptions, and dealing only with variants of some significance to readers of the plays as *literature*.

I am glad to be able to express my thanks for helpful suggestions to Dr M. C. Bradbrook, Dr Philip Gaskell, Professor R. G. Howarth, Mr A. N. L. Munby, Professor C. J. Sisson, and—"without wrong last to be named"—Professor F. P. Wilson; also to reviews of the 1927 edition by Sir W. W. Greg and Professors Mario Praz, Sisson, and Hazelton Spenser. Finally, Dr G. K. Hunter has kindly sent me some further additions to the endless list of Webster's borrowings.

July, 1957

---

[1] There exists a careful *Bibliography of Webster* by S. A. Tannenbaum (New York, 1941); and admirable Bibliographies of Renaissance Literature are printed yearly by *Studies in Philology*.

ABBREVIATIONS

A. WORKS BELIEVED WHOLLY OR PARTLY WEBSTER'S

A.Q.L.—*Anything for a Quiet Life.*

A.V.—*Appius and Virginia.*

C.C.—*A Cure for a Cuckold.*

Char.—The 32 *New Characters* in the 6th impression of Overbury's *Characters* (1615).

D.L.—*The Devil's Law-Case.*

D.M.—*The Duchess of Malfi* (1958 ed.).

F.M.I.—*The Fair Maid of the Inn.*

Ind. Malc.—Induction to *The Malcontent.*

Mon.Col.—*A Monumental Column.*

Mon.Hon.—*Monuments of Honour.*

N.Ho!—*Northward Ho!*

W.D.—*The White Devil* (1958 ed.).

W.Ho!—*Westward Ho!*

(*Wks.*—my edition of Webster's Works, 1927. References to *Sir T. Wyat*, *W.Ho!*, and *N.Ho!*, are from W. C. Hazlitt's edition, 1897.)

B. GENERAL

Bentley—G. E. Bentley, *The Jacobean and Caroline Stage*, Oxford, 1941-56.

Birch—T. Birch, *Court and Times of James I, Court and Times of Charles I*, 1848.

Brand, *Pop. Antiq.*—J. Brand, *Popular Antiquities*, 1913.

Chambers—E. K. Chambers, *The Elizabethan Stage*, Oxford, 1923.

Crawford—C. Crawford, *Collectanea*, 1906-7.

Dyce—A. Dyce, *Works of J. Webster*, 1830, revised 1857.

Hazlitt—W. C. Hazlitt, *Dramatic Works of J. Webster*, 1857, 1897.

H.D.S.—H. Dugdale Sykes, MS. notes on *W.D.*, *D.M.*, *D.L.*, *A.V.*

HLQ—*Huntington Library Quarterly.*

MLN—*Modern Language Notes.*

N.E.D.—*New (Oxford) English Dictionary.*

N.Q.—*Notes and Queries* (*N.Q.* 6. XI. 210=6th Series, vol. XI, p. 210).

Phil. Quart.—*Philological Quarterly.*

PMLA—*Publications of the Modern Language Association of America.*

Praz—Mario Praz, *Machiavelli in Inghilterra* (2nd ed.), 1943.

Sampson—M. W. Sampson, *The White Devil and The Duchess of Malfi*, Boston and London, 1904.

Sh.'s Eng.—*Shakespeare's England*, Oxford, 1917.

Stoll—E. E. Stoll, *J. Webster*, Boston, 1906.

St.Bibl.—*Studies in Bibliography.*

St.Phil.—*Studies in Philology.*

Tilley—M. P. Tilley, *Dictionary of Proverbial English in the 16th and 17th Centuries*, 1950.

T.L.S.—*Times Literary Supplement.*

(References to Shakespeare are from the Oxford edition; to Lyly's *Euphues* from E. Arber's edition, 1868; to Sidney's *Arcadia*, from the *Works*, ed. A. Feuillerat, 1922.)

BIOGRAPHICAL NOTE

(For details see *Wks.* 1. 49-56 and Bentley, v. 1239-56)

STRANGELY enough, less is now known of Webster than of Greek dramatists two thousand years older. He tells us (*Mon. Hon.*) that he was born free of the Merchant Taylors' Company. He *might* be the "Johannes Webster . . . generosus filius et heres apparens Johannis Webster de London generosi" admitted to the Middle Temple on Aug. 1st 1598.[1] He *might*, as Sisson and Howarth suggest, be the John Webster buried on March 3rd 1637/8 at St James's, Clerkenwell (where, probably, the poet's fellow-dramatists W. Rowley and Dekker had been laid in 1626 and 1632)—though Heywood's reference to Webster in *The Hierarchie of the blessed Angells* (licensed Nov. 7th 1634), in the past tense, has been taken to imply him already dead by 1634. But the only sure landmarks are some of his works.[2]

c. 1580? Born.

1602. Henslowe records payments to Webster (along with Munday,

---

[1] Mr Paul Clarkson of Baltimore tells me that in a count of legal terms and allusions in the drama of Webster's day (made by himself and a fellow-lawyer, Mr Clyde Warren) Ben Jonson heads the list with an average of 31 per play, closely followed by Webster with 29; whereas Shakespeare has only 13½. Certainly it would not be easy to equal the three trial-scenes of *W.D.*, *D.L.*, and *A.V.*; though Webster's love of legal lore seems a good deal warmer than his love of lawyers. (Cf. L. J. Sturge, *Webster and the Law*, *Shakespeare-Jahrbuch*, XLII. 148–57.)

Chambers and R. G. Howarth (who has devoted much research to Webster's obscure life) suggest that Webster was himself an actor; but I find this hard to reconcile with Webster's aloof allusion to actors at the end of *W.D.*, where he praises its acting "with the Joint testimony of some of their owne quality." (See *Wks.* 1. 51.) An odd way to talk if he belonged to that "quality" himself.

[2] J. P. Collier reported a marriage between John Webster and Isabell Sutton (July 25th 1590) as recorded in the register of St Leonard's, Shoreditch; not finding it there, I suggested that there seemed little motive for invention, and Collier might have given the wrong church (*Wks.* 1. 49); Prof. Howarth kindly tells me that Miss T. G. Herring, working for him in the Guildhall Library, has now rediscovered this entry, in the register of St Giles, Cripplegate. There seems no evidence, however, to link it with our dramatist.

Drayton, Middleton, Dekker, Chettle, Heywood, and Went-
worth Smith) for his share in various plays—*Caesar's Fall*,
"too shapes" (=*Caesar's Fall?*), *Lady Jane* (=*Sir T. Wyat?*),
Christmas comes but once a year.

1604. *Induction* to Marston's *Malcontent.* *Westward Ho!* (with
Dekker).

1605. *Northward Ho!* (with Dekker).

1607. *Sir T. Wyat, Westward Ho!*, and *Northward Ho!* published.

c. 1611–2. *The White Devil* (published 1612).

1612. *A Monumental Column* (on the death of Prince Henry: published
1613).

1612–4. *The Duchess of Malfi* (published 1623).

Before 1623. *The Guise* (lost).

1615. Thirty-two "New Characters" contributed by Webster to the
sixth edition of "Overbury's" *Characters.*

c. 1619? *The Devil's Law-Case* (published 1623).[1]

c. 1621. *Anything for a Quiet Life.* (Perhaps by Webster and
Middleton.)

1624. *The Late Murder of the Son upon the Mother, or Keep the Widow
Waking* (with Dekker, Ford, and Rowley—licensed in Sep-
tember. Lost).[2]

Monuments of Honour (Lord Mayor's Pageant—Oct. 29th).

c. 1624–5. *A Cure for a Cuckold* (with Rowley and ? Heywood).

---

[1] Dated by Bentley "1610" (v. 1250). But my doubts remain. See
Wks. II. 213–6, IV. 250–6. Apart from the evidence given there, it seems a
little hard to reconcile "1610" with the tone of the 1623 dedication to Sir
Thomas Finch—"Some of my other Works, as *The white Devill, The
Dutchesse of Malfi, Guise*, and others, you have formerly seene; I present
this humbly to kisse your hands, and to find your allowance". I wonder if
Sir Thomas would have been much gratified to be offered a dusty work out
of a drawer, thirteen years old—still older than those he had "formerly"
seen. True, *The Duchess of Malfi* was ten years old at its dedication to
Lord Berkeley. But *The Duchess* had made its name. *The Devil's Law-Case*
never did. (There are also in *D.L.* fainter echoes of Sidney's *Arcadia*, from
which Webster had borrowed so profusely in *D.M.* and *Mon.Col.*, but only
dubiously in the earlier *W.D.* of 1611–2.)

One *could* of course conjecture that Webster revised about 1619–20 a play
written about 1610; but, even so, metrical reasons would make me think he
rewrote it almost completely.

[2] On April 9th 1624 Nathaniel Tindall or Grindall stabbed his mother
Joan in Whitechapel; on Sept. 3 he was sentenced to the gallows. In July
1624 Anne Elsdon, a widow of sixty-two, assiduously plied with drink, was
tricked into a form of marriage, for her money, by a tobacconist of twenty-

c. 1625. *The Fair Maid of the Inn.* (Perhaps by Webster, Massinger, and Ford.)

c. 1626–7? *Appius and Virginia* (with Heywood?).[1]

Dec. 26th 1630. *The Duchess of Malfi* performed at the Cockpit (one of 21 plays given court performances by the King's Men, Sept. 30th 1630–Feb. 21st 1631).[2]

By Nov. 1634 or March 1638? Death.[3]

How Webster struck contemporaries, or what sort of person he was, we know even less. He collaborated freely: yet he seems somehow aloof. When writing in his own person, he remains stiff, proud, even a little pompous. His two great plays suggest a tragic pessimist; yet his other work leaves the impression of a mind perhaps sardonic and satirical,[4] but clouded with no particular gloom. Complimentary verses like those of Middleton, or Ford, or Sheppard tell us nothing of the man. Our only approach to a portrait is a caricature by the hostile Henry Fitzjeffrey of Lincoln's Inn.[5]

---

five, Tobias Audley; who was sent to Newgate (where he finally died). Both the tragic matricide and the farcical fraud were bundled together into this catchpenny melodrama for the Red Bull, regardless of poor Anne Elsdon's feelings, or of her family. Indeed a ballad about "keeping the widow waking" was sung, for publicity, under her very windows. Her resentful son-in-law, Benjamin Garfield, keeper of Bridewell, took legal action; to which we owe our knowledge. For Webster the episode seems hardly a "Monument of Honour". (See a fascinating chapter in C. J. Sisson, *Lost Plays of Shakespeare's Age*, 1936.)

[1] The dates assigned to this elusive drama have ranged from 1603 to 1634. See *Wks.* III. 121–30; Bentley, V. 1245–7.

[2] Bentley, I. 28. Of the other 20 plays only one was by Shakespeare— *A Midsummer Night's Dream.*

[3] Webster also wrote occasional verses (not impressive) for Munday's *Palmerin of England*, Part III (1602); S. Harrison's *Arches of Triumph* (1604); Heywood's *Apology for Actors* (1612); and Cockeram's *Dictionary* (1623). Further, an engraving in the Print Room of the B.M., which depicts the family of James I, has verses by Webster extolling seven of them; evidently composed between late 1624 and early 1625. See B. M. Wagner, *New Verses by J. Webster*, MLN. XLVI. 403-5.

[4] Cf. T. Bogard, *The Tragic Satire of J. Webster*, 1955.

[5] In a poem, "*Notes from Black-Fryers*" (satirizing various types in the audience), printed in *Certain Elegies done by Sundry Excellent Wits*, 1617. See *Wks.* I. 55.

But hist! with him[1] Crabbed (*Websterio*)
The *Play-wright, Cart-wright*[2]: whether? either! (*ho*—
No further. Looke as yee'd bee look't into:
Sit as ye woo'd be *Read: Lord*! who woo'd know him?
Was ever man so mangl'd with a *Poem*?
See how he drawes his mouth awry of late,
How he scrubs[3]: wrings his wrests: scratches his Pate.
A *Midwife*! helpe! By his *Braines coitus*,
Some *Centaure* strange: some huge *Bucephalus*,
Or *Pallas* (sure) ['s] ingendred in his *Braine*,
Strike, *Vulcan*, with thy hammer once againe.
This is the *Crittick* that (of all the rest)
I'de not have view mee, yet I feare him least,
Heer's not a word *cursively* I have *Writ*,
But hee'l *Industriously* examine it.
And in some 12. monthes hence (or there *about*)
Set in a shamefull sheete, my errors *out*.
But what care I! It *will* be so obscure,
That none shall understand him (I am sure).

Some traits seem recognizable in this crabbed, critical, difficult, costive figure. But it tells us little. The poet still lives for us, as his characters often die, "in a mist".

[1] *I.e.* Fantastick, a fashionable singer.
[2] "*Play-wright, Cart-wright*" suggests, I suppose, that the plays are lumbering products of laborious carpentry. But Howarth (*T.L.S.* 2/11/33) has indicated a possibly relevant point—that Webster's brother was actually in the coaching business. For William Hemminge, son of Shakespeare's fellow-actor, wrote an *Elegy on Randolph's Finger* (Randolph had lost his little finger in a duel), where occur these lines:

> that wᶜʰ soe ofte has toumbled ore a Verse
> Is toumbled now ytt selfe into a hearse,
> Borne to yttes grave, by Art, Invention,
> Thrice blessed Nature, Imitation.
> Ytt had byn drawne, and wee, In state aproche
> but websters brother wd nott lend a Coach:
> hee swore thay all weare hired to Convey
> the Malfy dutches sadly on her way.

It would be comically appropriate if our gloomy poet's brother turned out to have specialized in hiring out coaches for funerals—in short, to have been an undertaker. But this is guessing.

(G. C. Moore Smith, publishing the poem in 1923, dated it *c.* 1630–2. Its allusion to *The Duchess* might, I suppose, have been suggested by the court performance at Christmas, 1630.)

[3] Scratches himself.

THE DUCHESS OF MALFI

DATE

THE play must have been produced before Dec. 16th 1614: for on that day died William Ostler, who acted Antonio (cf. Wallace's letters to *The Times*, Oct. 2nd and 4th 1909).

Our other limit is rather less easy to fix; for it depends on the always risky evidence of metrical tests and parallel passages. But the metre certainly seems later than that of *The White Devil* (Appendix IV, *Wks.* IV. 250); and it is striking that *The Duchess of Malfi* should show repeated parallels with two works first published in 1612—Chapman's *Petrarch's Seven Penitential Psalms* and Donne's *An Anatomy of the World*, both the first part which had appeared in 1611 and its sequels of 1612 (for details see Commentary).

Further the frequent resemblances between the play and *A Monumental Column* (registered Dec. 25th 1612) and the quite extraordinary indebtedness visible in both to Sidney's *Arcadia* (this influence appears much less clearly in *The White Devil* and indeed has been denied there altogether; a new edition of the *Arcadia* appeared in 1613) make it natural to suppose that the two works were written fairly close together. It is perhaps just worth recording that of the most marked parallels between the elegy and the tragedy, Act I contains two, Act II two, Act III five, Act IV one, and Act V none; so that it would agree very prettily if Webster turned out to have been about half-way through the play when he wrote the poem. Further, Act III. has four borrowings from P. Matthieu's *Henry IV* (tr. Grimeston, 1612): the poem has over a dozen.

There are also some significant parallels with the "Overbury" *Characters*—not only with the *New Characters* of 1615, which are probably Webster's own work, but also, in two places (I. 1. 380-1; V. 2. 244: see Commentary), with the original *Characters* published as Overbury's in May 1614. But here again the evidence cannot be pressed too far. For the *Characters* are very likely to have circulated in MS; Webster may well have known Overbury; the passages in *The Duchess of Malfi* might be later insertions; and it is even possible that Webster might have had a hand in the 1614 collection of *Characters*, which were not exclusively by Overbury.

As for the suggested borrowing in Act IV from Campion's *Lords' Masque* (Feb. 14th 1613) which also contains a dance of madmen, the resemblance seems to me too vague and Elizabethan lunatics too common.

Still we may say that such evidence as there is points to the conclusion that *The Duchess of Malfi* was written after, though not very long after, the sister-tragedy it so much resembles, in 1612–4[1].

Something must however be said of that fearful warning against rash and dogmatic dating—the Concini allusion which opens the play. The first scene begins with a desultory discussion between Antonio and Delio of a recent salutary purging of the French Court by its King; and in this Vaughan first saw a reference to the dramatic murder of Concino Concini, Maréchal d'Ancre, on April 24th[2] 1617, which sent a wave of excitement over all Western Europe. His suggestion has since found general acceptance; and there is no reason to question its accuracy (see on I. 1. 8). Of course, however, critics pounced on the passage as proof positive that the whole play must be dated 1617–8 (Burbage, the original Ferdinand, having died on March 13th, 1619). Doubt was no more: and Professor Schelling wrote: "This puts to rest, once and for all, former surmises on the subject". In fact, however, as Rupert Brooke observes, "This eternal rest lasted nearly five[3] years"—until the discovery, that is, of the date of Ostler's death. It is simply a

---

[1] See also on IV. 2. 60.

[2] Stoll in his useful *John Webster* attempts (p. 25) to disprove this date of April 24th, on the bare evidence of two entries in the *Stationers' Register* and in the teeth of all the historians of the period, backed by contemporary records so precise that we know almost the exact minute when the fatal shots were fired. It is perfectly true that pamphlets on the murder are entered in the Register on April 17th and 23rd. But the explanation is the very simple one that England, not having adopted the Gregorian calendar, was ten days behind, so that April 24th (French) = April 14th (English) and the whole discrepancy vanishes.

For an admirable account of the Concini murder see Batiffol, *Louis XIII à Vingt Ans*, ch. 1.

[3] Really, thirteen. The suggestion was first made, not by Sampson (1904), but by Vaughan (1896).

case of a topical allusion being interpolated in a play at a later revival.

A revival, then, of *The Duchess of Malfi* may be supposed to have taken place in 1617, though it is frivolous to identify Webster's play with the "enterlude concerning the late Marquesse d'Ancre" of June 22nd 1617 (see Collier, *Annals of the Stage*, I. 391). Still this revival would in any case have occurred while the excitement was still high enough to make the allusion intelligible and interesting: probably, that is, not later than the end of 1617. The stream of English pamphlets on the subject in the *Stationers' Register* dries up in June; and interest must have waned after the execution of the Maréchal's wife in July 1617. This performance of *The Duchess* might be the one described by Orazio Busino (Feb. 7th 1618—see on *D.M.* III. 4) as if fairly recent[1].

A later revival is indicated by the second Actor-list to have occurred at some time after Taylor's replacement of Burbage (who died on March 13th 1619) and, probably, before Towley's death (June 1623); certainly, at all events, before the end of 1623, the year when the First Quarto was printed.' [2]

---

[1] He does not say he saw it himself, as Brooke asserts (p. 247): so that we cannot base any argument on the date of his arrival in England, Oct. 1617.

[2] The supposed allusion to Concini's death (1617) has been questioned by J. R. Brown (*Phil. Quart.* XXXI. 358-62). He suggests, rather, a reference to the evil counsellors of James I in 1614, transferred to France to baffle censorship. But surely a device so far-fetched might have equally baffled the audience? Imagine even an educated spectator listening to these lines in 1614. "When," he might mutter, "did all this happen? French favourites? I have heard of plenty—Agnes Sorel, Olivier Le Dain, Diane de Poitiers, Henri III's minions, and now this Maréchal d'Ancre. But were *they* 'judiciously' purged? God knows when, exactly, the Duchess of Malfi lived: *this* speech must be topical. But how? For to-day the French King is a mere boy; and the Queen-mother a mere creature of the d'Ancres and their sycophants. What the devil is the author driving at?" Indeed it would have been much as if an English drama of Hitler's day had begun: "Blessed Germany, where all is peace, justice, and freedom, and no one insults a Jew!" That could only have been bitterest irony. And of irony there is no question here.

But in 1617 an audience could have seized the point at once. Indeed on June 22nd, 1617, the Privy Council ordered an "enterlude" about the Marquis d'Ancre to be suppressed. Webster had already in 1612-4 shown interest in current French affairs by extensive borrowings from P. Matthieu's *Histoire de la Mort de Henry IV* (1611) in Grimeston's version of 1612.

HISTORICAL INTRODUCTION
WEBSTER'S SOURCES

In the diary of Giacomo the Notary, of Naples, among the records of battles, bread-riots, pestilences, and births of eight-legged cats, occurs this entry:

On Sunday November 17th, 1510, it was common talk throughout the city of Naples, that the illustrious Signora Joanna of Aragon, daughter of the late illustrious Don Enrico of Aragon, and sister of the most Reverend Monsignore the Cardinal of Aragon, having given out that she wished to make a pilgrimage to Santa Maria de Loreto, had gone thither with a retinue of many carriages and thence departed with Antonio de Bologna, son of Messer Antonino de Bologna, and gone with the aforesaid, saying that he was her husband, to Ragusa, leaving behind her one male child of ten, who was Duke of Amalfi[1].

Giacomo says no more; in the next year his record suddenly ends. But there is a strange thrill in coming on this dry contemporary confirmation of Webster's romantic story. For the true relation of the fate of the Duchess of Malfi has been curiously neglected by English scholarship despite its passion for sources. When it had been recorded that the story of the Duchess was derived from Bandello, because Bandello wrote fiction, it seemed to be assumed that he could not have written fact[2]. As it is, much more is known of the Duchess's life than of Webster's own.

---

[1] Notar Giacomo, *Cronica di Napoli* (printed at Naples, 1845), p. 331: "Adi. 17. de novembro 1510 dedomenica puplice perla Cita denapoli era fama como (*sic*) la illustre Signora Ioanna de aragonia duchessa de amalfe figliola del quondam illustre signore don herrico de aragonia et sorella carnale del Reuerendissimo Monsignore lo cardinale de aragonia hauendo data fama de volere andare ad sancta maria deloreto per deuocione nce (*sic*) ando con multi carriagi et dalla se partio con Antonio debolognia figliolo de messere Antonino debologna et andosene con el predicto con dire che era suo marito in ragosa laxando vno figliolo mascolo de eta de anni x quale era duca de amalfe scopis ornatus." (What the last two words mean I cannot say.)

[2] Thus Kiesow suggests that Bandello dated the story in his own time to lend it extra interest. And even Sugden's excellent *Topographical Dictionary to the Works of Shakespeare* as recently as 1925 makes the amazing statement that the Duchess's Malfi is on the east coast of the Adriatic, seven miles N.W. of Ragusa. For the historical facts the main authority is D. Morellini, *Giovanna d' Aragona* (Cesena, 1906).

She was the grand-daughter of Ferdinand or Ferrante I of
Naples, the second of her kings of the house of Aragon, a man
half fox, half wolf, who kept his enemies in cages and, as a
Machiavellian masterpiece, poisoned a guest after feasting him
royally for twenty-seven days. His enemies indeed asserted that
he was really no true scion of Aragon, but his mother's bastard
by a Moor of Valentia. One of his many mistresses, Diana
Guardati of Sorrento, bore Ferdinand a son, Enrico d' Aragona,
who in 1465 married Polissena Centelles and in 1473 was
created by his father Marchese di Gerace, a small town on the
underside of the Calabrian toe of Italy. Five years later, in
1478, he died, together with his major-domo and others of his
household, from eating poisonous fungi; and was lamented in
a naïve and curious poem which is the earliest known com-
position in the Calabrian dialect:

> Piangi, Cosenza, giniralimente,
> et tu, Calabria, a dirite ritorno
> a donni Arrichu, benigno e clemente,
> Ch' è mortu e trapassato, notte e iorno,
> coll' occhi corporali, amara mente,
> pir sin che sonarà l' ultimu cornu.

So runs one stanza; though whether the son of Ferdinand and
brother of Alfonso II of Naples, "the Abominable", was indeed
"benigno e clemente" we do not know. He left four children,
one of them born only after his death. Lodovico, the eldest, is
Webster's Cardinal; Caterina is out of our story; Carlo is Webster's
Ferdinand; and Giovanna, the future Duchess of Amalfi.

Lodovico's career was typical of the precocity common in
that age[1]. Proclaimed Marchese di Gerace as a child, in his early
teens (1489) he was astonishing the ambassadors of France,
Castile, Venice, Florence, and Milan by the skill by which he
broke four lances in the tilt. Three years later he wedded the
grand-daughter of Innocent VIII in the presence of the Pope
at Rome; and by the time he was twenty he was already a
widower and, renouncing his title in favour of his younger
brother Carlo, had become Cardinal of Aragon (1494). Two
years after, warlike as in the play, he was fighting the French
invaders at the side of the Great Captain, Gonsalvo di Cordova[2];

[1] See *Archivio Storico per le provincie Napoletane*, XIII. 130 ff.
[2] Notar Giacomo, pp. 201, 203.

but, unlike Webster's Cardinal, he died peacefully in Rome in 1519 and was richly interred in Santa Maria sopra la Minerva.

His sister Giovanna was married in 1490[1], as a girl of twelve or so, to Alfonso Piccolomini, son and heir of Antonio Piccolomini, first Duke of Amalfi, with great rejoicings—*"fu facta festa grande con danze et soni et farse"*. Antonio Piccolomini, nephew of Pius II, had been sent years before to help Ferdinand against the Angevins, and received in reward the Duchy of Amalfi, to which his son, the young Alfonso, succeeded in 1493. But Giovanna's husband did not long enjoy his dukedom, for he died of gout in 1498, the year of the burning of Savonarola. He left his Duchess with a daughter Caterina (who died in childbed) and a son not born till the next year, the future Alfonso II of Amalfi. Meanwhile she ruled the Duchy as Regent for her child and though there now began, with the French and Spanish invasions, what Guicciardini calls *"gli anni miserabili"*, she is said to have prospered and paid off the heavy debts her husband had incurred[2]. So all went well for years. But she was young—a girl of nineteen or twenty at her husband's death; and she had remained unmarried, whether for her child's sake, or because she cared for none of her own rank, or because it suited her brothers' ends to keep her so. At this point Antonio Bologna crossed her path.

Antonio Bologna, son of Antonino Bologna, came of a reputable house. Of his forbears Vannino Beccadelli had migrated from Bologna (whence their name) to Palermo in the fourteenth century: Vannino's son, Enrico, had been first magistrate at Palermo in the last decade of that century; and his grandson Antonio Beccadelli ("il Panormita"), our hero's grandfather, was one of the most distinguished literary figures of fifteenth century Italy, honoured in turn at the courts of Filippo Maria Visconti, the Emperor Sigismund, and Alfonso I of Naples, for whom his eloquence obtained from Padua that precious relic, an arm of Livy the historian[3].

[1] Leostello, *Effemeridi* in *Documenti per la storia* by G. Filangieri (Naples, 1883) p. 352.

[2] See M. Camera, *Memorie storico-diplomatiche di Amalfi* (Salerno, 1881), II. 28, 69, 78–82. C. needs checking: but gives some interesting details and documents.

[3] It is perhaps of some interest to Webster's fellow-countrymen that the learned "Panormita" knew a legend of his family's descent, 800 years before,

For details of the tragedy that followed we have to depend on Bandello (*Novelle*, 1. 26), whose faithfulness is borne out by the Corona manuscripts and Filonico, by Giacomo the Notary and the *Register of Deaths* at Milan.

Antonio Bologna, brought up at the Court of Naples and long major-domo of Federico, the last of its Aragonese dynasty, had followed his master to his exile in France. For in 1501 Federico, his Kingdom partitioned between his enemy Louis XII and his treacherous ally Ferdinand the Catholic, threw himself on the mercy of Louis, was given the Duchy of Anjou, and died at Tours towards the end of 1504. Returning after this to Naples, Antonio was offered the office of major-domo by the Duchess of Amalfi; devoted still to the house of Aragon, he willingly accepted it. Before long he and his mistress had fallen passionately in love and, dreading her brothers' anger, went through a secret marriage witnessed only by her waiting-woman. For years their relations were successfully concealed. Even the birth of a son remained undiscovered; but the birth of a second child started whispers which reached the brothers' ears, so that they set spies on the Duchess. Antonio growing alarmed withdrew with his two children to Ancona, to await the passing of the storm; but the Duchess, now expecting a third child, could not bear the loneliness of her palace. Like Bracciano seventy years later, she made a pretext of a pilgrimage to Loretto, whither she set out with a great retinue. Thence she proceeded to join Antonio in Ancona; and there threw off the mask before her astonished household. She would renounce her rank, she said, and henceforth live quietly with her husband in a private station. Her servants, foreseeing the storm, sent one of their number to the Cardinal of Aragon in Rome, and returned to Amalfi. For a little the lovers were left in peace at Ancona, where their third child was born; but the Cardinal of Aragon was putting pressure on Cardinal Gonzaga, Legate of Ancona under Julius II (who died in 1513). After "six or seven months" (summer of 1511), Antonio seeing that his efforts to combat the sentence of expulsion were bound soon to fail, obtained through a friend in Siena leave to take refuge there. Accordingly,

from an English Ambassador sent to the Pope, who was buried in San Giovanni in Monte at Bologna. It was also related that Galeazzo Beccadelli, a later ancestor, had been knighted at Forli by Edward I of England.

the moment the decree of "banishment from Ancona within
fifteen days" was issued, he was able to set out for his new home
before the brothers could conveniently arrange to have him way-
laid and murdered. ·But in Siena the same relentless pressure
recommenced. Through Cardinal Petrucci, his brother Borghese,
head of the Signiory at Siena, was induced to expel the refugees
(1512). (It is some consolation to know that five years later
Cardinal Petrucci was strangled in the Castle of St Angelo for
having tried to poison Leo X.)

Antonio and his family now turned (once more like Bracciano
and his Duchess) to seek refuge in Venice; but in the territory
of Forli they were overtaken by armed horsemen. The Duchess,
pleading that her brothers would not harm her in person, persuaded her husband to leave her and escape. So with his eldest
son and four servants he rode off and reached Milan; the Duchess,
with the other two children and her waiting woman, were
carried off to one of the castles of her Duchy. She was never
seen again.

Antonio, ignorant of her fate, lived on in Milan for more
than a year, first under the protection of Silvio Savello[1] (who
has lent his name to Webster's Silvio), while he was besieging
the French garrison of the Citadel of Milan on behalf of
Massimiliano Sforza (in the earlier part of 1513). Then, when
Silvio went out to fight at Crema (August 1513)[2], Antonio
attached himself to the Marchese di Bitonto, and finally to
Alfonso Visconti. Although the brothers had had Antonio's
property at Naples confiscated, the exile still lived in hopes of
appeasing them. In vain he was warned that his life was in
danger. "I had some reason to believe," says Girolamo Visconti,
who tells the story in Bandello, "that he was secretly given to
understand (by the brothers, who wished to keep· him within
reach) that he might even yet have his wife restored to him".
Next, a certain Neapolitan condottiere (probably Cesare Fiera-
mosca) related Antonio's history to a person whom Visconti
calls "il nostro Delio", and added that he had himself been
commissioned to have Antonio murdered; but, not regarding
himself as a hired assassin, had warned the victim of his danger.

[1] See Guicciardini (Florence, 1919), III. pp. 67, 92, 102: Gregorovius,
Rome in the Middle Ages, VII. 493.
[2] Cf. Marin Sanudo, *Diari* 16, col. 609: Guicciardini, III. 67.

Finally one day (in October 1513)[1] Delio and L. Scipione Attellano, who foreseeing Antonio's tragic end, had already thought of making a *novella* of his story, passed Antonio accompanied by two servants on his way to Mass at the church of S. Francesco. They noted dismay in his looks; and a few minutes later they heard an uproar. Antonio had been attacked and stabbed to death by a certain Lombard Captain, Daniel da Bozolo (Webster's Bosola), with three others. The assassins escaped unmolested from the territory of Milan.

The interest grows when it emerges that "Delio" (which is also the name assumed by Bandello in his sonnets) is probably Bandello himself, who was at this time a *protégé* of Ippolita Sforza and thus met in Milan not only Antonio[2], but another ill-fated figure of his *novelle*, the Countess of Celant. So that Webster's ultimate authority was probably one of the last persons to see his hero alive, and the Delio of the play is in origin Bandello himself. It throws, we may add, an ironic light on the standards of the day to find Bandello a few pages later (the separate *novelle* were of course only collected and published years afterwards) dedicating another of his tales with every expression of gratitude and esteem to the murderer, Lodovico Cardinal of Aragon. Yet there is, as we see, good reason to believe the story of the barbarous fate of the Duchess of Malfi to be essentially true[3].

[1] The date is established and the whole story confirmed by an entry in the *necrologio* of Milan (1450–1550), preserved in the *archivio di stato*—"Die Jovis sexto mensis Octobris 1513 Antonius de Bononia de Neapoli annorum xxx (he must surely have really been older) ex vulneribus". (Morellini, *Matteo Bandello*, p. 58 n.)

The Antonio Bologna whose epitaph at *Padua* is given in Nemeitz, *Inscriptionum singularium* (Leipzig, 1726), p. 298, is clearly a different person.

[2] Antonio is quoted as the narrator of another of the *novelle* (I. 5)—hardly the sort of story one would expect from a melancholy exile.

[3] The story is found also in the Corona MSS. of the Naples Library (so-called because a number of them are by Silvio and Ascanio Corona—*flor.* 1525: see D. Morellini in *Napoli Nobilissima*, XIV. 77). This version is apparently based mainly on Bandello, but omits items of more purely Milanese interest. According to them Antonio's surviving son was brought back to Naples and reared by his father's kin. An independent narrative, on the other hand, appears in Filonico's *Vita di Dorotea d' Avalos*, where the Duchess is said to have been taking to a religious life when she fell in love with Antonio, "vinta dalle tentazioni diaboliche". She fled to Ancona and was there poisoned with her children. (See also Ammirato, *Delle famiglie nobili napoletane* (Florence, 1651) II. "Bologna".)

The Duchess's son by her first husband became Duke of Amalfi and died in 1559, like his father, of gout. That his mother's misalliance did not rankle

From Bandello the tale passed to Belleforest, in whose second volume of *Histoires tragiques* it forms the first story[1]. Belleforest is a pedant and a prig. His characters all talk like great whales and their interminable speeches and soliloquies make even the Duchess's story dull; while the author's high moral tone compels him to pelt his unhappy heroine with a volley of references to Semiramis, Messalina, Faustina, even Pasiphaë, in order to express his disgust at her shameless behaviour in marrying a man she loved. "Shall I be of opinion that a homeless servaunt oughte to sollicite, nay rather suborne the Daughter of his Lorde without punishment, or that a vyle and abject person dare to mount upon a Prynces Bed?" (Painter's translation.) At the execrable impiety of the pretended pilgrimage to Loretto, his voice rises to a scream: "and yet you see this great and mighty Duchesse trot and run after the male, like a female Wolfe or Lionesse, (when they goe to sault) and forget the noble bloud of Aragon whereof she was descended, to couple hir self almost with the simplest person of the trimmest Gentlemen of Naples". Bandello is no Boccaccio: but he belongs to a different stage of civilisation from Belleforest. The Frenchman, sermons and all, was translated by William Painter in his *Palace of Pleasure* (1566–7: II. 23) during a varied career which ranged from the headmastership of Sevenoaks School to some highly successful embezzlement as clerk of Her Majesty's Ordnance. And so through the hands of a gentleman, a fool, and a knave the tale reached Webster.

The following are the main divergences of Belleforest and Painter from their source Bandello:

(1) It is the waiting-maid who suggests the pilgrimage to Loretto. (In Bandello, the Duchess: in Webster, Bosola.)

(2) Belleforest definitely calls the story a "*tragédie*"; of the marriage he remarks "*voici le premier acte de cette tragédie*"; Antonio's departure to Ancona completes the second act, his death the last.

(3) He changes Bandello's "Petrucci" to "Castruccio" (cf. Webster's Castruchio).

violently we may gather from the fact that he called one of his sons Antonio (and see Camera, II. 95–7, 99).

[1] A first volume of eighteen tales adapted from Bandello's *Novelle* by P. Boaistuau and Belleforest had appeared in 1559; this second, containing another eighteen by Belleforest alone, in 1565.

(4) Strangling is definitely mentioned as the manner of the Duchess's murder.

On these as well as on general grounds it seems likely that Webster used Belleforest's narrative in Painter's translation[1]. But it is interesting to see how very little Webster borrows from Painter's language, considering how freely he conveys from Montaigne and Sidney.

The following alterations are made by Webster in his turn[2] (apart from his important change of general attitude towards the Duchess, from the disapproval of Belleforest to complete sympathy):

(1) The previous warnings of the brothers are added to make the wooing-scene more dramatic.

(2) The Duchess's "guilt" is discovered at the birth of the first child, not the second. The manner—by the dropping of the horoscope—seems Webster's invention.

(3) The pretended peculation of Antonio is also Webster's addition. He says nothing of the stay at Siena. And the Duchess parts from Antonio before, not after, their pursuers appear.

(4) The tortures of the Duchess, the deaths of the brothers, and the manner of Antonio's murder (*i.e.* practically all IV and V) are new.

(5) Julia and her sub-plot are added. Castruchio has become her husband, instead of a Cardinal.

(6) Bosola, instead of being simply the final assassin, becomes the villain of the whole piece.

There remains however a further question—had Webster also seen the tragedy on the subject by Lope de Vega—*El Mayordomo de la Duquesa de Amalfi* (written before 1609: first printed (1618) in *Works*, vol. XI)? This play is based directly on Bandello, an edition of whom had been printed at Valladolid in 1603. It shows on the whole considerable divergences from Webster's work; whether it shows any considerable resemblances, opinion differs. The chief parallels are these—Lope's Duchess also bids Antonio "be covered", as a mark that he is now her

[1] For verbal indications of this see on I. 1. 73, 507–8; II. 5. 44–5, 87–91 (decisive); IV. 2. 259. It remains possible of course that Webster may also have read Bandello (see on II. 5. 46–9).

[2] Cf. Kiesow, *Die verschiedenen Bearbeitungen der Novelle von der Herzogin von Amalfi* in *Anglia* XVII. 199–258. (His attempt to reconstruct Bandello's chronology is, however, quite inaccurate.)

equal; she does so, however, in the wooing-scene. Secondly, Antonio's withdrawal to Ancona is screened in both plays by a pretence of dismissal in disgrace. In Lope he is indeed accused of a different offence—of seducing the Duchess's maid Libia, who answers to Cariola. But it is noteworthy that this stratagem has no foundation in the non-dramatic versions of the story; though of course some excuse for Antonio's departure was clearly needed by the plot. Thirdly, in Lope, the Duchess's brother Julio (Webster's Ferdinand; the pious Spaniard omits the wicked Cardinal) writes to Antonio inviting him back to a reconciliation. "Letters" of this tenour are vaguely mentioned in the prose stories; but the development of that suggestion is common to both dramatists. In Lope, however, Antonio is deceived, returns, and is poisoned by kissing Julio's hands. "Compare the death of Webster's Julia," argues Morellini, who believes in Lope's influence; but he forgets Isabella's similar death in *The White Devil*, to say nothing of the commonness of the idea in general. The Duchess herself is given poison, then a curtain is drawn revealing the heads of Antonio and her children. This certainly recalls the disclosure of the wax figures behind the traverse in Webster, which has no counterpart in Painter; though even here the influence of the *Arcadia* (see below) may be sufficient explanation. Finally, in Lope, the Duchess's son and heir, the young Duke, enters horrified at her murder and breathing vengeance[1]. This has no parallel in Webster's *Duchess of Malfi*: but it at once recalls the end of *The White Devil*[2], where Giovanni's appearance is quite contrary to the sources of that play. (The real Virginio Orsini was probably accessory to Vittoria's murder; certainly not hostile like Giovanni.)

What is the answer? It is difficult to feel sure. Coincidence and the logical necessities of the plot may be sufficient to account for the resemblances. And it is certainly asking a good deal to expect us to believe that Webster was seriously influenced by a Spanish play which had not yet appeared in print. That seems to me the real difficulty, though it has not deterred some

[1] A sequel called *La Venganza de la Duquesa de Amalfi* by Diego Muxet de Solis appeared in 1624.
[2] For another very slight trace of conceivable influence by Lope de Vega see on *W.D.* III. 2. 178–83.

scholars. Webster's indebtedness to this far feebler play remains, I think, very dubious—and in any case unimportant.

There are also certain separate sources for various incidents in the play. The description of the Duke's lycanthropia in v. 2 is largely based on Grimeston's translation (1607: pp. 364–7) of S. Goulart's *Histoires admirables* (1600 and 1606); so that Webster had doubtless read also the same writer's brief account of the Duchess of Malfi, which has however no independent interest, being clearly based on Belleforest[1].

Again, for the tormenting of the Duchess in Act IV with wax-figures representing her husband and children as dead, Webster drew to some extent on Sidney's account in his *Arcadia* of the persecution of Philoclea and Pamela by their aunt Cecropia, who frightens each of them with the seeming death of the other —Pamela is apparently beheaded, and Philoclea's head is shown in a basin. This influence is decisively confirmed by verbal borrowings as well (see Commentary on the scene).

As for the shutting in of the Duchess with madmen, a similar idea in a comic form recurs in several Elizabethan plays, in Dekker's *Honest Whore* (Part I. iv. 3) and again in *Northward Ho!* where a character who probably represented the poet Chapman, is so treated in jest.

I may perhaps add here, not as sources, but as parallels that may well have been present in the minds of Webster and his audience, two contemporary or almost contemporary episodes of real life. I know that such supposed historical allusions are dangerous. Miss Winstanley in her pursuit of them has reached the point of finding the Porter in *Macbeth* to be really Guy Fawkes, and Ariel Henry of Navarre. And it is too easy to discover in an Elizabethan dramatist, as Taine says of La Fontaine, "des souvenirs qu'il avait et des intentions qu'il n'avait pas". But it is only with "souvenirs" that I am here concerned; and certainly in the scene of the Duchess among the madmen,

---

[1] Like another short *résumé* of no particular importance, which Webster may or may not have seen, in T. Beard's *Theatre of God's Judgments* (1579), II. 322 ("Of Whoredoms committed under the colour of Marriage").

There are also passing references to the story in the *Forest of Fancy* (1579), sig. N 1, in Whetstone's *Heptameron of Civil Discourses* (1582), 5th day, and in Greene's *Card of Fancy* (1584), p. 119 (the first and last of these call Antonio "Ulrico"); and some critics have, not very convincingly, conjectured "the lady of Malfy" for "the lady of the Strachey" in *Twelfth Night*, II. 5. 44.

we are strongly reminded of the story of the fate of Torquato
Tasso at the hands of another Italian duke. Tasso was shut up
in the madhouse of Sta Anna in 1579 by Alfonso d' Este,
Duke of Ferrara. The real reason was the simple and sufficient
one that the poet had become insane. But by the beginning
of the seventeenth century there had begun to grow up the
famous legend of the singer caged by the tyrant, with hints of
an unhappy romance behind. Thus in 1609 we have d'Alessandro
in his *Studio sulle Fonti della Gerusalemme* writing mysteriously:

Essendo stato tredici anni in corte del signor Duca di Ferrara, al
fine per malignità di altrui cadde in disgrazia a detto Signore, in tanto
che per ordine di quello sette anni dimorò nelle carceri di Ferrara—
nè saprei dire più la causa della sua prigione, che cagione per la quale
Ovidio fu relegato in Ponto da Cesare Augusto.

Now this is indeed *ignotum per ignotius*: for the cause of
Ovid's banishment is itself a mystery. Still, the allusion here is
clearly to a love-affair with a princess of high rank, such as
Ovid is supposed to have had with the younger Julia: and later
narrators of the story were only to tell more explicitly and in
detail the fatal passion of Tasso for Leonora d' Este, Alfonso's
sister. My only point is that here we have an Italian Court,
a Duke's sister entangled with a lover by birth beneath her, and
the imprisonment of the victim of family-pride among madmen.
The resemblance may surely have occurred to Webster, who
actually quotes a phrase of Tasso in the play.

There is also a second parallel, of Webster's own day, which
deserves passing mention. For while his audience watched *The
Duchess of Malfi*, some of them must have remembered the real
tragedy which was creeping to its close in the Tower, a few
minutes' walk away—whether Webster himself had thought of
it or not. For there in the Tower, imprisoned for the last three
years and with a mind now unhinged, lay Lady Arabella Stuart,
the cousin of the King, in punishment for her offence in wedding
Lord William Seymour. The pair had married secretly in the
summer of 1610. Seymour's birth, however, was not too low,
but too high; for he happened to be the one man in England
whom James dreaded as his cousin's husband, since he strengthened
yet further her claim to the crown. So they were both im-
prisoned, as soon as the secret came out, a few weeks after the
marriage. In 1611 they escaped from the Tower, but Arabella

was recaptured by her pursuers in mid-Channel, while she lingered there in her anxiety to assure herself of the safety of her husband's vessel. She was brought back to the Tower, went mad in her misery, and died in 1615: while Lord Seymour sheltered helplessly in Paris, like Antonio in Milan. I do not wish to exaggerate the resemblances, though it will be seen that there are several: but it is perhaps a little surprising that the authorities did not feel the subject of the persecuted Duchess a dangerous one for popular sympathy.

THE PLAY

The Duchess of Malfi seems the work of a dramatist definitely older, in mind as well as in years, than the creator of *The White Devil.* There is here a sadder, tenderer, less violent mood, of which the scenes where Giovanni mourns a lost mother and Cornelia a lost son, alone give a foretaste in the earlier play. The characters of *The Duchess of Malfi* come before us less brightly coloured, in a less dazzling world. The action pulses at less of a fever heat; and instead of the sunlight a-glitter on a flashing Mediterranean, we seem to watch the cypress shadows on the hillsides of Amalfi lengthen slowly towards the coming night. It is in the shadow of night, indeed, that scene after scene takes place: and a twilight seems to lie across the characters themselves. The innocent Antonio goes shuddering like a guilty soul through that harsh world where Paolo Giordano Orsini shouldered so unhesitatingly his superb and insolent way. Antonio sheds no man's blood: he shudders at the sight of his own. And in his Duchess likewise there is a tenderness such as Vittoria never knew. Hers is a sadder and more pensive, though not less undaunted, soul; and at the last, in her prison darkness gibbered around by madmen, she sits before us silently with the sad and terrible patience of a Mater Dolorosa. Here is no heroine who starts up before the tribunal in Rome to meet her day of judgment with defiance, in the proud consciousness that upon her are the eyes of the Ambassadors of Christendom and behind them the wide theatre of the world. And while

---

[1] Perhaps Pepys's mental disturbance was partly the cause of this unfavourable judgment: for a performance of the play on Sept. 30th 1662 is much more pleasantly recorded, and he had found it "pretty good" to read (Nov. 2nd and 6th 1666).

Vittoria dies, like a Roman Emperor, standing, her gentler counterpart. bows her head to the murderer's cord and kneels humbly before that cold star-lit heaven whence no hand stoops to save. The Duchess is the sister, indeed, of Isabella rather than Vittoria[1]. On the minor characters also the same twilight has fallen. Francisco Duke of Florence would never have died raving with the remorse of Duke Ferdinand, though the death of a dozen sisters lay crimson upon his soul. The bitter Monticelso toyed with no mistresses; we cannot hear him sue for mercy like the Cardinal of Aragon, or pray in death only to be laid by and forgotten. Even the black Zanche died like a queen, where the unhappy Cariola scratches and screams and lies to gain a moment longer of life. And, last of all, Bosola with his vexed refrain of "honest", his melancholy, his belated, ineffectual repentances, is but one more example, when we set him beside Flamineo, of the change of key which marks Webster's treatment of this, his second and last great work. It is not on its inferiority to *The White Devil* (though it does seem to me inferior) that I wish here to dwell; but simply on the deep difference of tone which goes together with the innumerable parallels of situation and idea to be found in these twin plays. And if *The Duchess of Malfi* is on the whole the weaker work, yet there are compensations. If the vigour is less, there is a new and gentler grace in the moments when Webster allows his tortured figures a little span of happiness. For we shall find nothing in *The White Devil* like that exquisite wooing of Antonio by the Duchess or the happy jesting of the married lovers on the eve of ruin. Here are new colours for Webster: it is as if these gleams of sudden sun cast a momentary rainbow across the driving spray of his fierce and wind-swept sea. And, again, with the relaxation of the writer's passionate energy, comes the deeper meditativeness of those passages of poetry which, far more justly than any garishness of dancing maniacs and dead men's hands, have made *The Duchess of Malfi* grow into the memories of men. There is no character in *The White Devil*

---

[1] To Kiesow the Duchess is "eine Schöpfung echt germanischen Geistes—der Typus für die Liebe germanischer Frauen." One may well object that the Duchess is not a "Typus", but a charming individual. But it illustrates the difference: not even Teutonic criticism (be it said without any disparagement of that indefatigable German scholarship which has done so much for our English drama) has yet tried to annex Vittoria.

Echo scene

that we can imagine brooding like Antonio over the ruined church at Milan with a sadness that recalls at once that of Hamlet over Yorick's skull and, with a strange anticipation, the *Elegy* of Gray. And similarly with the Echo-scene that follows. In itself but one instance among hundreds of a tiresome fashion of Renaissance ingenuity, in Webster's hands it becomes at once a thing apart from its tediously conceited fellows. If we ask what Webster could do that his contemporaries could not, the answer lies not in horror-scenes, but in such things as this. Yet this scene too could hardly have found a place in *The White Devil*; and if we ask what forms there its nearest counterpart, perhaps we may answer that Echo is the ghostly sister of the boy Giovanni—this Echo that cries its simple, artificial answers with the pathetic cleverness of a child, as it too laments a Duchess foully slain.

> *Del.* I told you 'twas a pretty one: You may make it
> A Huntes-man, or a Faulconer, a Musitian,
> Or a Thing of Sorrow.
> *Eccho. A Thing of Sorrow.*
> *Ant.* I sure: that suites it best.
> *Eccho. That suites it best.*

There is indeed something far ghostlier about this dream-scene than about any robust, top-booted apparition in *The White Devil*; as befits what is essentially the ghostlier play[1]. And it is as from a trance, at the end of it, that Antonio wakes to the real darkness round him, there to recall at last that essential courage which lies at the heart of both Webster's great plays alike.

And yet here too there is a difference. With the Duchess and Antonio it is the enduring courage of the martyr; not, as with Vittoria and Brachiano, the high spirit of the soldier who hews his way to death through the thickest of the battle. For, after all, what is left in such a world worth fighting for? This busy trade of life, which appears so vain only in the final moments of *The White Devil*, has the sense of its vanity, the doubt of all its values, stamped here on every page. Antonio, at the very

---

[1] This quality of *The Duchess of Malfi* makes particularly happy and appropriate Mr Waley's choice of it for transposition into the ghostly form of a Nō play. See Commentary on *D.M.* III. 4.

moment when love declares itself before him, questions, even though it be half-playfully, the worth of love itself and of the life it hands on to posterity. Imagine Brachiano, with his mistress before him, playing the theorizing sceptic thus! Here are no longer those strong hearts whose covenant with the world was so hard to break, to whom the name of death was "infinitely terrible". To the Duchess death has become the best gift her brothers can give; to Antonio, the yearned-for release from his long pain.

Such is the atmosphere, I feel, of *The Duchess of Malfi*—a profound, unalterable sadness. Melancholy has shrouded it in her shadow. Her name passes perpetually like a watchword across the lips of these sentinels who gaze wanly into the hopeless night and look only for relief. Bosola is "melancholy"; and Antonio and the Duchess become so; and her brother Ferdinand goes mad with it; and the Cardinal is haunted by it with the vision of a thing armed with a rake, that seems to strike at him from the fish-ponds in his garden, as he broods on the flames of Hell. We come indeed to feel that this phantom of insane melancholia pursues, like a hereditary curse, the last generation of the House of Aragon in Amalfi. And of such a tragedy the melancholy madmen are after all a fitting chorus: they are more than a mere episode in this play whose conclusion is not only death, but madness. Unity of tone—that one unity which the Romantics at their best have continued to respect—is surely accomplished here.

The creation of this atmosphere, its poetry, and two or three supreme scenes—these are the greatness of *The Duchess of Malfi*. The characters are less outstanding: and the plot has obvious weaknesses. It is indeed ridiculous to say with Charles Kingsley of the Duchess, that she is not a "person" at all. In her brief moments of sunshine, before the night closes on her, the Duchess shows vivid colours, though delicate ones. If in the gloom of the end there remains to her only the grey of fortitude, lit up at moments with the dull red of anger, there is surely no lack of reality in the charming, gay, spontaneous young sovereign of the earlier acts, whose "half-blush" so gracefully becomes her in the sudden wave of unneeded shame that follows her successful wooing. Happily we have emerged from an age when that wooing was felt to be "painful", and it was necessary to defend or excuse this figure of fresh, high-spirited youth for loving with the body as well as with the soul.

The fatal error of the Duchess—fault we cannot call it—is that she ever fell in love with Antonio. Weakness is the least dramatic of human qualities; and the play, as well as his mistress, suffers from its presence in him. We do not demand that every character shall be cast in heroic mould: but we blush uncomfortably at the scene where Antonio enters, pistol in hand, after the Duke has safely retired, only to bluster where he should have acted. The dagger left by Ferdinand has a handle, he cries to his mistress, as well as a point: but whose hand should grasp that hilt if not his own? We come to feel that Antonio is not good enough for the woman he has won. Perilous as his position was, hard as it might have been to ride out into the night after Duke Ferdinand and meet sword to sword the brother of his mistress, or to try to raise Amalfi in its Duchess's name, none the less a stouter heart would have found a better end. It is not physical cowardice: we have Bosola's word for it, in one of those Elizabethan speeches made by one character about another which are clearly meant to be taken by the audience as true, that Antonio was a good soldier. It is the initiative, the generalship that is fatally lacking. Antonio was better at managing horses than men. Because of this weakness he saves himself, always, only "by halves"; until in the end his life becomes worse than death. Soldier, courtier, lover, poet—only the poet in him succeeds in not leaving us cold. If we care for him beyond that, it is for his mistress's sake. Such as he is, for all his sensitiveness, a juster and a happier fate would have wedded him, not to the Duchess, but to Cariola.

After the Duchess, the only character that holds us is Bosola. He too has some of the weakness of his victim Antonio; his soul, unlike Flamineo's, is perpetually a house of Beelzebub divided against itself, and doomed thereby to fall. Conscience is sour in his mouth: and he is more human, not more real, than the reptile Flamineo simply in this, that his conscience turns his sting upon himself. His mixture of punctilio and unscrupulousness may seem unreal to the modern reader; it is not so to those who have a better knowledge of that age when *bravi* like the assassin of Troilo Orsini, with an artist's disinterestedness, refused all reward when their work was done.

We have even the story of a cut-throat who, being hired by one Italian to kill another, was offered a higher price by the victim to go back and murder his employer: he accepted; but insisted none the less, to the victim's horror, that his original contract must first be honourably fulfilled. So Bosola, while clearly sympathising with the Duchess and to some extent with Antonio, continues to earn his pay. He would be really honest, were he sure that such a thing as honesty existed. His mouth grows bitter with a genuine anger at the vices of courts which seem to belie all human goodness. Yet though unlike Flamineo he feels pity, he remains as helpless as Hamlet, his distant kinsman in the family of Malcontents, to carry it into effect. He is cynical, yet furious against hypocrisy; his insight avails to show him only his own and the world's degradation; too proud to flatter, he stoops to be a tool; and only when it is too late he deserts the side of sin, to earn the wages of death. The curse of the Stoic poet is upon him: his vision torments him with regret for the beauty of that goodness he has flung away. He dies as he lived:

> In a mist, I know not how.

Flamineo too dies "in a mist": but he did not live in one.

As for Duke Ferdinand, he is mainly what the plot requires him to be, an angry tyrant. Only a sudden flash here and there quickens the spectator's imagination to try to fathom him more deeply. It has been suggested to me that he is really in love with his sister. This is an ingenious idea, though it seems to me out of the question that Webster meant his audience to take that view. The analysis Ferdinand gives of his own motives at the end of Act IV, though muddled, is clearly intended to be accepted as true. An Elizabethan audience was simple[1] and would certainly have swallowed it. And if we to-day are apt to feel that his alleged motives are inadequate, it is partly that Webster has failed to make us conceive vividly enough the importance of the "infinite mass of treasure", by giving it more prominence; partly, that we find it difficult to imagine the violence of family pride in a sixteenth-century Spaniard or

---

[1] Cf. Tailor, *The Hog hath lost his Pearl*, I. I: "*Player.* I hope you have made no dark sentence in't; for, I'll assure you, our audience commonly are very simple, idle-headed people, and if they should hear what they understand not, they would quite forsake our house".

Italian. We have to realise that these things were different in an age and land in which, for instance, the six sons of Lelio Massimo, on their father's second marriage, entered the bridal-chamber next morning and shot the bride in bed, because she was a cast-off mistress of Marcantonio Colonna.

I do not believe, then, that Webster meant us to hunt for more motives in Ferdinand's heart than he has set in Ferdinand's mouth. And yet, when one reads *The Fair Maid of the Inn*, with its brother confessedly half-enamoured of his sister and passionately jealous of her lover[1], and then turns back to the frenzies with which Ferdinand (unlike the Cardinal) hears of his sister's seduction, the agonized remorse with which he sees her dead, it is hard to be positive that some such motive had never crossed Webster's own mind. It is merely a suggestion, and an inessential one; it can be taken or left; but it does not seem to me impossible in the part-author of *The Fair Maid of the Inn*, the friend and collaborator of John Ford.

The weakness of the play, however, lies clearly in its plot. It lives too long, when it outlives the heroine. Imagine if in *The White Devil* Vittoria had died before Brachiano; and yet even that would have been less fatal. The play goes well enough at first. The opening Act contains the exposition and then the fatal wooing; Act II the discovery of the Duchess's "guilt"; Act III the discovery also of Antonio's, followed by the lovers' flight; and Act IV the death of the Duchess. So far so good; unfortunately, as William Archer suavely puts it, "the play still drags its festering length through another Act", which consists of Antonio's murder, followed by the necessary poetic justice on the brothers and Bosola in their turn. Thus though there is less sub-plot, less irrelevant complication, than in *The White Devil*, the plot of *The Duchess of Malfi* has the far worse defect of reaching its natural end before the play. And yet, despite *longueurs*, even here Webster retains his gift of putting his most living poetry in the mouths of dying men. Its plot as a whole has added nothing to the greatness of *The Duchess of Malfi*: but neither can it destroy it. We turn back from the critics, from Lamb with his outcries of admiration, from Archer with his nibbling pedantries, from Stoll and Kiesow with their vision of

[1] Mainly in Ford and Massinger's part of the play: but cf. II. 4, which is Webster's; and again *D.L.* V. 2. 36.

the play as a warning of the awful results of marrying beneath one, to the poet himself.

> 'Tis weakenesse,
> Too much to thinke what should have bin done.

Let us be thankful for what has been—for this picture of a spirit that faces the cold shining of the stars with none of Pascal's terror before their infinite silence, and the mopping and mowing of the demented world around it with a calm that prosperity could not give, nor disaster take away.

Note.—There still seems to persist in some critics a notion that we are to think the Duchess in some way blameworthy for wedding Antonio, and in some degree deserving of her fate. There are people whose mouths are always watering for "poetic justice", with the same paltry puritanism as enraged Job in his comforters. But life is often poignant with injustice; why not poetry?

No doubt it could be argued that the Duchess to some extent forgot her duty to her subjects in Amalfi; but this aspect does not enter Webster's mind. No doubt she was rash; but life can bring crises when—

> He either fears his fate too much,
> Or his deserts are small,
> That dares not put it to the touch,
> To gain or lose it all.

Surely, since fairy-tales began, honest human sympathy has gone out to the young adventurer who wins his princess; even though he might be a squire of low degree. Neither Boccaccio nor Keats pursed their lips at the Isabella of "The Pot of Basil" for loving her rich brothers' employee. Webster's own view of his characters stands, I think, clear enough in the portraits of Duke, Cardinal, and Duchess painted in i. i. 153–214; and his ultimate verdict I take to be the same as Cariola's—

> Whether the spirit of greatnes, or of woman
> Raigne most in her, I know not, but it shewes
> A fearefull madnes. I owe her much of pitty.

"Madness", perhaps; but a madness in no way ignoble.

THE
TRAGEDY
OF THE DVTCHESSE
Of Malfy.

As it was Prefented priuatly, at the Black-
Friers; and publiquely at the Globe, By the
Kings Maiefties Seruants.

The perfeĉt and exaĉt Coppy, with diuerfe
things Printed, that the length of the Play would
not beare in the Prefentment.

VVritten by *John Webfter.*

Hora.——*Si quid——*
——*Candidus Imperti fi non his vtere mecum.*

LONDON:

Printed by NICHOLAS OKES, for IOHN
WATERSON, and are to be fold at the
figne of the Crowne, in *Paules*
Church-yard, 1 6 2 3.

The Actors Names.

BOSOLA, *J. Lowin.*
FERDINAND, 1 *R. Burbidge.* 2 *J. Taylor.*
CARDINALL, 1 *H. Cundaile.* 2 *R. Robinson.*
ANTONIO, 1 *W. Ostler.* 2 *R. Benfeild.*
DELIO, *J. Underwood.*
FOROBOSCO, *N. Towley.*
MALATESTE.
The *Marquesse of* Pescara, *J. Rice.*
SILVIO, *T. Pollard.*
[CASTRUCHIO.]
[RODERIGO.]
[GRISOLAN.]
The *severall mad men, N. Towley. J. Underwood, &c.*
The DUTCHESSE, *R. Sharpe.*
The CARDINALS Mis. *J. Tomson.*
The DOCTOR,⎫
CARIOLA,   ⎬ *R. Pallant.*
COURT OFFICERS.
[*Old Lady.*]
Three *young Children.*
Two *Pilgrimes.*
[*Ladies, Executioners, and Attendants.*]

TO THE RIGHT HONORABLE, *GEORGE*

HARDING, *Baron* Barkeley, *of* Barkeley
Castle and Knight of the Order of the *Bathe*
To the Illustrious Prince C H A R L E S.

My Noble Lord,

T*HAT I may present my excuse, why, (being a stranger to your Lordshippe) I offer this Poem to your Patronage, I plead this warrant; Men (who never saw the Sea, yet desire to behold that regiment of waters,) choose some eminent River, to guide them thither; and make that as it were, their Conduct, or* Postilion: *By the like ingenious meanes, has your* fame *arrived at my knowledge, receiving it from some of worth, who both in* contemplation, *and* practise, *owe to your* Honor *their clearest service. I do not altogether looke up at your* Title: *The ancien'st* Nobility, *being but a* rellique *of time past, and the truest* 10 Honor *indeede beeing for a man to conferre* Honor *on himselfe, which your* Learning *strives to propagate, and shall make you arrive at the* Dignity *of a great* Example. *I am confident this worke is not unworthy your* Honors *perusal for by such* Poems *as this,* Poets *have kist the hands of* Great Princes, *and drawne their gentle eyes to looke downe upon their sheetes of paper, when the* Poets *themselves were bound up in their winding-sheetes. The like curtesie from your* Lordship, *shall make you live in your grave, and* laurell *spring out of it; when the ignorant scorners of the* Muses *(that like wormes in* Libraries, *seeme to live onely to destroy* 20 learning*) shall wither, neglected, and forgotten. This worke and my selfe I humbly present to your approved censure. It being the utmost of my wishes, to have your Honorable selfe my weighty and perspicuous* Comment: *which grace so done me, shall ever be acknowledged*

> *By your Lordships*
> *in all duty and*
> *Observance,*

John Webster.

In the just Worth, of that well Deserver,
M[r]. JOHN WEBSTER, *and Upon this*
Maister-peece of Tragœdy.

I N this Thou imitat'st one Rich, and Wise,
   That sees His Good Deedes done before he dies;
   As He by Workes, Thou by this Worke of Fame,
Hast well provided for thy Living Name;
To trust to others Honorings, is Worth's Crime,
Thy Monument is rais'd in thy Life Time;
And 'tis most just; for every Worthy Man
Is his owne Marble; and his Merit can
Cut Him to any Figure, and expresse
More Art, then Deaths Cathedrall Pallaces,
Where Royall Ashes keepe their Court: thy Note
Be ever Plainnes, 'tis the Richest Coate:
Thy Epitaph onely the Title *bee,*
Write, Dutchesse, *that will fetch a teare for thee,*
For who e're saw this Dutchesse *live, and dye,*
That could get off under a Bleeding Eye?

10

In Tragædiam.

Ut Lux ex Tenebris ictu percussa TONANTIS;
Illa, (*Ruina Malis*) *claris fit vita Poetis.*

Thomas Middletonus,
Poëta & Chron:
Londinensis.

To his friend M^r. *John Webster*
Upon his Dutchesse
of *Malfy.*

I Never saw thy Dutchesse, till the day,
That She was lively body'd in thy Play;
How'ere she answer'd her low-rated Love,
Her brothers anger did so fatall proove,
Yet my opinion is, she might speake more;
But never (in her life) so well before.

WIL: ROWLEY.

To the Reader of the Authour,
and his Dutchesse of *Malfy.*

CRowne Him a Poet, whom nor Rome, *nor* Greece,
Transcend in all theirs, for a Master-peece:
In which, whiles words and matter change, and Men
Act one another; Hee, from whose cleare Pen
They All tooke life, To Memory hath lent
A lasting Fame, to raise his Monument.

JOHN FORD

Actus Primus. Scena Prima.

[Amalfi. The Palace of the Duchess.]

[Enter Antonio and Delio.]

DELIO.

YOU are wel-come to your Country (deere *Antonio*)
   You have bin long in *France*, and you returne
   A very formall French-man, in your habit.
How doe you like the French Court?
  ANT. I admire it—
In seeking to reduce both State, and People
To a fix'd Order, the[ir] juditious King
Begins at home: Quits first his Royall Pallace
Of flattring Sicophants, of dissolute,
And infamous persons—which he sweetely termes   10
His Masters Master-peece (the worke of Heaven)
Considring duely, that a Princes Court
Is like a common Fountaine, whence should flow
Pure silver-droppes in generall: But if 't chance
Some curs'd example poyson't neere the head,
"Death, and diseases through the whole land spread.
And what is't makes this blessed government,
But a most provident Councell, who dare freely
Informe him the corruption of the times?
Though some oth'Court hold it presumption   20
To instruct Princes what they ought to doe,
It is a noble duety to informe them
What they ought to fore-see: Here comes *Bosola* [Enter Bosola.]
The onely Court-Gall: yet I observe his rayling
Is not for simple love of Piety:
Indeede he rayles at those things which he wants,
Would be as leacherous, covetous, or proud,
Bloody, or envious, as any man,
If he had meanes to be so: Here's the Cardinall. [Enter Cardinal.]
  BOS. I doe haunt you still.   30
  CAR. So.

Bos. I have done you better service then to be slighted thus: miserable age, where onely the reward of doing well, is the doing of it!

Car. You inforce your merrit to[o] much.

Bos. I fell into the Gallies in your service, where, for two yeares together, I wore two Towells in stead of a shirt, with a knot on the shoulder, after the fashion of a Romaine Mantle: Slighted thus? I will thrive some way: black-birds fatten best 40 in·hard weather: why not I, in these dogge dayes?

Car. Would you could become honest—

Bos. With all your divinity, do but direct me the way to it—I have knowne many travell farre for it, and yet returne as arrant knaves, as they went forth; because they carried themselves alwayes along with them; [Exit Cardinal.] Are you gon? Some fellowes (they say) are possessed with the divell, but this great fellow, were able to possesse the greatest Divell, and make him worse.

Ant. He hath denied thee some suit?

50 Bos. He, and his brother, are like Plum-trees (that grow crooked over standing-pooles) they are rich, and ore-laden with Fruite, but none but Crowes, Pyes, and Catter-pillers feede on them: Could I be one of their flattring Panders, I would hang on their eares like a horse-leach, till I were full, an[d] then droppe off: I pray leave me.

Who wold relie upon these miserable dependances, in expectation to be advanc'd to-morrow? what creature ever fed worse, then hoping *Tantalus*? nor ever died any man more fearefully, then he that hop'd for a pardon: There are rewards for hawkes, 60 and dogges, ∧ when they have done us service; but for a Souldier, that hazards his Limbes in a battaile, nothing but a kind of Geometry, is his last Supportation.

Del. Geometry?

Bos. I, to hang in a faire paire of slings, take his latter-swinge in the world, upon an honorable pare of Crowtches, from hospitall to hospitall—fare ye well Sir. And yet do not you scorne us, for places in the Court, are but [like] beds in the hospitall, where this mans head lies at that mans foote, and so lower, and lower.   [*Exit.*]

70 Del. I knew this fellow (seaven yeares) in the Gallies, For a notorious murther, and 'twas thought

The Cardinall suborn'd it: he was releas'd
By the French Generall (*Gaston de Foux*)
When he recover'd *Naples*.
    A n t. 'Tis great pitty
He should be thus neglected—I have heard
He's very valiant: This foule mellancholly
Will poyson all his goodnesse, for (i'le tell you)
If too immoderate sleepe be truly sayd
To be an inward rust unto the soule;   80
It then doth follow want of action
Breeds all blacke male-contents, and their close rearing
(Like mothes in cloath) doe hurt for want of wearing.

     [*Enter Silvio, Castruchio, Roderigo, & Grisolan.*]

    D e l. The Presence 'gins to fill, you promis'd me
To make me the partaker of the natures
Of some of your great Courtiers.
    A n t. The Lord Cardinall's
And other strangers', that are now in Court?—
I shall: here comes the great *Calabrian* Duke. [*Enter Ferdinand.*]
    F e r d. Who tooke the Ring oftnest?   90
    S i l. *Antoni*[o] *Bologna* (my Lord.)
    F e r d. Our Sister Duchesse' great Master of her houshold?
Give him the Jewell: when shall we leave this sportive-action,
and fall to action indeed?
    C a s t. Me thinkes (my Lord) you should not desire to go to
war, in person.
    F e r. Now, for some gravity: why (my Lord?)
    C a s t. It is fitting a Souldier arise to be a Prince, but not
necessary a Prince descend to be a Captaine.
    F e r d. Noe?   100
    C a s t. No, (my Lord) he were far better do it by a Deputy.
    F e r d. Why should he not as well sleepe, or eate, by a Deputy?
This might take idle, offensive, and base office from him, whereas
the other deprives him of honour.
    C a s t. Beleeve my experience: that Realme is never long in
quiet, where the Ruler, is a Souldier.
    F e r d. Thou toldst me thy wife could not endure fighting.
    C a s t. True (my Lord.)

F[ER]D. And of a jest, she broke of a Captaine she met, full
110 of wounds: I have forgot it.

CAST. She told him (my Lord) he was a pittifull fellow, to
lie, like the Children of *Ismael*, all in Tents.

FERD. Why, there's a wit were able to undoe all the Chyr-
urgeons o'the City, for although Gallants should quarrell, and
had drawne their weapons, and were ready to goe to it; yet her
perswasions would make them put up.

CAST. That she would (my Lord)—How doe you like my
Spanish Gennit?

ROD. He is all fire.

120 FERD. I am of *Pliney's* opinion, I thinke he was begot by
the wind, he runs, as if he were ballass'd with Quick-silver.

SIL. True (my Lord) he reeles from the Tilt often.

ROD. GRIS. Ha, ha, ha.

FERD. Why do you laugh? Me thinks you that are Courtiers
should be my touch-wood, take fire, when I give fire; that is,
laugh when I laugh, were the subject never so wity—

CAST. True (my Lord) I my selfe have heard a very good
jest, and have scorn'd to seeme to have so silly a wit, as to understand it.

130 FERD. But I can laugh at your Foole (my Lord.)

CAST. He cannot speake (you know) but he makes faces, my
lady cannot abide him.

FERD. Noe?

CAST. Nor endure to be in merry Company: for she saies
too much laughing, and too much Company, fils her too full of
the wrinckle.

FERD. I would then have a Mathematicall Instrument made
for her face, that she might not laugh out of compasse: I shall
shortly visit you at *Millaine* (Lord *Silvio*.)

140 SIL. Your Grace shall arrive most wel-come.

FERD. You are a good Horse-man (*Antonio*) you have excellent Riders in *France*—what doe you thinke of good Horse-
man-ship?

ANT. Noblely (my Lord)—as out of the Grecian-horse,
issued many famous Princes: So, out of brave Horse-man-ship,
arise the first Sparkes of growing resolution, that raise the minde
to noble action.

FERD. You have be-spoake it worthely.

Sil. Your brother, the Lord Cardinall, and sister Dutchesse.
     [*Enter Cardinal, Duchess, Cariola, & Julia.*]
Card. Are the Gallies come about?   150
Gris. They are (my Lord.)
Ferd. Here's the Lord *Silvio*, is come to take his leave.
Del. Now (Sir) your promise: what's that Cardinall?
I meane his Temper? they say he's a brave fellow,
Will play his five thousand crownes, at Tennis, Daunce,
Court Ladies, and one that hath fought single Combats.
Ant. Some such flashes superficially hang on him, for forme:
but observe his inward Character: he is a mellancholly Church-
man: The Spring in his face, is nothing but the Ingendring of
Toades: where he is jealous of any man, he laies worse plots 160
for them, then ever was impos'd on *Hercules*: for he strewes
in his way Flatter[er]s, Panders, Intelligencers, Athiests, and a
thousand such politicall Monsters: he should have beene Pope:
but in stead of comming to it by the primative decensie of the
church, he did bestow bribes, so largely, and so impudently, as
if he would have carried it away without heavens knowledge.
Some good he hath done.
Del. You have given too much of him: what's his brother?
Ant. The Duke there? a most perverse, and turbulent
     Nature—
What appeares in him mirth, is meerely outside,   170
If he laugh hartely, it is to laugh
All honesty out of fashion.
Del. Twins?
Ant. In qualitie:
He speakes with others Tongues, and heares mens suites,
With others Eares: will seeme to sleepe o'th bench
Onely to intrap offenders, in their answeres;
Doombes men to death, by information,
Rewards, by heare-say.
Del. Then the Law to him   180
Is like a fowle blacke cob-web, to a Spider—
He makes it his dwelling, and a prison
To entangle those shall feede him.
Ant. Most true:
He nev'r paies debts, unlesse they be [shrewd] turnes,
And those he will confesse that he doth owe.

Last: for his brother, there, (the Cardinall)
They that doe flatter him most, say Oracles
Hang at his lippes: and verely I beleeve them:
190 For the Divell speakes in them.
　　But for their sister, (the right noble Duchesse)
You never fix'd you[r] eye on three faire Meddalls,
Cast in one figure, of so different temper:
For her discourse, it is so full of Rapture,
You onely will begin, then to be sorry
When she doth end her speech: and wish (in wonder)
She held it lesse vaine-glory, to talke much,
Then [you] pennance, to heare her: whilst she speakes,
She throwes upon a man so sweet a looke,
200 That it were able raise one to a Galliard
That lay in a dead palsey; and to doate
On that sweete countenance: but in that looke,
There speaketh so divine a continence,
As cuts off all lascivious, and vaine hope.
Her dayes are practis'd in such noble vertue,
That sure her nights (nay more her very Sleepes)
Are more in Heaven, then other Ladies Shrifts.
Let all sweet Ladies breake their flattring Glasses,
And dresse themselves in her.
210　　DEL. Fye *Antoni*[o],
You play the wire-drawer with her commendations.
　　ANT. I'll case the picture up: onely thus much—
All her particular worth growes to this somme:
She staines the time past: lights the time to come—
　　CARIOLA. You must attend my Lady, in the gallery,
Some halfe an houre hence.
　　ANT. I shall.　　　　　　[*Exeunt Antonio & Delio.*]
　　FERD. Sister, I have a suit to you:
　　DUCH. To me, Sir?
220　　FERD. A Gentleman here: *Daniel de Bosola*:
One, that was in the Gallies.
　　DUCH. Yes, I know him:
　　FERD. A worthy fellow h'is: pray let me entreat for
The provisorship of your horse.
　　DUCH. Your knowledge of him,
Commends him, and prefers him.

FERD. Call him heither,   [*Exit Servant.*]
Wee [are] now upon parting: Good Lord *Silvio*
Do us commend to all our noble friends
At the League[r].   230
    SIL. Sir, I shall.
    [DUCH.] You are for *Millaine*?
    SIL. I am:
    DUCH. Bring the Carroches: we'll bring you down to the
        Haven.   [*Exeunt, except Card. & Ferd.*
    CAR. Be sure you entertaine that *Bosola*
For your Intelligence: I would not be seene in't.
And therefore many times I have slighted him,
When he did court our furtherance: as this Morning.
    FERD. *Antonio*, the great Master of her houshold
Had beene farre fitter: 240
    CARD. You are deceiv'd in him,
His Nature is too honest for such businesse,
He comes: I'll leave you: [*Exit. Enter Bosola.*]
    BOS. I was lur'd to you.
    FERD. My brother here (the Cardinall) could never abide you.
    BOS. Never since he was in my debt.
    FERD. May be some oblique character in your face,
Made him suspect you?
    BOS. Doth he study Phisiognomie?
There's no more credit to be given to th'face,   250
Then to a sicke mans uryn, which some call
The Physitians whore, because she cozens him:
He did suspect me wrongfully:
    FERD. For that
You must give great men leave to take their times:
Distrust, doth cause us seldome be deceiv'd;
You see, the oft shaking of the Cedar-Tree
Fastens it more at roote.
    BOS. Yet take heed:
For to suspect a friend unworthely,   260
Instructs him the next way to suspect you,
And prompts him to deceive you.
    [F]ERD. There's gold.
    BOS. So:
What followes? (Never raind such showres as these

Without thunderbolts i'th taile of them;) whose throat must I cut?

FERD. Your inclination to shed blood rides post
Before my occasion to use you: I give you that
To live i'th Court, here: and observe the Duchesse,
270 To note all the particulars of her haviour:
What suitors doe sollicite her for marriage
And whom she best affects: she's a yong widowe,
I would not have her marry againe.

Bos. No, Sir?

FERD. Doe not you aske the reason: but be satisfied,
I say I would not.

Bos. It seemes you would create me
One of your familiars.

FERD. Familiar? what's that?

280   Bos. Why, a very quaint invisible Divell, in flesh:
An Intelligencer.

FERD. Such a kind of thriving thing
I would wish thee: and ere long, thou maist arrive
At a higher place by't.

Bos. Take your Divels
Which Hell calls Angels: these curs'd gifts would make
You a corrupter, me an impudent traitor,
And should I take these, they'll'd take me [to] Hell.

FER. Sir, I'll take nothing from you, that I have given:
290 There is a place, that I procur'd for you
This morning: (the Provisor-ship o'th' horse)—
Have you heard o[n']t?

Bos. Noe.

FER. 'Tis yours, is't not worth thankes?

Bos. I would have you curse your selfe now, that your bounty
(Which makes men truly noble) ere should make
Me a villaine: oh, that to avoid ingratitude
For the good deed you have done me, I must doe
All the ill man can invent: Thus the Divell
300 Candies all sinnes [o'er]: and what Heaven termes vild,
That names he complementall.

FER. Be your selfe:
Keepe your old garbe of melencholly: 'twill expresse
You envy those that stand above your reach,
Yet strive not to come neere'em: This will gaine

Accesse, to private lodgings, where your selfe
May (like a pollitique dormouse—.
   Bos. As I have seene some,
Feed in a Lords dish, halfe asleepe, not seeming
To listen to any talke: and yet these Rogues   310
Have cut his throat in a dreame: whats my place?
The Provisor-ship o'th horse? say then my corruption
Grew out of horse-doong: I am your creature.
   Ferd. Away!
   Bos. Let good men, for good deeds, covet good fame,
Since place, and riches oft are bribes of shame—
Sometimes the Divell doth preach.   *Exit Bosola.*
            [*Enter Cardinal, Duchess, & Cariola.*]
   Card. We are to part from you: and your owne discretion.
Must now be your director.
   Ferd. You are a Widowe: 320
You know already what man is: and therefore
Let not youth...high promotion, eloquence—
   Card. No, nor any thing without the addition, *Honor*,
Sway your high blood.
   Ferd. Marry? they are most luxurious,
Will wed twice.
   Card. O fie!
   Ferd. Their livers are more spotted
Then *Labans* sheepe.
   Duch. Diamonds are of most value   330
They say, that have past through most Jewellers hands.
   Ferd. Whores, by that rule, are precious:
   Duch. Will you heare me?
I'll never marry:
   Card. So most Widowes say:
But commonly that motion lasts no longer
Then the turning of an houreglasse—the funeral Sermon,
And it, end both together.
   Ferd. Now heare me:
You live in a ranke pasture here, i'th Court—   340
There is a kind of honney-dew, that's deadly:
'Twill poyson your fame; looke [to]'t: be not cunning:
For they whose faces doe belye their hearts,
Are Witches, ere they arrive at twenty yeeres,

I: and give the divell sucke.

DUCH. This is terrible good councell:

FERD. Hypocrisie is woven of a fine small thred,
Subtler, then *Vulcans* Engine: yet (beleev²t)
Your darkest actions: nay, your privat'st thoughts,
350 Will come to light.

CARD. You may flatter your selfe,
And take vour owne choice: privately be married
Under the E[a]ves of night...

FERD. Think't the best voyage
That ere you made; like the irregular Crab,
Which though't goes backward, thinkes that it goes right,
Because it goes its owne way: but observe;
Such weddings, may more properly be said
To be executed, then celibrated.

360 CARD. The marriage night
Is the entrance into some prison.

FERD. And those joyes,
Those lustfull pleasures, are like heavy sleepes
Which doe fore-run mans mischiefe.

CARD. Fare you well.
Wisdome begins at the end: remember it.   [*Exit*.]

DUCH. I thinke this speech betweene you both was studied,
It came so roundly off.

FERD. You are my sister,
370 This was my Fathers poyniard: doe you see,
I'll'd be loth to see't looke rusty, 'cause 'twas his:
I would have you to give ore these chargeable Revels;
A Vizor, and a Masque are whispering roomes
That were nev'r built for goodnesse: fare ye well:
And woemen like that part, which (like the Lamprey)
Hath nev'r a bone in't.

DUCH. Fye Sir!

FERD. Nay,
I meane the Tongue: varietie of Courtship;
380 What cannot a neate knave with a smooth tale,
Make a woman beleeve? farewell, lusty Widowe.   [*Exit*.]

DUCH. Shall this move me? if all my royall kindred
Lay in my way unto this marriage:
I'll'd make them my low foote-steps: And even now,

Even in this hate (as men in some great battailes
By apprehending danger, have atchiev'd
Almost impossible actions: I have heard Souldiers say so),
So I, through frights, and threatnings, will assay
This dangerous venture: Let old wives report
I wincked, and chose a husband: *Cariola*,   390
To thy knowne secricy, I have given up
More then my life, my fame:
   CAR[IOL]A. Both shall be safe:
For I'll conceale this secret from the world
As warily as those that trade in poyson,
Keepe poyson from their children.
   DUCH. Thy protestation
Is ingenious, and hearty: I beleeve it.
Is *Antonio* come?
   CARIOLA. He attends you: 400
   DUCH. Good deare soule,
Leave me: but place thy selfe behind the Arras,
Where thou maist over-heare us: wish me good speed   [*Cariola*
For I am going into a wildernesse,   *withdraws behind*
Where I shall find nor path, nor friendly clewe   *the arras.*
To be my guide—I sent for you, Sit downe: *The Duchess*
Take Pen and Incke, and write: are you ready?   *draws the*
   ANT. Yes: *traverse*
   DUCH. What did I say?   *revealing Antonio.*]
   ANT. That I should write some-what.   410
   DUCH. Oh, I remember:
After [these] triumphs, and this large expence
It's fit (like thrifty husbands) we enquire
What's laid up for to-morrow:
   ANT. So please your beauteous Excellence.
   DUCH. Beauteous?
Indeed I thank you: I look yong for your sake.
You have tane my cares upon you.
   ANT. I'le fetch your Grace
The particulars of your revinew, and expence.   420
   DUCH. Oh, you are an upright treasurer: but you mistooke,
For when I said I meant to make enquiry,
What's layd up for to-morrow: I did meane
What's layd up yonder for me.

Ant. Where?

Duch. In Heaven,
I am making my will, (as 'tis fit Princes should
In perfect memory) and I pray Sir, tell me
Were not one better make it smiling, thus?
430 Then in deepe groanes, and terrible ghastly lookes,
As if the guifts we parted with, procur'd
That violent distr[a]ction?

Ant. Oh, much better.

Duch. If I had a husband now, this care were quit:
But I intend to make yo[u] Over-seer;
What good deede, shall we first remember? say.

Ant. Begin with that first good deed began i'th'world,
After mans creation, the Sacrament of marriage—
I'ld have you first provide for a good husband,
440 Give him all.

Duch. All?

Ant. Yes, your excellent selfe.

Duch. In a winding sheete?

Ant. In a cople.

Duch. St. Win[i]frid, that were a strange will.

Ant. 'Twere strange
If there were no will in you to marry againe.

Duch. What doe you thinke of marriage?

Ant. I take't, as those that deny Purgatory,
450 It locally containes, or heaven, or hell,
There's no third place in't.

Duch. How doe you affect it?

Ant. My banishment, feeding my mellancholly,
Would often reason thus.

Duch. Pray let's heare it.

Ant. Say a man never marry, nor have children,
What takes that from him? onely the bare name
Of being a father, or the weake delight
To see the little wanton ride a cocke-horse
460 Upon a painted sticke, or heare him chatter
Like a taught Starling.

Duch. Fye, fie, what's all this?
One of your eyes is blood-shot, use my Ring to't,
They say 'tis very soveraigne, 'twas my wedding Ring,

And I did vow never to part with it,
But to my second husband.
    ANT. You have parted with it now.
    DUCH. Yes, to helpe your eye-sight.
    ANT. You have made me starke blind.
    DUCH. How?   470
    ANT. There is a sawcy, and ambitious divell
Is dauncing in this circle.
    DUCH. Remoove him.
    ANT. How?
    DUCH. There needs small conjuration, when your finger
May doe it: thus, is it fit?
    ANT. What sayd you?   *he kneeles*
    DUCH. Sir,
This goodly roofe of yours, is too low built,
I cannot stand upright in't, nòr discourse,   480
Without I raise it higher: raise your selfe,
Or if you please, my hand to helpe you: so.
    ANT. Ambition (Madam) is a great mans madnes,
That is not kept in chaines, and close-pent-roomes,
But in faire lightsome lodgings, and is girt
With the wild noyce of pratling visitan[t]s,
Which makes it lunatique, beyond all cure—
Conceive not, I am so stupid, but I ayme
Whereto your favours tend: But he's a foole
That (being a-cold) would thrust his hands i'th'fire   490
To warme them.
    DUCH. So, now the ground's broake,
You may discover what a wealthy Mine,
I make you Lord [of].
    ANT. Oh my unworthinesse.
    DUCH. You were ill to sell your selfe,
This darkning of your worth, is not like that
Which trades-men use i'th'City—their false lightes
Are to rid bad wares off: and I must tell you
If you will know where breathes a compleat man,   500
(I speake it without flattery) turne your eyes,
And progresse through your selfe.
    ANT. Were there nor heaven, nor hell,
I should be honest: I have long serv'd vertue,

And nev'r tane wages of her.

DUCH. Now she paies it—
The misery of us, that are borne great!—
We are forc'd to wo[o], because none dare wo[o] us:
And as a Tyrant doubles with his words,
510 And fearefully equivocates: so we
Are forc'd to expresse our violent passions
In ridles, and in dreames, and leave the path
Of simple vertue, which was never made
To seeme the thing it is not: Goe, go brag
You have left me heartlesse—mine is in your.bosome,
I hope 'twill multiply love there: You doe tremble:
Make not your heart so dead a peece of flesh
To feare, more then to love me: Sir, be confident,
What is't distracts you? This is flesh, and blood, (Sir,)
520 'Tis not the figure cut in Allablaster
Kneeles at my husbands tombe: Awake, awake (man)
I do here put of[f] all vaine ceremony,
And onely doe appeare to you a yong widow
That claimes you for her husband, and like a widow,
I use but halfe a blush in't.

ANT. Truth speake for me,
I will remaine the constant Sanctuary
Of your good name.

DUCH. I thanke you (gentle love)
530 And 'cause you shall not come to me in debt,
(Being now my Steward) here upon your lippes
I signe your *Quietus est*: This you should have beg'd now,
I have seene children oft eate sweete-meates thus,
As fearefull to devoure them too soone.

ANT. But for your Brothers?

DUCH. Do not thinke of them,
All discord, without this circumference,   [*she puts her arms*
Is onely to be pittied, and not fear'd: *about him.*]
Yet, should they know it, time will easily
540 Scatter the tempest.

ANT. These words should be mine,
And all the parts you have spoke, if some part of it
Would not have savour'd flattery.

DUCH. Kneele.   [*Cariola shows herself.*]

ANT. Hah?

DUCH. Be not amaz'd, this woman's of my Councell,
I have heard Lawyers say, a contract in a Chamber,
(*Per verba* [de] *presenti*) is absolute marriage:
Blesse (Heaven) this sacred Gordian, which let violence
Never untwine.   550

ANT. And may our sweet affections, (like the Sphears)
Be still in motion.

DUCH. Quickning, and make
The like soft Musique.

ANT. That we may imitate the loving Palmes
(Best Embleme of a peacefull marriage)
That nev'r bore fruite devided.

DUCH. What can the Church force more?

ANT. That Fortune may not know an accident
Either of joy, or sorrow, to devide   560
Our fixed wishes.

DUCH. How can the Church build faster?
We now are man, and wife, and 'tis the Church
That must but eccho this: Maid, stand apart,
I now am blinde.

ANT. What's your conceit in this?

DUCH. I would have you leade your Fortune by the hand,
Unto your marriage bed:
(You speake in me this, for we now are one)
We'll onely lie, and talke together, and plot   570
T'appease my humorous kindred; and if you please
(Like the old tale, in *Alexander* and *Lodowicke*)
Lay a naked sword betweene us, keepe us chast:
Oh, let me shrowd my blushes in your bosome,
Since 'tis the treasury of all my secrets.

CAR. Whether the spirit of greatnes, or of woman
Raigne most in her, I know not, but it shewes
A fearefull madnes. I owe her much of pitty.   *Exeunt.*

ACTUS II. SCENA I.

[The Same.]

[Enter Bosola & Castruchio.]

Bos. You say you would faine be taken—for an eminent
Courtier?

Cast. 'Tis the very maine of my ambition.

Bos. Let me see, you have a reasonable good face for't
already, and your night-cap expresses your eares sufficient largely
—I would have you learne to twirle the strings of your band
with a good grace; and in a set speech, (at th'end of every
sentence,) to hum, three, or foure times, or blow your nose (till
it smart againe,) to recover your memory—when you come to
10 be a president in criminall causes, if you smile upon a prisoner,
hang him, but if you frowne upon him, and threaten him, let
him be sure to scape the Gallowes.

Cast. I would be a very merrie president—

Bos. Do not sup a nights, 'twill beget you an admirable wit.

Cast. Rather it would make me have a good stomake to
quarrel, for they say, your roaring-boyes eate meate seldome,
and that makes them so valiant: but how shall I know whether
the people take me for an eminent fellow?

Bos. I will teach a tricke to know it—give out you lie a-
20 dying, and if you heare the common people curse you, be sure
you are taken for one of the prime night-caps— *[Enter Old Lady.]*
You come from painting now?

Old Lady. From what?

Bos. Why, from your scurvy face-physicke—to behold thee
not painted enclines somewhat neere a miracle: These...in thy
face here, were deepe rutts, and foule sloughes the last progresse:
There was a Lady in *France*, that having had the small pockes,
flead the skinne off her face, to make it more levell; and whereas
before she look'd like a Nutmeg-grater, after she resembled an
30 abortive hedge-hog.

Old Lady. Do you call this painting?

Bos. No, no, but [I] call [it] carreening of an old morphew'd
Lady, to make her disembogue againe—There's rough-cast
phrase to your plastique.

Information Literacy

Introduction to Research Da

EASTERN CONNECTICUT STATE UNIVERSITY

J. Eugene Smith Library

ADMISSIONS   ACADEMICS   ADMINISTRATION   ATHLETI

Text Only Version

About the Library

Hours

Important Phone Numbers

Departments

Staff Directory

Policies

Library Home

Pathways to:
Major Eastern Sites

Search the catalog:
[   ] Search

Find Information

Online Catalog - CONSULS

Databases (articles, images)

Journal Locator

Government Documents

Course Reserves

Research Guides

Getting Help

Ask a Librarian

Getting Started

Login to your libra

PIN Codes

Suggestion Box

Services

Alumni/Community Resources

EasternOnline Resources

Borrowing

Faculty Resources

Interlibrary Loan

Reserve Forms

Information Lite

EASTERN
CONNECTICUT
STATE UNIVERSITY

OLD LADY. It seemes you are well acquainted with my closset?

BOS. One would suspect it for a shop of witch-craft, to finde in it the fat of Serpents; spawne of Snakes, Jewes spittle, and their yong children['s] ordures—and all these for the face: I would sooner eate a dead pidgeon, taken from the soles of the 40 feete of one sicke of the plague, then kisse one of you fasting: here are two of you, whose sin of your youth is the very patrimony of the Physition, makes him renew his foote-cloth with the Spring, and change his high-priz'd curtezan with the fall of the leafe: I do wonder you doe not loath your selves—observe my meditation now:
What thing is in this outward forme of man
To be belov'd? we account it ominous,
If Nature doe produce a Colt, or Lambe,
A Fawne, or Goate, in any limbe resembling   50
A Man; and flye from't as a prodegy.
Man stands amaz'd to see his deformity,
In any other Creature but himselfe.
But in our owne flesh, though we beare diseases
Which have their true names onely tane from beasts,
As the most ulcerous Woolfe, and swinish Meazeall;
Though we are eaten up of lice, and wormes,
And though continually we beare about us
A rotten and dead body, we delight
To hide it in rich tissew—all our feare,   60
(Nay all our terrour) is, least our Phisition
Should put us in the ground, to be made sweete.
Your wife's gone to *Rome*: you two cople, and get you
To the wels at *Leuca*, to recover your aches. [*Exeunt Castruchio*
I have other worke on foote: I observe our Duchesse   *& Old*
Is sicke a dayes, she puykes, her stomacke seethes,   *Lady.*]
The fins of her eie-lids looke most teeming blew,
She waines i'th'cheeke, and waxes fat i'th'flanke;
And (contrary to our *Italian* fashion,)
Weares a loose-bodied Gowne—there's somewhat in't,   70
I have a tricke, may chance discover it
(A pretty one)—I have bought some Apricocks,
The first our Spring yeelds.   [*Enter Delio & Antonio.*]

DEL. And so long since married?

You amaze me.

A n t. Let me seale your lipps for ever,
For did I thinke, that any thing but th'ayre
Could carry these words from you, I should wish
You had no breath at all: [to Bosola] Now Sir, in your contem-
        plation?

80 You are studdying to become a great wise fellow?

B o s. Oh Sir, the opinion of wisedome is a foule tettor, that
runs all over a mans body: if simplicity direct us to have no
evill, it directs us to a happy being: For the subtlest folly proceedes from the subtlest wisedome: Let me be simply honest.

A n t. I do understand your in-side.

B o s. Do you so?

A n t. Because you would not seeme to appeare to th'world
Puff'd up with your preferment: You continue
This out o[f flashion mellancholly—leave it, leave it.

90 B o s. Give me leave to be honest in any phrase, in any complement whatsoever—shall I confesse my selfe to you? I looke
no higher then I can reach: they are the gods, that must ride
on winged horses, a Lawyers mule of a slow pace will both suit
my disposition, and businesse: For (marke me) when a mans
mind rides faster then his horse can gallop, they quickly both
tyre.

A n t. You would looke up to Heaven, but I thinke
The Divell, that rules i'th'aire, stands in your light.

B o s. Oh (Sir) you are Lord of the ascendant, chiefe man
100 with the Duchesse, a Duke was your cosen German, remov'd:
Say you were lineally descended from King *Pippin*, or he himselfe,
what of this? search the heads of the greatest rivers in the World,
you shall finde them but bubles of water: Some would thinke
the soules of Princes were brought forth by some more weighty
cause, then those of meaner persons—they are deceiv'd, there's
the same hand to them: The like passions sway them, the same
reason, that makes a Vicar goe to Law for a tithe-pig, and undoe
his neighbours, makes them spoile a whole Province, and batter
downe goodly Cities, with the Cannon. [*Enter Duchess & Ladies.*]

110 D u c h. Your arme *Antonio*, do I not grow fat?
I am exceeding short-winded: *Bosola*,
I would have you (Sir) provide for me a Littor,
Such a one, as the Duchesse of *Florence* roade in.

Bos. The Duchesse us'd one, when she was great with childe.

Duch. I thinke she did: come hether, mend my ruffe—
Here, when? thou art such a tedious Lady; and
Thy breath smells of Lymmon pils, would thou hadst done—
Shall I sound under thy fingers? I am so troubled
With the mother.

Bos. [aside] I feare to[o] much.   120

Duch. I have heard you say, that the French Courtie[r]s
Weare their hats on fore the King.

Ant. I have seene it.

Duch. In the Presence?

Ant. Yes:

[Duch.] Why should not we bring up that fashion?
'Tis ceremony more then duty, that consists
In the remooving of a peece of felt:
Be you the example to the rest o'th' Court,
Put on your hat first.   130

Ant. You must pardon me:
I have seene, in colder countries then in *France*,
Nobles stand bare to th'Prince; and the distinction
M[e]thought show'd reverently.

Bos. I have a present for your Grace.

Duch. For me sir?

Bos. Apricocks (Madam.)

Duch. O sir, where are they?
I have heard of none to yeare.

Bos. [aside] Good, her colour rises.   140

Duch. Indeed I thanke you: they are wondrous faire ones:
What an unskilfull fellow is our Gardiner!
We shall have none this moneth.

Bos. Will not your Grace pare them?

Duch. No, they tast of muske (me thinkes) indeed they doe:

Bos. I know not: yet I wish your Grace had parde 'em:

Duch. Why?

Bos. I forgot to tell you the knave Gardner,
(Onely to raise his profit by them the sooner)
Did ripen them in horse-doung.   150

Duch. O you jest:
You shall judge: pray tast one.

Ant. Indeed Madam,

I doe not love the fruit.

DUCH. Sir, you are loath
To rob us of our dainties: 'tis a delicate fruit,
They say they are restorative?

BOS. 'Tis a pretty
Art: this grafting.

160   DUCH. 'Tis so: a bettring of nature.

BOS. To make a pippin grow upon a crab,
A dampson on a black thorne: [aside] how greedily she eats them!
A whirlewinde strike off these bawd-farthingalls,
For, but for that, and the loose-bodied gowne,
I should have discover'd apparently
The young spring-hall cutting a caper in her belly.

DUCH. I thanke you (Bosola:) they were right good ones,
If they doe not make me sicke.

ANT. How now Madame?

170   DUCH. This greene fruit . . . and my stomake are not friends—
How they swell me!

BOS. [aside] Nay, you are too much swell'd already.

DUCH. Oh, I am in an extreame cold sweat.

BOS. I am very sorry: [Exit.]

DUCH. Lights to my chamber: O, good Antonio,
I feare I am undone.   Exit Duchesse

DEL. Lights there, lights!

ANT. O my most trusty Delio, we are lost:
I feare she's falne in labour: and ther's left
180 No time for her remove.

DEL. Have you prepar'd
Those Ladies to attend her? and procur'd
That politique safe conveyance for the Mid-wife
Your Duchesse plotted?

ANT. I have:

DEL. Make use then of this forc'd occasion:
Give out that Bosola hath poyson'd her,
With these Apricocks: that will give some colour
For her keeping close.

190   ANT. Fye, fie, the Physitians
Will then flocke to her.

DEL. For that you may pretend
She'll use some prepar'd Antidote of her owne,

Least the Physitians should repoyson her.

ANT. I am lost in amazement: I know not what to think on't.

Ex.

SCENA II.

[The Same.]

[Enter Bosola & old Lady.]

BOS. *[aside]* So, so: ther's no question but her teatchines and most vulterous eating of the Apricocks, are apparant signes of breeding—*[to the old Lady]* now?

OLD LADY. I am in hast (Sir.)

BOS. There was a young wayting-woman, had a monstrous desire to see the Glasse-house.

OLD LA. Nay, pray let me goe:

BOS. And it was onely to know what strange instrument it was, should swell up a glasse to the fashion of a womans belly.

OLD LA. I will heare no more of the Glasse-house—you   10 are still abusing woemen?

BOS. Who—I? no, onely (by the way now and then) mention your fraileties. The Orrenge tree bear[s] ripe and greene fruit, and blossoms altogether: And some of you give entertainment for pure love: but more, for more precious reward. The lusty Spring smels well: but drooping Autumne tasts well: If we have the same golden showres, that rained in the time of *Jupiter* the Thunderer: you have the same *Dan[a]es* still, to hold up their laps to receive them: didst thou never study the *Mathematiques*?

OLD LA. What's that (Sir?)   20

BOS. Why, to know the trick how to make a many lines meete in one center: Goe, goe; give your foster-daughters good councell: tell them, that the Divell takes delight to hang at a womans girdle, like a false rusty watch, that she cannot discerne how the time passes.   *[Exit Old Lady. Enter Antonio, Delio,*

ANT. Shut up the Court gates: *Roderigo, & Grisolan.]*

ROD. Why sir? what's the danger?

ANT. Shut up the Posternes presently: and call All the Officers o'th' Court.

GRIS. I shall instantly: *[Exit.]* 30

ANT. Who keepes the key o'th' Parke-gate?

ROD. *Forobosco.*

ANT. Let him bring't presently.

[*Re-enter Grisolan with Servants.*]

SERVANT. Oh, Gentlemen o'th' Court, the fowlest treason.

BOS. [*aside*] If that these Apricocks should be poysond, now;
Without my knowledge!

SERV. There was taken even now
A Switzer in the Duchesse Bed-chamber.

2. SERV. A Switzer?

40   SERV. With a Pistoll in his great cod-piece.

BOS. H[a], ha, ha.

SERV. The cod-piece was the case for't.

2. SER. There was a cunning traitor.
Who would have search'd his cod-piece?

SERV. True, if he had kept out of the Ladies chambers:
And all the mowldes of his buttons, were leaden bullets.

2. SERV. Oh wicked Caniball: a fire-lock in's cod-piece?

SERV. 'Twas a French plot, upon my life.

2. SER. To see what the Divell can doe!

50   ANT. All the Office[r]s here?

SERV. We are:

ANT. Gentlemen,
We have lost much Plate you know; and but this evening
Jewels, to the value of foure thousand Duckets
Are missing in the Du[tc]hesse Cabinet—
Are the Gates shut?

SER. Yes.

ANT. 'Tis the Duchesse pleasure
Each Officer be lock'd into his chamber

60 Till the Sun-rysing: and to send the keyes
Of all their chests, and of their outward doores
Into her bed-chamber: She is very sicke.

ROD. At her pleasure.

ANT. She intreates you take't not ill: The Innocent
Shall be the more approv'd by it.

BOS. Gentleman o'th' Wood-yard, where's your Switzer now?

SERV. By this hand, 'twas creadably reported by one o'th'
Black-guard.   [*Exeunt except Antonio & Delio.*]

DEL. How fares it with the Dutchesse?

ANT. She's expos'd

70 Unto the worst of torture, paine, and feare;

DEL. Speake to her all happy comfort.

ANT. How I do play the foole with mine own danger!
You are this night (deere friend) to poast to Rome,
My life lies in your service.

DEL. Doe not doubt me—

ANT. Oh, 'Tis farre from me: and yet feare presents me
Somewhat that look[s] like danger.

DEL. Beleeve it,
'Tis but the shadow of your feare, no more:
How superstitiously we mind our evils!   80
The throwing downe salt, or crossing of a Hare;
Bleeding at nose, the stumbling of a horse:
Or singing of a Criket, are of powre
To daunt whole man in us: Sir, fare you well:
I wish you all the joyes of a bless'd Father;
And (for my faith) lay this unto your brest,
Old friends (like old swords) still are trusted best. [*Exit. Enter*

CARIOLA. Sir, you are the happy father of a sonne,   *Car.*
Your wife commends him to you.   *with a child.*]

ANT. Blessed comfort: 90
For heaven-sake tend her well: I'll presently
Goe set a figure for's Nativitie.   *Exeunt.*

SCENA III.

[*The Same. Outside the Palace.*]

[*Enter Bosola, with a dark lanthorn.*]

BOS. Sure I did heare a woman shreike: list, hah!
And the sound came (if I receiv'd it right)
From the Dutchesse lodgings: ther's some stratagem
In the confyning all our Courtiers
To their severall wards: I must have part of it,
My Intelligence will freize else: List againe—
It may be 'twas the mellencholly bird,
(Best friend of silence, and of solitarines)
The Oowle, that schream'd so: hah? *Antonio?*

[*Enter Antonio with a candle, his sword drawn.*]

ANT. I heard some noyse: [who's] there? what art thou?
    speake.   10

Bos. *Antonio?* Put not your face; nor body
To such a forc'd expression of feare—
I am *Bosola*; your friend.
    Ant. *Bosola?*
(This Moale do's undermine me) heard you not
A noyce even now?
    Bos. From whence?
    Ant. From the *Duchesse* lodging.
    Bos. Not I: did you?
20   Ant. I did: or else I dream'd.
    Bos. Let's walke towards it.
    Ant. No: It may be, 'twas
But the rising of the winde:
    Bos. Very likely:
Me thinkes 'tis very cold, and yet you sweat.
You looke wildly.
    Ant. I have bin setting a figure
For the Dutchesse Jewells;
    Bos. Ah: and how falls your question?
30 Doe you find it radicall?
    Ant. What's that to you?
'Tis rather to be question'd what designe
(When all men were commanded to their lodgings)
Makes you a night-walker.
    Bos. In sooth I'll tell you:
Now all the Court's asleepe, I thought the Divell
Had least to doe here; I came to say my prayers,
And if it doe offend you I doe so,
You are a fine Courtier.
40   Ant. [*aside*] This fellow will undoe me;
You gave the Dutchesse Apricocks to-day,
Pray heaven they were not poysond?
    Bos. Poysond? a spanish figge
For the imputation.
    Ant. Traitors are ever confident,
Till they are discover'd: There were Jewels stolne too—
In my conceit, none are to be suspected
More then your selfe.
    Bos. You are a false steward.
50   Ant. Sawcy slave! I'll pull thee up by the rootes;

Bos. May be the ruyne will crush you to peeces.

Ant. You are an impudent snake indeed (sir)—

Are you scarce warme, and doe you shew your sting?

    [Bos.]   .   .   .

Ant. You Libell well (sir.)

Bos. No (sir,) copy it out:

And I will set my hand to't.

Ant. My nose bleedes:

One that were superstitious, would count

This ominous: when it meerely comes by chance.   60

Two letters, that are wrought here, for my name

Are drown'd in blood:

Meere accedent: for you (sir) I'll take order:

I'th morne you shall be safe: [aside] 'tis that must colour

Her lying-in: sir, this doore you passe not:

I doe not hold it fit, that you come neere

The Dutchesse lodgings, till you have [quit] your selfe;

[aside] *The Great are like the Base; nay, they are the same,*

When they seeke shamefull waies, to avoid shame.   Ex.

Bos. *Antonio* here about, did drop a Paper—   70

Some of your helpe (falce-friend)—oh, here it is:

What's here? a childes Nativitie calculated!

> *The Dutchesse was deliver'd of a Sonne, 'tweene the houres twelve, and one, in the night*: Anno Dom: 1504. (*that's this yeere*) *decimo nono Decembris,* (*that's this night*) *taken according to the Meridian of Malfy* (*that's our Dutchesse: happy discovery!*). *The Lord of the first house, being combust in the ascendant, signifies short life:* and Mars *being in a human signe, joyn'd to the taile of the Dragon, in the eight house, doth threaten a violent death;* Cæte[r]a non scrutantur.   80

Why now 'tis most apparant: This precise fellow

Is the Dutchesse Bawde: I have it to my wish:

This is a parcell of Intelligency

Our Courtiers were [cas'de-up] for? It needes must follow,

That I must be committed, on pretence

Of poysoning her: which I'll endure, and laugh at:

If one could find the father now! but that

Time will discover; Old *Castruchio*

I'th morning poasts to Rome; by him I'll send

A Letter, that shall make her brothers Galls   90

Ore-flowe their Livours—this was a thrifty way.
Though Lust doe masque in ne[v]*'r so strange disguise,*
She's oft found witty, but is never wise. [*Exit.*]

SCENA IIII.

[*Rome. The Cardinal's Palace.*]

[*Enter Cardinal and Julia.*]

CARD. Sit: thou art my best of wishes—pre-thee tell me
What tricke didst thou invent to come to Rome,
Without thy husband?
JUL. Why, (my Lord) I told him
I came to visit an old Anchorite
Heare, for devotion.
CARD. Thou art a witty false one:
I meane to him.
JUL. You have prevailed with me
10 Beyond my strongest thoughts: I would not now
Find you inconstant.
CARD. Doe not put thy selfe
To such a voluntary torture: which proceedes
Out of your owne guilt.
JUL. How (my Lord?)
CARD. You feare
My constancy, because you have approov'd
Those giddy and wild turning[s] in your selfe.
JUL. Did you ere find them?
20 CARD: Sooth generally for woemen,
A man might strive to make glasse male-able,
Ere he should make them fixed.
JUL. So, (my Lord)!—
CARD. We had need goe borrow that fantastique glasse
Invented by *Galileo* the Florentine,
To view another spacious world i'th' Moone,
And looke to find a constant woman there.
JUL. This is very well (my Lord.)
CARD. Why do you weepe?
30 Are teares your justification? the selfe-same teares
Will fall into your husbands bosome, (Lady)

With a loud protestation, that you love him
Above the world: Come, I'll love you wisely,
That's jealously, since I am very certaine
You cannot me make cuckould.

    JUL. I'll go home
To my husband.

    CARD. You may thanke me, (Lady)
I have taken you off your mellancholly pearch,
Boare you upon my fist, and shew'd you game,   40
And let you flie at it: I pray the[e] kisse me—
When thou wast with thy husband, thou wast watch'd
Like a tame Ellephant: (still you are to thanke me)
Thou hadst onely kisses from him, and high feeding,
But what delight was that? 'twas just like one
That hath a little fingring on the Lute,
Yet cannot tune it: (still you are to thanke me.)

    JUL. You told me of a piteous wound i'th'heart,
And a sicke livour, when you woed me first,
And spake like one in physicke.   50

    CARD. Who's that?   *[Enter Servant.]*
Rest firme, for my affection to thee,
Lightning mooves slow to't.

    SER. (Madam) a Gentleman
That's come post from *Malfy*, desires to see you.

    CAR. Let him enter, I'll with-draw.   *Exit.*

    SER. He sayes,
Your husband (old *Castruchio*) is come to *Rome*,
Most pittifully tyr'd with riding post.   *[Exit. Enter Delio.]*

    JUL. Signior *Delio*? 'tis one of my old Suitors.   60

    DEL. I was bold to come and see you.

    JUL. Sir, [you] are wel-come.

    DEL. Do you lie here?

    JUL. Sure, your owne experience
Will satisfie you no—our Romane Prelates
Do not keepe lodging, for Ladies.

    DEL. Very well:
I have brought you no comendations from your husband,
For I know none by him.

    JUL. I heare he's come to *Rome*?   70

    DEL. I never knew man, and beast, of a horse, and a knight,

So weary of each other—if he had had a good backe,
He would have undertooke to have borne his horse,
His breech was so pittifully sore.

    JUL. Your laughter,
Is my pitty.

    DEL. Lady, I know not whether
You want mony, but I have brought you some.

    JUL. From my husband?

80   DEL. No, from mine owne allowance.

    JUL. I must heare the condition, ere I be bound to take it.

    DEL. Looke on't, 'tis gold, hath it not a fine colour?

    JUL. I have a Bird more beautifull.

    DEL. Try the sound on't.

    JUL. A Lute-string far exceeds it,
It hath no smell, like Cassia, or Cyvit,
Nor is it phisicall, though some fond Doctors
Perswade us seeth'[t] in Cullisses—I'le tell you,
This is a Creature bred by——   [*Enter Servant.*]

90   SER. Your husband's come,
Hath deliver'd a letter to the Duke of *Calabria*,
That, to my thinking hath put him out of his wits.   [*Exit.*]

    JUL. Sir, you heare,
'Pray let me know your busines, and your suite,
As briefely as can be.

    DEL. With good speed, I would wish you
(At such time, as you are non-resident
With your husband) my mistris.

    JUL. Sir, I'le go aske my husband if I shall,
100 And straight returne your answere.   *Exit.*

    DEL. Very fine—
Is this her wit, or honesty that speakes thus?
I heard one say the Duke was highly mov'd
With a letter sent from *Malfy*: I doe feare
Antonio is betray'd: how fearefully
Shewes his ambition now, (unfortunate Fortune)!—
"They passe through whirle-pooles, and deepe woes doe shun,
Who the event weigh, ere the action's done.   *Exit.*

SCENA V.

[The Same.]

[Enter] Cardinall, and Ferdinand, with a letter.

FERD. I have this night dig'd up a man-drake.

CAR. Say you?

FERD. And I am growne mad with't.

CAR. What's the pro[deg]y?

FERD. Read there—a sister dampn'd—she's loose i'th'hilts:
Growne a notorious Strumpet.

CAR. Speake lower.

FERD. Lower?
Rogues do not whisper't now, but seeke to publish't,
(As servants do the bounty of their Lords)   10
Aloud; and with a covetuous searching eye,
To marke who note them: Oh confusion sease her,
She hath had most cunning baudes to serve her turne,
And more secure conveyances for lust,
Then Townes of garrison, for Service.

CARD. Is't possible?
Can this be certaine?

FERD. Rubarbe, oh, for rubarbe
To purge this choller—here's the cursed day
To prompt my memory, and here'it shall sticke   20
Till of her bleeding heart, I make a spunge
To wipe it out.

CARD. Why doe you make your selfe
So wild a Tempest?

FERD. Would I could be one,
That I might tosse her pallace 'bout her eares,
Roote up her goodly forrests, blast her meades,
And lay her generall territory as wast,
As she hath done her honors.

CARD. Shall our blood   30
(The royall blood of *Arragon*, and *Castile*)
Be thus attaincted?

FERD. Apply desperate physicke—
We must not now use Balsamum, but fire,
The smarting cupping-glasse, for that's the meane

To purge infected blood, (such blood as hers:)
There is a kind of pitty in mine eie,
I'll give it to my hand-kercher; and now 'tis here,
I'll bequeath this to her Bastard.

40   CARD. What to do?

FERD. Why, to make soft lint for his mother['s] wounds,
When I have hewed her to peeces.

CARD. Curs'd creature—
Unequall nature, to place womens hearts
So farre upon the left-side!

FERD. Foolish men,
That ere will trust their honour in a Barke,
Made of so slight, weake bull-rush, as is woman,
Apt every minnit to sinke it!

50   CAR. Thus Ignorance, when it hath purchas'd honour,
It cannot weild it.

FERD. Me thinkes I see her laughing,
Excellent *Hyenna*—talke to me somewhat, quickly,
Or my imagination will carry me
To see her, in the shamefull act of sinne.

CARD. With whom?

FERD. Happily, with some strong-thigh'd Bargeman;
Or one [o']th'wood-yard, that can quoit the sledge,
Or tosse the barre, or else some lovely Squire

60 That carries coles up, to her privy lodgings.

CARD. You flie beyond your reason.

FERD. Goe to (Mistris.)
'Tis not your whores milke, that shall quench my wild-fire,
But your whores blood.

CARD. How idlely shewes this rage!—which carries you,
As men convai'd by witches, through the ayre,
On violent whirle-windes—this intemperate noyce,
Fitly resembles deafe-mens shrill discourse,
Who talke aloud, thinking all other men

70 To have their imperfection.

FERD. Have not you,
My palsey?

CARD. Yes—I can be angry
Without this rupture—there is not in nature
A thing, that makes man so deform'd, so beastly,

As doth intemperate anger: chide your selfe—
You have divers men, who never yet exprest
Their strong desire of rest, but by unrest,
By vexing of themselves: Come, put your selfe
In tune.   80

    FERD. So—I will onely study to seeme
The thing I am not: I could kill her now,
In you, or in my selfe, for I do thinke
It is some sinne in us, Heaven doth revenge
By her.

    CARD. Are you starke mad?

    FERD. I would have their bodies
Burn't in a coale-pit, with the ventage stop'd,
That their curs'd smoake might not ascend to Heaven:
Or dippe the sheetes they lie in, in pitch or sulphure,   90
Wrap them in't, and then light them like a match:
Or else to boile their Bastard to a cullisse,
And give't his leacherous father, to renew
The sinne of his backe.

    CARD. I'll leave you.

    FERD. Nay, I have done,
I am confident, had I bin damn'd in hell,
And should have heard of this, it would have put me
Into a cold sweat: In, in, I'll go sleepe—
Till I know who leapes my sister, i'll not stirre: 100
That knowne, i'll finde Scorpions to string my whips,
And fix her in a generall ecclipse.   *Exeunt.*

ACTUS III. SCENA I.

[Amalfi. The Palace of the Duchess.]

[Enter Antonio and Delio.]

    ANT. Our noble friend (my most beloved *Delio*)
Oh, you have bin a stranger long at Court,
Came you along with the Lord *Ferdinand*?

    DEL. I did Sir, and how faires your noble *Duchesse*?

    ANT. Right fortunately well: She's an excellent
Feeder of pedegrees: since you last saw her,
She hath had two children more, a sonne, and daughter.

DEL. Me thinkes 'twas yester-day: Let me but wincke,
And not behold your face, which to mine eye
10 Is somewhat leaner, verily I should dreame
It were within this halfe houre.

ANT. You have not bin in Law, (friend *Delio*)
Nor in prison, nor a Suitor at the Court
Nor beg'd the reversion of some great mans place,
Nor troubled with an old wife, which doth make
Your time so inse[n]cibly hasten.

DEL. 'Pray Sir tell me,
Hath not this newes arriv'd yet to the eare;
Of the Lord *Cardinall*?

20 ANT. I feare it hath,
The Lord *Ferdinand*, (that's newly come to Court,)
Doth beare himselfe right dangerously.

DEL. Pray why?

ANT. He is so quiet, that he seemes to sleepe
The tempest out (as Dormise do in Winter)——
Those houses, that are haunted, are most still,
Till the divell be up.

DEL. What say the common people?

ANT. The common-rable, do directly say
30 She is a Strumpet.

DEL. And your graver heades,
(Which would [b]e pollitique) what censure they?

ANT. They do observe, I grow to infinite purchase
The leaft-hand way, and all suppose the Duchesse
Would amend it, if she could: For, say they,
Great Princes, though they grudge their Officers
Should have such large, and unconfined meanes
To get wealth under them, will not complaine
Least thereby they should make them odious
40 Unto the people—for other obligation
Of love, or marriage, betweene her and me,
They never dreame [of]. [*Enter Ferdinand, Duchess, & Bosola.*]

DEL. The Lord *Ferdinand*
Is going to bed.

FERD. I'll instantly to bed,
For I am weary: I am to ∧ be-speake
A husband for you.

DUCH. For me (Sir?)—'pray who is't?

FERD. The great Count *Malateste.*

DUCH. Fie upon him,   50
A Count! he's a meere sticke of sugar-candy,
(You may looke quite thorough him)—when I choose
A husband, I will marry for your honour.

FERD. You shall do well in't: How is't (worthy *Antonio?*)

DUCH. But (Sir) I am to have private conference with you,
About a scandalous report, is spread
Touching mine honour.

FERD. Let me be ever deafe to't:
One of Pasquils paper-bullets, court calumney,
A pestilent ayre, which Princes pallaces   60
Are seldome purg'd [of]: Yet, say that it were true,
I powre it in your bosome, my fix'd love
Would strongly excuse, extenuate, nay deny
Faults, [were] they apparant in you: Goe be safe
In your owne innocency.

DUCH. [aside] Oh bless'd comfort—
This deadly aire is purg'd.   *Exeunt, [except Ferdinand & Bosola].*

FERD. Her guilt treads on
Hot burning cultures: Now *Bosola,*
How thrives our intelligence?   70

BOS. (Sir) uncertainly—
'Tis rumour'd she hath had three bastards, but
By whom, we may go read i'th'Starres.

FERD. Why some
Hold opinion, all things are written there.

BOS. Yes, if we could find Spectacles to read them—
I do suspect, there hath bin some Sorcery
Us'd on the Duchesse.

FERD. Sorcery?—to what purpose?

BOS. To make her doate on some desertles fellow,   80
She shames to acknowledge.

FERD. Can your faith give way
To thinke there's powre in potions, or in Charmes,
To make us love, whether we will or no?

BOS. Most certainely.

FERD. Away, these are meere gulleries, horred things
Invented by some cheating mounte-banckes

To abuse us: Do you thinke that hearbes, or charmes
Can force the will? Some trialls have bin made
90 In this foolish practise; but the ingredients
Were lenative poysons, such as are of force
To make the patient mad; and straight the witch
Sweares (by equivocation) they are in love.
The witch-craft lies in her rancke b[l]ood: this night
I will force confession from her: You told me
You had got (within these two dayes) a false key
Into her Bed-chamber.
    Bos. I have.
    Ferd. As I would wish.
100   Bos. What doe you intend to doe?
    Ferd. Can you ghesse?
    Bos. No:
    Ferd. Doe not aske then:
He that can compasse me, and know my drifts,
May say he hath put a girdle 'bout the world,
And sounded all her quick-sands.
    Bos. I doe not
Thinke so.
    Ferd. What doe you thinke then, pray?
110   Bos. That you
Are your owne Chronicle too much: and grosly
Flatter your selfe.
    Ferd. Give me thy hand, I thanke thee:
I never gave Pention but to flatterers,
Till I entertained thee: farewell,
That Friend a Great mans ruine strongely checks,
Who railes into his beliefe, all his defects.   *Exeunt.*

SCENA II.

[*The Bed-chamber of the Duchess.*]

[*Enter Duchess, Antonio, & Cariola.*]

    Dutch. Bring me the Casket hither, and the Glasse;
You get no lodging here, to-night (my Lord.)
    Ant. Indeed, I must perswade one:
    Duch. Very good!

I hope in time 'twill grow into a custome,
That Noblemen shall come with cap, and knee,
To purchase a nights lodging, of their wives.

    A n t. I must lye here.

    D u t c h. Must? you are a Lord of Misse-rule.

    A n t. Indeed, my Rule is onely in the night.   10

    D u t c h. To what use will you put me?—

    A n t. Wee'll sleepe together:

    D u t c h. Alas, what pleasure can two Lovers find in sleepe?

    C a r. My Lord, I lye with her often: and I know
She'll much disquiet you:

    A n t. See, you are complain'd of.

    C a r. For she's the sprawlingst bedfellow.

    A n t. I shall like her the better for that

    C a r. Sir, shall I aske you a question?

    A n t. I pray thee *Cariola*.   20

    C a r. Wherefore still when you lie with my Lady
Doe you rise so early?

    A n t. Labouring men
Count the Clocke oftnest *Cariola*,
Are glad when their task's ended.

    D u c h. I'll stop your mouth.   [*kisses him.*]

    A n t. Nay, that's but one, *Venus* had two soft Doves
To draw her Chariot: I must have another: [*kisses her.*]
When wilt thou marry, *Cariola*?

    C a r. Never (my Lord.)   30

    A n t. O fie upon this single life: forgoe it:
We read how *Daphne*, for her peevish [f]light
Became a fruitlesse Bay-tree: *Siri[n]x* turn'd
To the pale empty Reede: *Anaxar[e]te*
Was frozen into Marble: whereas those
Which married, or prov'd kind unto their friends
Were, by a gracious influence, transhap'd
Into the Oliffe, Pomgranet, Mulbery:
Became Flowres, precious Stones, or eminent Starres.

    C a r. This is a vaine Poetry: but I pray you tèll me,   40
If there were propos'd me, Wisdome, Riches, and Beauty,
In three severall young men, which should I choose?

    A n t. 'Tis a hard question: This was *Paris'* case
And he was blind in't, and there was great cause:

For how was't possible he could judge right,
Having three amorous Goddesses in view,
And they starcke naked? 'twas a Motion
Were able to be-night the apprehention
Of the seveerest Counsellor of Europe.
50 Now I looke on both your faces, so well form'd,
It puts me in mind of a question, I would aske.
    CAR. What is't?
    ANT. I doe wonder why hard-favour'd Ladies
For the most part, keepe worse-favour'd waieting women,
To attend them, and cannot endure faire-ones.
    DUCH. Oh, that's soone answer'd.
Did you ever in your life know an ill Painter
Desire to have his dwelling next doore to the shop
Of an excellent Picture-maker? 'twould disgrace
60 His face-making, and undoe him: I pre-thee
When were we so merry? my haire tangles.
    ANT. 'Pray-thee (*Cariola*) let's steale forth the roome,
And let her talke to her selfe: I have divers times
Serv'd her the like—when she hath chafde extreamely:
I love to see her angry: softly *Cariola. Exeunt [Antonio & Cariola]*.
    DUCH. Doth not the colour of my haire 'gin to change?
When I waxe gray, I shall have all the Court
Powder their haire, with Arras, to be like me:
You have cause to love me, I entred you into my heart   [*Enter*
70 Before you would vouchsafe to call for the keyes.   *Ferdinand*
We shall one day have my brothers take you napping: *unseen.*]
Me thinkes his Presence (being now in Court)
Should make you keepe your owne Bed: but you'll say
Love mixt with feare, is sweetest: I'll assure you
You shall get no more children till my brothers
Consent to be your Ghossips: have you lost your tongue?   [*She*
'Tis welcome: *turns & sees Ferdinand.*]
For know whether I am doomb'd to live, or die,
I can doe both like a Prince.   *Ferdinand gives*
80   FERD. Die then, quickle: *her a ponyard.*
Vertue, where art thou hid? what hideous thing
Is it, that doth ecclipze thee?
    DUCH. 'Pray sir heare me:
    FERD. Or is it true, thou art but a bare name,

Ahd no essentiall thing?
    DUCH. Sir!
    FERD. Doe not speake.
    DUCH. No sir:
I will plant my soule in mine eares, to heare you.
    FERD. Oh most imperfect light of humaine reason,   90
That mak'st [us] so unhappy, to foresee
What we can least prevent: Pursue thy wishes:
And glory in them: there's in shame no comfort,
But to be past all bounds, and sence of shame.
    DUCH. I pray sir, heare me: I am married—
    FERD. So!
    DUCH. Happily, not to your liking: but for that
Alas: your sheeres doe come untimely now
To clip the birds wings, that's already flowne:
Will you see my Husband?   100
    FERD. Yes, if I could change
Eyes with a Basilisque:
    DUCH. Sure, you came hither
By his con[fe]deracy.
    FERD. The howling of a Wolfe
Is musicke to the[e] (schrech-Owle) pre'thee peace:
What ere thou art, that hast enjoy'd my sister,
(For I am sure thou hearst me) for thine owne sake
Let me not know thee: I came hither, prepar'd
To worke thy discovery: yet am now perswaded   110
It would beget such violent effects
As would damp[n]e us both: I would not for ten Millions
I had beheld thee: therefore use all meanes
I never may have knowledge of thy name;
Enjoy thy lust still, and a wret[c]hed life,
On that condition: And for thee (vilde woman,)
If thou doe wish thy Leacher may grow old
In thy Embracements, I would have thee build
Such a roome for him, as our Anchorites
To holier use enhabite: Let not the Sunne   120
Shine on him, till he's dead: Let Dogs, and Monkeys
Onely converse with him, and such dombe things
To whom Nature denies use to sound his name.
Doe not keepe a Paraqueto, least she learne it;

If thou doe love him, cut out thine owne tongue
Least it bewray him.
    DUCH. Why might not I marry?
I have not gone about, in this, to create
Any new world, or custome.
130   FERD. Thou art undone:
And thou hast taine that massiy sheete of lead
That hid thy husbands bones, and foulded it
About my heart.
    DUTCH. Mine bleedes for't.
    FERD. Thine? thy heart?
What should I nam't, unlesse a hollow bullet
Fill'd with unquenchable wild-fire?
    DUTCH. You are, in this
Too strict: and were you not my Princely brother
140   I would say to[o] wilfull: My reputation
Is safe.
    FERD. Dost thou know what reputation is?
I'll tell thee—to small purpose, since th'instruction
Comes now too late:
Upon a time Reputation, Love, and Death,
Would travell ore the world: and it was concluded
'That they should part, and take three severall wayes:
Death told them, they should find him in great Battailes:
Or Cities plagu'd with plagues: Love gives them councell
150   To enquire for him 'mongst unambitious shepheards,
Where dowries were not talk'd of: and sometimes
'Mongst quiet kindred, that had nothing left
By their dead Parents: stay (quoth Reputation)
Doe not forsake me: for it is my nature
If once I part from any man I meete,
I am never found againe: And so, for you:
You have shooke hands with Reputation,
And made him invisible: So fare you well.
I will never see you more.
160   DUTCH. Why should onely I,
Of all the other Princes of the World
Be cas'de-up, like a holy Relique? I have youth,
And a litle beautie.
    FERD. So you have some Virgins,

That are Witches: I will never see thee more.   *Exit. Enter*
                              Antonio with a Pistoll, [& *Cariola.*]

DUTCH. You saw this apparition?

ANT. Yes: we are
Betraid; how came he hither? I should turne   [*he points the*
This, to thee, for that.   *pistol at Cariola.*]

CAR. Pray sir doe: and when   170
That you have cleft my heart, you shall read there,
Mine innocence:

DUTCH. That Gallery gave him entrance.

ANT. I would this terrible thing would come againe,
That (standing on my Guard) I might relate
My warrantable love: ha, what meanes this?

DUTCH. He left this with me: *she shewes the*

ANT. And it seemes, did wish   *poniard.*
You would use it on your selfe?

DUTCH. His Action seem'd   180
To intend so much.

ANT. This hath a handle to't,
As well as a point—turne it towards him, and
So fasten the keene edge, in his rancke gall: [*Knocking within.*]
How now? who knocks? more Earthquakes?

DUTCH. I stand
As if a Myne, beneath my feete, were ready
To be blowne up.

CAR. 'Tis *Bosola*:

DUTCH. Away!—   190
Oh misery, me thinkes unjust actions
Should weare these masques, and curtaines; and not we:
You must instantly part hence: I have fashion'd it already.
                              Ex. Ant. [*Enter Bosola.*]

BOS. The Duke your brother is ta'ne up in a whirlewind—
Hath tooke horse, and's rid poast to Rome.

DUTCH. So late?

BOS. He told me, (as he mounted into th'sadle,)
You were undone.

DUTCH. Indeed, I am very neere it.

BOS. What's the matter?   200

DUTCH. *Antonio*, the master of our house-hold
Hath dealt so falsely with me, in's accounts:

My brother stood engag'd with me for money
Ta'ne up of certaine Neopolitane Jewes,
And *Antonio* lets the Bonds be forfeyt.

    Bos. S[t]range: [*aside*] this is cunning:

    Dutch. And hereupon
My brothers Bills at Naples are protested
Against: call up our Officers.

210   Bos. I shall.   *Exit.* [*Enter Antonio.*]

    Dutch. The place that you must flye to, is *Ancona*—
Hire a house there. I'll send after you
My Treasure, and my Jew[e]lls: our weake safetie
Runnes upon engenous wheeles: short sillables,
Must stand for periods: I must now accuse you
Of such a fained crime, as *Tasso* calls
Magnanima Mensogna: a Noble Lie,
'Cause it must shield our honors: harke they are comming.

                     [*Enter Bosola & Officers.*]

    Ant. Will your Grace heare me?

220   Dutch. I have got well by you: you have yeelded me
A million of losse; I am like to inherit
The peoples curses for your Stewardship:
You had the tricke, in Audit time to be sicke,
Till I had sign'd your *Quietus*; and that cur'de you
Without helpe of a Doctor. Gentlemen,
I would have this man be an example to you all:
So shall you hold my favour: I pray let him;
For h'as done that (alas) you would not thinke of,
And (because I intend to be rid of him)

230 I meane not to publish: use your fortune else-where.

    Ant. I am strongely arm'd to brooke my over-throw,
As commonly men beare with a hard yeere:
I will not blame the cause on't; but doe thinke
The necessitie of my malevolent starre
Procures this, not her humour: O the inconstant,
And rotten ground of service, you may see:
'Tis ev'n like him, that in a winter night
Takes a long slumber, ore a dying fire;
As loth to part from't: yet parts thence as cold,

240 As when he first sat downe.

    Dutch. We doe confi[s]cate

(Towards the satisfying of your accounts)
All that you have.

ANT. I am all yours: and 'tis very fit
All mine should be so.

DUTCH. So, sir; you have your Passe.

ANT. You may see (Gentlemen) what 'tis to serve
A Prince with body, and soule.　　　　　　　　*Exit.*

BOS. Heere's an example, for extortion; what moysture is
drawne out of the Sea, when fowle weather comes, powres downe, 250
and runnes into the Sea againe.

DUTCH. I would know what are your opinions
Of this *Antonio.*

2. OFFI. He could not abide to see a Pigges head gaping—
I thought your Grace would finde him a Jew:

3. OFFI. I would you had bin his Officer, for your owne
sake.

4. OFFI. You would have had more money.

1. OFFI. He stop'd his eares with blacke wooll: and to those
came to him for money said he was thicke of hearing.　　260

2. OFFI. Some said he was an hermophrodite, for he could
not abide a woman.

4. OFFI. How scurvy prowd he would looke, when the
Treasury was full: Well, let him goe:

1. OFFI. Yes, and the chippings of the Buttrey fly after
him, to scowre his gold Chaine.

DUTCH. Leave us: what doe you thinke of these?　*Exeunt*

BOS. That these are Rogues; that in's prosperitie, [*Officers*].
But to have waited on his fortune, could have wish'd
His durty Stirrop rivited through their noses:　　　　　270
And follow'd after's Mule, like a Beare in a Ring.
Would have prostituted their daughters, to his Lust:
Made their first-borne Intelligencers: thought none happy
But such as were borne under his bless'd Plannet
And wore his Livery: and doe these Lyce drop off now?
Well, never looke to have the like againe;
He hath left a sort of flattring rogues behind him,
Their doome must follow: Princes pay flatterers,
In their owne money: Flatterers dissemble their vices,
And they dissemble their lies, that's Justice:　　　　　280
Alas, poore gentleman!—

DUCH. Poore! he hath amply fill'd his cofers.

BOS. Sure he was too honest: *Pluto* the god of riches,
When he's sent (by *Jupiter*) to any man
He goes limping, to signifie that wealth
That comes on god's name, comes slowly, but when he's sent
[On] the divells arrand, he rides poast, and comes in by scuttles:
Let me shew you, what a most unvalu'd jewell,
You have (in a wanton humour) throwne away,
290 To blesse the man shall find him: He was an excellent
Courtier, and most faithfull, a souldier, that thought it
As beastly to know his owne value too little,
As devillish to acknowledge it too much,
Both his vertue, and forme, deserv'd a farre better fortune:
His discourse rather delighted to judge it selfe, then shew it selfe.
His breast was fill'd with all perfection,
And yet it seem'd a private whispring roome.
It made so little noyse of't.

DUCH. But he was basely descended.

300   BOS. Will you make your selfe a mercinary herald,
Rather to examine mens pedegrees, then vertues?
You shall want him,
For know an honest states-man to a Prince,
Is like a Cedar, planted by a Spring,
The Spring bathes the trees roote, the gratefull tree
Rewards it with his shadow: you have not done so—
I would sooner swim to the *Bermootha's* on
Two Polititians' rotten bladders, tide
Together with an Intelligencers hart-string
310 Then depend on so changeable a Princes favour.
Fare-thee-well (*Antonio*) since the mallice of the world
Would needes downe with thee, it cannot be sayd yet
That any ill happened unto thee,
Considering thy fall was accompanied with vertue.

DUCH. Oh, you render me excellent Musicke.

BOS. Say you?

DUCH. This good one that you speake of, is my husband.

BOS. Do I not dreame? can this ambitious age
Have so much goodnes in't, as to prefer
320 A man, meerely for worth: without these shadowes
Of wealth and painted honors? possible?

DUCH. I have had three children by him.

BOS. Fortunate Lady,
For you have made your private nuptiall bed
The humble, and faire Seminary of peace,
No question but: many an unbenific'd Scholler
Shall pray for you, for this deed, and rejoyce
That some preferment in the world can yet
Arise from merit. The virgins of your land
(That have no dowries) shall hope your example　　330
Will raise them to rich husbands: Should you want
Souldiers 'twould make the very *Turkes* and *Moores*
Turne Christians, and serve you for this act.
Last, the neglected Poets of your time,
In honour of this trophee of a man,
Rais'd by that curious engine, (your white hand)
Shall thanke you, in your grave, for't; and make that
More reverend then all the Cabinets
Of living Princes: For *Antonio*—
His fame shall likewise flow from many a pen,　　340
When Heralds shall want coates, to sell to men.

DUCH. As I taste comfort, in this friendly speech,
So would I finde concealement.

BOS. O the secret of my Prince,
Which I will weare on th'in-side of my heart.

DUCH. You shall take charge of all my coyne, and jewels,
And follow him, for he retires himselfe
To *Ancona*.

BOS. So.

DUCH. Whither, within few dayes,　　350
I meane to follow thee.

BOS. Let me thinke:
I would wish your Grace, to faigne a Pilgrimage
To our Lady of *Loretto*, (scarce seaven leagues
From faire *Ancona*)—so may you depart
Your Country, with more honour, and your flight
Will seeme a Princely progresse, retaining
Your usuall traine about you.

DUCH. Sir, your direction
Shall lead me, by the hand.　　360

CAR. In my opinion,

She were better progresse to the bathes at *Leuca*,
Or go visit the *Spaw*
In *Germany*, for (if you will beleeve me)
I do not like this jesting with religion,
This faigned Pilgrimage.

　　DUCH. Thou art a superstitious foole,
Prepare us instantly for our departure:
Past sorrowes, let us moderately lament them,
370 For those to come, seeke wisely, to prevent them. *Exit* [*Duchess,*
　　BOS. A Polititian is the divells quilted anvell,　　　　　*with*
He fashions all sinnes on him, and the blowes　　　　*Cariola*].
Are never heard—he may worke in a Ladies Chamber,
(As here for proofe)—what rests, but I reveale
All to my Lord? oh, this base quality
Of Intelligencer! why, every Quality i'th'world
Preferres but gaine, or commendation:
Now for this act, I am certaine to be rais'd,
"And men that paint weedes, (to the life) are prais'd. *Exit.*

SCENA III.

[*Rome. The Cardinal's Palace.*]

[*Enter*] *Cardinall, Ferdinand, Mallateste, Pescara, Silvio, Delio.*

　　CARD. Must we turne Souldier then?
　　MAL. The Emperour,
Hearing your worth that way, (ere you attain'd
This reverend garment,) joynes you in commission
With the right fortunate souldier, the Marquis of *Pescara*,
And the famous *Lanoy*.
　　CARD. He that had the honour
Of taking the *French* King Prisoner?
　　MAL. The same—
10 Here's a plot drawne, for a new Fortification,
At *Naples*.
　　FERD. This great Count *Mala*[teste], I perceive
Hath got employment?
　　DEL. No employment (my Lord)—
A marginall note in the muster-booke, that he is
A voluntary Lord.

FERD. He's no Souldier?

DEL. He has worne gun-powder, in's hollow tooth,
For the tooth-ache.

SIL. He comes to the leaguer, with a full intent,   20
To eate fresh beefe, and garlicke, meanes to stay
Till the sent be gon, and straight returne to Court.

DEL. He hath read all the late service,
As the City Chronicle relates it,
And keepe[s] two Painters going, onely to expresse
Battailes in modell.

SIL. Then he'l fight by the booke.

DEL. By the Almanacke, I thinke,
To choose good dayes, and shun the Criticall.
That's his mistris' skarfe.   30

SIL. Yes, he protests
He would do much for that taffita—

DEL. I thinke he would run away from a battaile
To save it from taking prisoner.

SIL. He is horribly afraid,
Gun-powder will spoile the perfume on't—

DEL. I saw a Duch-man breake his pate once
For calling him pot-gun—he made his head
Have a boare in't, like a musket.

SIL. I would he had made a touch-hole to't.   40
He is indeede a guarded sumpter-cloath
Onely for the remoove of the Court.   [Enter Bosola.]

PES. Bosola arriv'd? what should be the businesse?
Some falling out amongst the Cardinalls.
These factions amongst great men, they are like
Foxes—when their heads are devided
They carry fire in their tailes, and all the Country
About them, goes to wracke for't.

SIL. What's that Bosola?

DEL. I knew him in Padua, a fantasticall scholler,   50
Like such, who studdy to know how many knots
Was in Hercules club, of what colour Achilles beard was,
Or whether Hector were not troubled with the tooth-ach—
He hath studdied himselfe halfe bleare-ei'd, to know
The true semitry of Cæsars nose by a shooing-horne,
And this he did

To gaine the name of a speculative man.

PES. Marke Prince *Ferdinand*,

A very *Salamander* lives in's eye,

60 To mocke the eager violence of fire.

SIL. That Cardinall hath made more bad faces with his oppression

Then ever *Michael Angelo* made good ones,

He lifts up's nose, like a fowle Por-pisse before

A storme—

PES. The Lord *Ferdinand* laughes.

DEL. Like a deadly Cannon,

That lightens ere it smoakes.

PES. These are your true pangues of death,

The pangues of life, that strugle with great states-men—

70 DEL. In such a deformed silence, witches whisper

Their charmes.

CARD. Doth she make religion her riding hood

To keepe her from the sun, and tempest?

FERD. That: that damnes her: Me thinkes her fault, and
beauty

Blended together, shew like leaprosie—

The whiter, the fowler: I make it a question

Whether her beggerly brats were ever christned.

CARD. I will instantly sollicite the state of *Ancona*

To have them banish'd.

80   FERD. You are for *Loretto*?

I shall not be at your Ceremony: fare you well,

Write to the Duke of *Malfy*, my yong Nephew,

She had by her first husband, and acquaint him,

With's mothers honesty.

BOS. I will.

FERD. *Antonio!*

A slave, that onely smell'd of yncke, and coumpters,

And nev'r in's litfle, look'd like a Gentleman,

But in the audit time—go, go presently,

90 Draw me out an hundreth and fifty of our horse,

And meete me at the fort-bridge.   *Exeunt.*

SCENA IIII.

[*Loretto.*]

[*Enter*] *Two Pilgrimes to the Shrine of our Lady of* Loretto.

1. PILG. I have not seene a goodlier Shrine then this,
Yet I have visited many.
    2. PILG. The Cardinall of *Arragon*   X
Is, this day, to resigne his Cardinals hat,
His sister Duchesse likewise is arriv'd
To pay her vow of Pilgrimage—I expect
A noble Ceremony.
    1. PILG. No question:——They come.
Here the Ceremony of the Cardinalls enstalment, in the habit
[*of*] *a Souldier: perform'd in delivering up his Crosse, Hat,*
Robes, and Ring, at the Shrine; and investing him with
Sword, Helmet, Sheild, and Spurs: Then Antonio, *the*
Duchesse, *and their Children, (having presented themselves*
at the Shrine) are (by a forme of Banishment in dumbe-shew,
expressed towards them by the Cardinall, and the State of
Ancona) banished: During all which Ceremony, this Ditty
is sung (to very sollemne Musique) by divers Church-men;
and then Exeunt.

Armes, and Honors, decke thy story,
To thy Fames eternall glory,   10
Adverse Fortune ever flie-thee,   The Au-
No disastrous fate come nigh-thee.   thor dis-
                                  claimes
I alone will sing thy praises,   this Ditty
Whom to honour vertue raises;   to be his.
And thy study, that divine-is,
Bent to Marshiall discipline-is:
Lay aside all those robes lie by thee,
Crown thy arts, with armes: they'll beutifie thee.

O worthy of worthiest name, adorn'd in this manner,
Lead bravely thy forces on, under wars warlike banner: 20
O mayst thou prove fortunate, in all Marshiall courses,
Guide thou still, by skill, in artes, and forces:

Victory attend thee nigh, whilst fame sings loud thy powres,
Triumphant conquest crowne thy head, and blessings powre
    downe showres.

  1. PILG. Here's a strange turne of state—who would have
    thought
So great a Lady, would have match'd her selfe
Unto so meane a person? yet the Cardinall
Beares himselfe much too cruell.
  2. PILG. They are banish'd.
30 1. PILG. But I would aske what power hath this state
Of *Ancona*, to determine of a free Prince?
  2. PILG. They are a free state sir, and her brother shew'd
How that the Pope fore-hearing of her loosenesse,
Hath seaz'd into th'protection of the Church
The Dukedome, which she held as dowager.
  1. PIL. But by what justice?
  2. PILG. Sure I thinke by none,
Only her brothers instigation.
  1. PILG. What was it, with such violence he tooke
40 Of[f] from her finger?
  2. PIL. 'Twas her wedding ring,
Which he vow'd shortly he would sacrifice
To his revenge.
  1. PILG. Alasse *Antonio*,
If that a man be thrust into a well,
No matter who sets hand to't, his owne weight
Will bring him sooner to th'bottome: Come, let's hence.
Fortune makes this conclusion generall,
"All things do helpe th'unhappy man to fall.   *Exeunt.*

SCENA V.

[*Near Loretto.*]

[*Enter*] *Antonio, Duchesse, Children, Cariola, Servants.*

DUCH. Banish'd *Ancona*!
  ANT. Yes, you see what powre
Lightens in great mens breath.
  DUCH. Is all our traine
Shrunke to this poore remainder?

ANT. These poore men,
(Which have got little in your service) vow
To take your fortune: But your wiser buntings
Now they are fledg'd, are gon.
    DUCH. They have done wisely—   10
This puts me in minde of death, Physitians thus,
With their hands full of money, use to give ore
Their Patients.
    ANT. Right the fashion of the world—
From decaide fortunes, every flatterer shrinkes,
Men cease to build, where the foundation sinkes.
    DUCH. I had a very strange dreame to-night.
    ANT. What was't?
    DUCH. Me thought I wore my Coronet of State,
And on a sudaine all the Diamonds   20
Were chang'd to Pearles.
    ANT. My Interpretation
Is, you'll weepe shortly, for to me, the pearles
Doe signifie your teares:
    DUTCH. The Birds, that live i'th field
On the wilde benefit of Nature, live
Happier then we; for they may choose their Mates,
And carroll their sweet pleasures to the Spring: [*Enter Bosola*
    BOS. You are happily ore-ta'ne.   *with a letter.*]
    DUCH. From my brother?   30
    BOS. Yes, from the Lord *Ferdinand* . . . your brother,
All love, and safetie—
    DUTCH. Thou do'st blanch mischiefe—
Wouldst make it white: See, see; like to calme weather
At Sea, before a tempest, false hearts speake faire
To those they intend most mischiefe.
        [*Reads*] A Letter.
Send Antonio *to me; I want his head in a busines:*
A politicke equivocation—
He doth not want your councell, but your head;
That is, he cannot sleepe till you be dead.   40
And here's annother Pitfall, that's strew'd ore
With Roses: marke it, 'tis a cunning one.
I stand ingaged for your husband, for severall debts at Naples: *let*
not that trouble him, I had rather have his heart, then his mony.

And I beleeve so too.

    Bos. What doe you beleeve?

    Dutch. That he so much distrusts my husbands love,
He will by no meanes beleeve his heart is with him
Untill he see it: The Divell is not cunning enough
50 To circumvent us in Ridles.

    Bos. Will you reject that noble, and free league
Of amitie, and love which I present you?

    Dutch. Their league is like that of some politick Kings
Onely to make themselves of strength, and powre
To be our after-ruine: tell them so;

    Bos. And what from you?

    Ant. Thus tell him: I will not come.

    Bos. And what of this?

    Ant. My brothers have dispers'd
60 Blood-hounds abroad; which till I heare are muzell'd,
No truce, though hatch'd with nere such politick skill
Is safe, that hangs upon our enemies will.
I'll not come at them.

    Bos. This proclaimes your breeding.
Every small thing drawes a base mind to feare:
As the Adamant drawes yron: fare you well sir,
You shall shortly heare from's.   *Exit.*

    Dutch. I suspect some Ambush:
Therefore by all my love...I doe conjure you
70 To take your eldest sonne, and flye towards *Millaine*;
Let us not venture all this poore remainder
In one unlucky bottom.

    Ant. You councell safely:
Best of my life, farewell: Since we must part,
Heaven hath a hand in't: but no otherwise,
Then as some curious Artist takes in sunder
A Clocke, or Watch, when it is out of frame
To bring't in better order.

    Dutch. I know not which is best,
80 To see you dead, or part with you: Farewell Boy.
Thou art happy, that thou hast not understanding
To know thy misery: For all our wit
And reading, brings us to a truer sence
Of sorrow: In the eternall Church, Sir,

I doe hope we shall not part thus.

ANT. Oh, be of comfort,
Make Patience a noble fortitude:
And thinke not how unkindly we are us'de:
"Man (like to *Cassia*) is prov'd best, being bruiz'd.

DUTCH. Must I like to a slave-borne Russian,   90
Account it praise to suffer tyranny?
And yet (O Heaven) thy heavy hand is in't.
I have seene my litle boy oft scourge his top,
And compar'd my selfe to't: naught made me ere
Go right, but Heavens scourge-sticke.

ANT. Doe not weepe:
Heaven fashion'd us of nothing: and we strive,
To bring our selves to nothing: farewell *Cariola*,
And thy sweet armefull: if I doe never see thee more,
Be a good Mother to your litle ones,   100
And save them from the Tiger: fare you well.

DUCH. Let me looke upon you once more: for that speech
Came from a dying father: your kisse is colder
Then that I have seene an holy Anchorite
Give to a dead mans skull.

ANT. My heart is turnde to a heavy lumpe of lead,
With which I sound my danger: fare you well. *Exit,* [*with son.*]

DUCH. My Laurell is all withered.

CAR. Looke (Madam) what a troope of armed men
Make toward us.   *Enter Bosola with a Guard,* [*with Vizards.*] 110

DUCH. O, they are very welcome:
When Fortunes wheele is over-charg'd with Princes,
The waight makes it move swift. I wo[u]ld have my ruine
Be sudden: I am your adventure, am I not?

BOS. You are, you must see your husband no more—

DUCH. What Divell art thou, that counterfeits heavens
    thunder?

BOS. Is that terrible? I would have you tell me whether
Is that note worse, that frights the silly birds
Out of the corne; or that which doth allure them
To the nets? you have hearkned to the last too much.   120

DUCH. O misery: like to a rusty ore-char[g]'d Cannon,
Shall I never flye in peeces? come: to what Prison?

BOS. To none:

Duch. Wh(i)ther then?

Bos. To your Pallace.

Duch. I have heard that *Charons* boate serves to convay
All ore the dismall Lake, but brings none backe againe.

Bos. Your brothers meane you safety, and pitie.

Dutch. Pitie!

130 With such a pitie men preserve alive
Pheasants, and Quailes, when they are not fat enough
To be eaten.

Bos. These are your children?

Dutch. Yes:

Bos. Can they pratle?

Dutch. No:
But I intend, since they were borne accurs'd;
Cursses shall be their first language.

Bos. Fye (Madam)

140 Forget this base, low-fellow.

Dutch. Were I a man:
I'll'd beat that counterfeit face, into thy other—

Bos. One of no Birth.

Dutch. Say that he was borne meane...
Man is most happy, when's owne actions
Be arguments, and examples of his Vertue.

Bos.. A barren, beggerly vertue.

Dutch. I pre-thee who is greatest, can you tell?
Sad tales befit my woe: I'll tell you one.

150 A Salmon, as she swam unto the Sea,
Met with a Dog-fish; who encounters her
With this rough language: why art thou so bold
To mixe thy selfe with our high state of floods
Being no eminent Courtier, but one
That for the calmest, and fresh time o'th' yeere
Do'st live in shallow Rivers, rank'st thy selfe
With silly Smylts, and Shrympes? and darest thou
Passe by our Dog-ship, without reverence?
O (Quoth the Salmon) sister, be at peace:

160 Thanke *Jupiter*, we both have pass'd the Net—
Our value never can be truely knowne,
Till in the Fishers basket we be showne,
I'th' Market then my price may be the higher,

Even when I am neerest to the Cooke, and fire.
So, to Great men, the Morrall may be stretched.
"Men oft are valued high, when th'are most wretch[e]d.
But come: wh[i]ther you please: I am arm'd 'gainst misery:
Bent to all swaies of the Oppressors will.
There's no deepe Valley, but neere some great Hill.   *Ex.*

ACTUS IIII. SCENA I.

[Amalfi. The Palace of the Duchess.]

[Enter Ferdinand & Bosola.]

FERD. How doth our sister Dutchesse beare her selfe
In her imprisonment?
    BOS. Nobly: I'll describe her:
She's sad, as one long us'd to't: and she seemes
Rather to welcome the end of misery
Then shun it: a behaviour so noble,
As gives a majestie to adversitie:
You may discerne the shape of lovelinesse
More perfect, in her teares, then in her smiles;
She will muse foure houres together: and her silence,   10
(Me thinkes) expresseth more, then if she spake.
    FERD. Her mellancholly seemes to be fortifide
With a strange disdaine.
    BOS. 'Tis so: and this restraint
(Like English Mastiffes, that grow feirce with tying)
Makes her too passionately apprehend
Those pleasures she's kept from.
    FERD. Curse upon her!
I will no longer study in the booke
Of anothers heart: informe her what I told you. *Exit.* [*Enter*   20
    BOS. All comfort to your Grace;   *Duchess & Attendants.*]
    DUTCH. I will have none:
'Pray-thee, why do'st thou wrap thy poysond Pilles
In Gold, and Sugar?
    BOS. Your elder brother the Lord *Ferdinand*
Is come to visite you: and sends you word,
'Cause once he rashly made a solemne vowe

Never to see you more; he comes i'th' night:
And prayes you (gently) neither Torch, nor Taper
30 Shine in your Chamber: he will kisse your hand:
And reconcile himselfe: but, for his vowe,
He dares not see you:
    DUCH. At his pleasure:
Take hence the lights: he's come. [*Exeunt Servants with lights;*
    FERD. Where are you? DUTCH. Here sir: *enter Ferd.*]
    FERD. This darkenes suites you well.
    DUTCH. I would aske you pardon:
    FERD. You have it;
For I account it the honorabl'st revenge
40 Where I may kill, to pardon: where are your Cubbs?
    DUCH. Whom! FERD. Call them your children;
For though our nationall law distinguish Bastards
From true legitimate issue: compassionate nature
Makes them all equall.
    DUCH. Doe you visit me for this?
You violate a Sacrament o'th' Church
Shall make you howle in hell for't.
    FERD. It had bin well,
Could you have liv'd thus alwayes: for indeed
50 You were too much i'th' light: But no more—
I come to seale my peace with you: here's a hand,   *gives her*
To which you have vow'd much love: the Ring upon't   *a dead*
You gave.   *mans*
    DUCH. I affectionately kisse it: *hand.*
    FERD. 'Pray doe: and bury the print of it in your heart:
I will leave this Ring with you, for a Love-token:
And the hand, as sure as the ring: and doe not doubt
But you shall have the heart too: when you need a friend,
Send it to him, that ow'de it: you shall see
60 Whether he can ayd you.
    DUTCH. You are very cold.
I feare you are not well after your travell:
Hah? lights: oh horrible!
    FERD. Let her have lights enough.   *Exit.* [*Re-enter*
                                                 Servants with lights.]
    DUTCH. What witch-craft doth he practise, that he hath left
A dead-mans hand here?————*Here is discover'd, (behind a*

Travers;) the artificiall figures of Antonio, *and his children;*
appearing as if they were dead.

Bos. Looke you: here's the peece, from which 'twas ta'ne;
He doth present you this sad spectacle,
That now you know directly they are dead,
Hereafter you may (wisely) cease to grieve   70
For that which cannot be recovered.

Duch. There is not betweene heaven, and earth one wish
I stay for after this: it wastes me more,
Then were't my picture, fashion'd out of wax,
Stucke with a magicall needle, and then buried
In some fowle dung-hill: and yond's an excellent property
For a tyrant, which I would account mercy—

Bos. What's that?

Dutch. If they would bind me to that liveles truncke,
And let me freeze to death.   80

Bos. Come, you must live.

Dutch. That's the greatest torture soules feele in hell,
In hell: that they must live, and cannot die:
Portia, I'll new kindle thy Coales againe,
And revive the rare, and almost dead example
Of a loving wife.

Bos. O fye: despaire? remember
You are a Christian.

Dutch. The Church enjoynes fasting:
I'll starve my selfe to death.   90

Bos. Leave this vaine sorrow;
Things being at the worst, begin to mend: the Bee
When he hath shot his sting into your hand
May then play with your eye-lyd.

Dutch. Good comfortable fellow
Perswade a wretch that's broke upon the wheele
To have all his bones new set: entreate him live,
To be executed againe: who must dispatch me?
I account this world a tedious Theatre,
For I doe play a part in't 'gainst my will.   100

Bos. Come, be of comfort, I will save your life.

Dutch. Indeed I have not leysure to tend so small a busines.

Bos. Now, by my life, I pitty you.

Dutch. Thou art a foole then,

To wast thy pitty on a thing so wretch'd
As cannot pitty it[self]: I am full of daggers:
Puffe: let me blow these vipers from me.
What are you?   [*she turns suddenly to a Servant.*]
    S ER. One that wishes you long life.
110   D UCH. I would thou wert hang'd for the horrible curse
Thou hast given me: I shall shortly grow one
Of the miracles of pitty: I'll goe pray: No,
I'll goe curse:
    B OS. Oh fye!
    D UTCH. I could curse the Starres.
    B OS. Oh fearefull!
    D UTCH. And those three smyling seasons of the yeere
Into a Russian winter: nay the world
To its first Chaos.
120   B OS. Looke you, the Starres shine still:
    D UTCH. Oh, but you must remember, my curse hath a great
        way to goe:
Plagues, (that make lanes through largest families)
Consume them!
    B OS. Fye Lady!
    D UTCH. Let them like tyrants
Never be remembred, but for the ill they have done:
Let all the zealous prayers of mortefied
Church-men forget them—
    B OS. O uncharitable!
130   D UTCH. Let heaven, a little while, cease crowning Martirs
To punish them:
Goe, howle them this: and say `I long to bleed—
"It is some mercy, when men kill with speed.
              Exit, [*with Servants: re-enter Ferdinand.*]
    F ERD. Excellent; as I would wish: she's plagu'd in Art.
These presentations are but fram'd in wax,
By the curious Master in that Qualitie,
Vincentio Lauriola, and she takes them
For true substantiall Bodies.
    B OS. Why doe you doe this?
140   F ERD. To bring her to despaire.
    B OS. 'Faith, end here:
And go no farther in your cruelty—

Send her a penetentiall garment, to put on,
Next to her delicate skinne, and furnish her
With beades, and prayer bookes.
    FERD. Damne her, that body of hers,
While that my blood ran pure in't, was more worth
Then that which thou wouldst comfort, (call'd a soule)—
I will send her masques of common Curtizans,
Have her meate serv'd up by baudes, and ruffians,   150
And ('cause she'll needes be mad) I am resolv'd
To remove forth the common Hospitall
All the mad-folke, and place them neere her lodging:
There let them practise together, sing, and daunce,
And act their gambols to the full o'th'moone:
If she can sleepe the better for it, let her,
Your worke is almost ended.
    BOS. Must I see her againe?
    FERD. Yes.   BOS. Never.
    FERD. You must.   160
    BOS. Never in mine owne shape,
That's forfeited, by my intelligence,
And this last cruell lie: when you send me next,
The businesse shalbe comfort.
    FERD. Very likely!—
Thy pity is nothing of kin to thee: *Antonio*
Lurkes about *Millaine*, thou shalt shortly thither,
To feede a fire, as great as my revenge,
Which nev'r will slacke, till it have spent his fuell—
"Intemperate agues, make Physitians cruell.   *Exeunt.*   170

SCENA II.

[*The Same.*]

[*Enter Duchess & Cariola.*]

    DUCH. What hideous noyse was that?
    CARI. 'Tis the wild consort
Of Mad-men (Lady) which your Tyrant brother
Hath plac'd about your lodging: This tyranny,
I thinke was never practis'd till this howre.
    DUCH. Indeed I thanke him: nothing but noyce, and foily

Can keepe me in my right wits, whereas reason
And silence, make me starke mad: Sit downe,
Discourse to me some dismall Tragedy.

10   CARI. O 'twill encrease your mellancholly.
     DUCH. Thou art deceiv'd,
To heare of greater griefe, would lessen mine—
This is a prison? CARI. Yes, but you shall live
To shake this durance off. DUCH. Thou art a foole,
The Robin red-brest, and the Nightingale,
Never live long in cages. CARI. Pray drie your eyes.
What thinke you of, Madam? DUCH. Of nothing:
When I muse thus, I sleepe.
     CARI. Like a mad-man, with your eyes open?

20   DUCH. Do'st thou thinke we shall know one another,
In th'other world? CARI. Yes, out of question.
     DUCH. O that it were possible we might
But hold some two dayes conference with the dead,
From them, I should learne somewhat, I am sure
I never shall know here: I'll tell thee a miracle—
I am not mad yet, to my cause of sorrow.
Th'heaven ore my head, seemes made of molt[e]n brasse,
The earth of flaming sulphure, yet I am not mad:
I am acquainted with sad misery,

30 As the tan'd galley-slave is with his Oare,
Necessity makes me suffer constantly,
And custome makes it easie—who do I looke like now?
     CARI. Like to your picture in the gallery,
A deale of life in shew, but none in practise:
Or rather like some reverend monument
Whose ruines are even pittied. DUCH. Very proper:
And Fortune seemes onely to have her eie-sight,
To behold my Tragedy:
How now, what noyce is that?   [Enter Servant.

40   SERVANT. I am come to tell you,
Your brother hath entended you some sport:
A great Physitian, when the Pope was sicke
Of a deepe mellancholly, presented him
With severall sorts of mad-men, which wilde object
(Being full of change, and sport,) forc'd him to laugh,
And so th'impost-hume broke: the selfe same cure,

The Duke intends on you.

    DUCH. Let them come in.

    SER. There's a mad Lawyer, and a secular Priest,
A Doctor that hath forfeited his wits   50
By jealousie: an Astrologian,
That in his workes, sayd such a day o'th'moneth
Should be the day of doome; and fayling of't,
Ran mad: an English Taylor, crais'd i'th'braine,
With the studdy of new fashion: a gentleman usher
Quite beside himselfe, with care to keepe in minde,
The number of his Ladies salutations,
Or "how do you", she employ'd him in each morning:
A Farmer too, (an excellent knave in graine)
Mad, 'cause he was hindred transportation,   60
And let one Broaker (that's mad) loose to these,
You'ld thinke the divell were among them.

    DUCH. Sit *Cariola*: let them loose when you please,
For I am chain'd to endure all your tyranny. [*Enter Madmen.*]

        Here (by a Mad-man) this song is sung, to a dismall
        kind of Musique.

        O let us howle, some heavy note,
          some deadly-dogged howle,
        Sounding, as from the threatning throat,
          of beastes, and fatall fowle.
        As Ravens, Schrich-owles, Bulls, and Beares,
          We'll b[e]ll, and bawle our parts,   70
        Till yerk-some noyce have cloy'd your eares,
          and corasiv'd your hearts.
        At last when as our quire wants breath,
          our bodies being blest,
        We'll sing like Swans, to welcome death,
          and die in love and rest,

    1. MAD-MAN. [*Astrologer.*] Doomes-day not come yet? I'll draw it neerer by a perspective, or make a glasse, that shall set all the world on fire upon an instant: I cannot sleepe, my pillow is stuff't with a littour of Porcupines.   80

    2. MAD. [*Lawyer.*] Hell is a meere glasse-house, where the divells are continually blowing up womens soules, on hollow yrons, and the fire never goes out.

3. MAD. [*Priest.*] I will lie with every woman in my parish the tenth night: I will tithe them over, like hay-cockes.

4. MAD. [*Doctor.*] Shall my Pothecary out-go me, because I am a Cuck-old? I have found out his roguery: he makes allom of his wives urin, and sells it to Puritaines, that have sore throates with over-strayning.

90   1. MAD. I have skill in Harroldry.

2. Hast?

1. You do give for your creast a wood-cockes head, with the Braines pickt out on't, you are a very ancient Gentleman.

3. Greeke is turn'd Turke, we are onely to be sav'd by the Helvetian translation.

1. Come on Sir, I will lay the law to you.

2. Oh, rather lay a corazive—the law will eate to the bone.

3. He that drinkes but to satisfie nature is damn'd.

4. If I had my glasse here, I would shew a sight should make
100 all the women here call me mad Doctor.

1. What's he, a rope-maker?   [*pointing at the Priest.*]

2. No, no, no, a snufling knave, that while he shewes the tombes, will have his hand in a wenches placket.

3. Woe to the Caroach, that brought home my wife from the Masque, at three a clocke in the morning, it had a large Feather-bed in it.

4. I have paired the divells nayles forty times, roasted them in Ravens egges, and cur'd agues with them.

3. Get me three hundred milch bats, to make possets, to
110 procure sleepe.

4. All the Colledge may throw their caps at me, I have made a Soape-boyler costive, it was my master-peece:——*Here the Daunce consisting of 8. Mad-men, with musicke answerable thereunto, after which,* Bosola (*like an old man*) *enters.*

DUCH. Is he mad to[o]?

SER. 'Pray question him: I'll leave you. [*Exeunt Servant &*
BOS. I am come to make thy tombe.   *Madmen.*]

DUCH. Hah, my tombe?
Thou speak'st, as if I lay upon my death bed,
Gasping for breath: do'st thou perceive me sicke?

BOS. Yes, and the more dangerously, since thy sicknesse is
120 insensible.

DUCH. Thou art not mad sure, do'st know me?

Bos. Yes.   Duch. Who am I?

Bos. Thou art a box of worme-seede, at best, but a salvatory of greene mummey: what's this flesh? a little cruded milke, phantasticall puffe-paste: our bodies are weaker then those paper prisons boyes use to keepe flies in: more contemptible: since ours is to preserve earth-wormes: didst thou ever see a Larke in a cage? such is the soule in the body: this world is like her little turfe of grasse, and the Heaven ore our heades, like her looking glasse, onely gives us a miserable knowledge of the small com- 130 passe of our prison.

Duch. Am not I, thy Duchesse?

Bos. Thou art some great woman sure, for riot begins to sit on thy fore-head (clad in gray haires) twenty yeares sooner, then on a merry milkemaydes. Thou sleep'st worse, then if a mouse should be forc'd to take up her lodging in a cats eare: a little infant, that breedes it's teeth, should it lie with thee, would crie out, as if thou wert the more unquiet bed-fellow.

Duch. I am Duchesse of *Malfy* still.

Bos. That makes thy sleepes so broken: 140
"Glories (like glowe-wormes) afarre off, shine bright,
But look'd to neere, have neither heate, nor light.

Duch. Thou art very plaine.

Bos. My trade is to flatter the dead, not the living—
I am a tombe-maker.

Duch. And thou com'st to make my tombe?

Bos. Yes.

Duch. Let me be a little merry—
Of what stuffe wilt thou make it?

Bos. Nay, resolve me first, of what fashion?   150

Duch. Why, do we grow phantasticall in our death-bed?
Do we affect fashion in the grave?

Bos. Most ambitiously: Princes images on their tombes
Do not lie, as they were wont, seeming to pray
Up to heaven: but with their hands under their cheekes,
(As if they died of the tooth-ache)—they are not carved
With their eies fix'd upon the starres; but as
Their mindes were wholy bent upon the world,
The selfe-same way they seeme to turne their faces.

Duch. Let me know fully therefore the effect   160
Of this thy dismall preparation,

This talke, fit for a charnell?

BOS. Now, I shall—   [*Enter Executioners with*]
Here is a present from your Princely brothers,   *a Coffin,*
And may it arrive wel-come, for it brings   *Cords, and*
Last benefit, last sorrow.   *a Bell.*

DUCH. Let me see it—
I have so much obedience, in my blood,
I wish it in ther veines, to do them good.

170   BOS. This is your last presence Chamber.

CARI. O my sweete Lady.

DUCH. Peace, it affrights not me.

BOS. I am the common Bell-man,   [*Takes up the Bell.*]
That usually is sent to condemn'd persons
The night before they suffer:

DUCH. Even now thou said'st,
Thou wast a tombe-maker?

BOS. 'Twas to bring you
By degrees to mortification: Listen.   [*Rings his bell.*]

180   *Hearke, now every thing is still—*
The Schritch-Owle, and the whistler shrill,
Call upon our Dame, aloud,
And bid her quickly don her shrowd:
Much you had of Land and rent,
Your length in clay's now competent.
A long war disturb'd your minde,
Here your perfect peace is sign'd—
Of what is't fooles make such vaine keeping?
Sin their conception, their birth, weeping:
190   *Their life, a generall mist of error,*
Their death, a hideous storme of terror—
Strew your haire, with powders sweete:
Don cleane linnen, bath your feete,
And (the foule feend more to checke)
A crucifixe let blesse your necke,
'Tis now full tide, 'tweene night, and day,
End your groane, and come away.

CARI. Hence villaines, tyrants, murderets: alas!
What will you do with my Lady? call for helpe.

200   DUCH. To whom, to our next neighbours? they are mad-
folkes.

Bos. Remoove that noyse.

Duch. Farwell *Cariola*,
In my last will, I have not much to give—
A many hungry guests have fed upon me,
Thine will be a poore reversion.

Cari. I will die with her.

Duch. I pray-thee looke thou giv'st my little boy
Some sirrop, for his cold, and let the girle
Say her prayers, ere she sleepe.　Now what you please,　[*Cariola*
What death?　　　　　　　　　　　　　　　*is forced off.*] 210

Bos. Strangling, here are your Executioners.

Duch. I forgive them:
The apoplexie, cathar, or cough o'th'loongs,
Would do as much as they do.

Bos. Doth not death fright you?

Duch. Who would be afraid on't?
Knowing to meete such excellent company
In th'other world.

Bos. Yet, me thinkes,
The manner of your death should much afflict you,　　　　220
This cord should terrifie you?　Duch. Not a whit—
What would it pleasure me, to have my throate cut
With diamonds? or to be smothered
With Cassia? or to be shot to death, with pearles?
I know death hath ten thousand severall doores
For men, to take their *Exits*: and 'tis found
They go on such strange geometricall hinges,
You may open them both wayes: any way, (for heaven sake)
So I were out of your whispering: Tell my brothers,
That I perceive death, (now I am well awake)　　　　230
Best guift is, they can give, or I can take—
I would faine put off my last womans-fault,
I'ld not be tedious to you.

Exec. We are ready.

Duch. Dispose my breath, how please you, but my body
Bestow upon my women, will you?　Exec. Yes.

Duch. Pull, and pull strongly, for your able strength,
Must pull downe heaven upon me:
Yet stay, heaven gates are not so highly arch'd
As Princes pallaces—they that enter there　　　　240

Must go upon their knees: Come violent death,   [*She kneels.*]
Serve for *Mandragora*, to make me sleepe;
Go tell my brothers, when I am laid out,   *They*
They then may feede in quiet.   *strangle her.*

Bos. Where's the waiting woman?
Fetch her: Some other strangle the children: [*Re-enter Execu-*
Looke you, there sleepes your mistris.   *tioner with Cariola.*]

Cari. Oh you are damn'd
Perpetually for this: My turne is next,
250 Is't not so ordered? Bos. Yes, and I am glad
You are so well prepar'd for't.

Cari. You are deceiv'd Sir,
I am not prepar'd for't, I will not die,
I will first come to my answere; and know
How I have offended. Bos. Come, dispatch her:
You kept her counsell, now you shall keepe ours.

Cari. I will not die, I must not, I am contracted
To a young Gentle-man.

Exec. Here's your wedding Ring.
260 Car. Let me but speake with the Duke: I'll discover
Treason to his person.

Bos. Delayes: throttle-her.

Exec. She bites: and scratches:

Car. If you kill me now
I am damn'd: I have not bin at Confession
This two yeeres: Bos. When!

Car. I am quicke with child.

Bos. Why then,
Your credit's sav'd: beare her into th' next roome:
        [*They strangle her, and bear her away. Enter Ferdinand.*]
270 Let this lie still. Ferd. Is she dead?

Bos. Shee is what
You'll'd have her: But here begin your pitty— *Shewes the*
Alas, how have these offended?   *children strangled.*

Ferd. The death
Of young Wolffes, is never to be pittied.

Bos. Fix your eye here: Ferd. Constantly.

Bos. Doe you not weepe?
Other sinnes onely speake; Murther shreikes out:
The Element of water moistens the Earth,

But blood flies upwards, and bedewes the Heavens.   280
   FERD. Cover her face: Mine eyes dazell: she di'd yong.
   BOS. I thinke not so: her infelicitie
Seem'd to have yeeres too many.
   FERD. She, and I were Twinnes:
And should I die this instant, I had liv'd
Her Time to a Mynute.
   BOS. It seemes she was borne first:
You have bloodely approv'd the auncient truth,
That kindred commonly doe worse ag[r]ee
Then remote strangers.   290
   FERD. Let me see her face againe;
Why didst not thou pitty her? what an excellent
Honest man might'st thou have bin
If thou hadst borne her to some Sanctuary!
Or (bold in a good cause) oppos'd thy selfe
With thy advanced sword above thy head,
Betweene her Innocence, and my Revenge!
I bad thee, when I was distracted of my wits,
Goe kill my dearest friend, and thou hast don't.
For let me but examine well the cause;   300
What was the meanenes of her match to me?
Onely I must confesse, I had a hope
(Had she continu'd widow) to have gain'd
An infinite masse of Treasure by her death:
And that was the mayne cause; her Marriage—
That drew a streame of gall quite through my heart;
For thee, (as we observe in Tragedies
That a good Actor many times is curss'd
For playing a villaines part) I hate thee for't:
And (for my sake) say thou hast done much ill, well: 310
   BOS. Let me quicken your memory: for I perceive
You are falling into ingratitude: I challenge
The reward due to my service.
   FERD. I'll tell thee,
What I'll give thee— BOS. Doe:
   FERD. I'll give thee a pardon
For this murther:
   BOS. Hah? FERD. Yes: and 'tis
The largest bounty I can studie to doe thee.

320 By what authority did'st thou execute
This bloody sentence? Bos. By yours—
    Ferd. Mine? was I her Judge?
Did any ceremoniall forme of Law,
Doombe her to not-Being? did a compleat Jury
Deliver her conviction up i'th Court?
Where shalt thou find this [j]udgement registerd
Unlesse in hell? See: like a bloody foole
Th'hast forfeyted thy life, and thou shalt die for't.
    Bos. The Office of Justice is perverted quite
330 When one Thiefe hangs another: who shall dare
To reveale this? Ferd. Oh, I'll tell thee:
The Wolfe shall finde her Grave, and scrape it up:
Not to devoure the corpes, but to discover
The horrid murther.
    Bos. You; not I, shall quake for't.
    Ferd. Leave me:
    Bos. I will first receive my Pention.
    Ferd. You are a villaine:
    Bos. When your Ingratitude
340 Is Judge, I am so. Ferd; O horror!
That not the feare of him, which bindes the divels
Can prescribe man obedience.
Never looke upon me more. Bos. Why fare thee well:
Your brother, and your selfe, are worthy men;
You have a paire of hearts, are hollow Graves,
Rotten, and rotting others: and your vengeance,
(Like two chain'd bullets) still goes arme in arme—
You may be Brothers: for treason, like the plague,
Doth take much in a blood: I stand like one
350 That long hath ta'ne a sweet, and golden dreame.
I am angry with my selfe, now that I wake.
    Ferd. Get thee into some unknowne part o'th' world
That I may never see thee. Bos. Let me know
Wherefore I should be thus neglected? sir,
I serv'd your tyranny: and rather strove,
To satisfie your selfe, then all the world;
And though I loath'd the evill, yet I lov'd
You that did councell it: and rather sought
To appeare a true servant, then an honest man.

FERD. I'll goe hunt the Badger, by Owle-light: 360
'Tis a deed of darkenesse.   *Exit.*
    BOS. He's much distracted: Off my painted honour!—
While with vaine hopes, our faculties we tyre,
We seeme to sweate in yce, and freeze in fire;
What would I doe, we[r]e this to doe againe?
I would not change my peace of conscience
For all the wealth of Europe: She stirres; here's life:
Returne (faire soule) from darkenes, and lead mine
Out of this sencible Hell: She's warme, she breathes:
Upon thy pale lips I will melt my heart   370
To store them with fresh colour: who's there?
Some cordiall drinke! Alas! I dare not call:
So, pitty would destroy pitty: her Eye opes,
And heaven in it seemes to ope, (that late was shut)
To take me up to mer[c]y.
    DUTCH. *Antonio.*
    BOS. Yes (Madam) he is living,
The dead bodies you saw, were but faign'd statues;
He's reconcil'd to your brothers: the Pope hath wrought
The attonement.   380
    DUTCH. Mercy!   *she dies.*
    BOS. Oh, she's gone againe: there the cords of life broake:
Oh sacred Innocence, that sweetely sleepes
On Turtles feathers: whil'st a guilty conscience
Is a blacke Register, wherein is writ
All our good deedes, and bad: a Perspective
That showes us hell; that we cannot be suffer'd
To doe good when we have a mind to it!
This is manly sorrow:
These teares, I am very certaine, never grew   390
In my Mothers Milke. My estate is suncke below
The degree of feare: where were these penitent fountaines,
While she was living?
Oh, they were frozen up: here is a sight
As direfull to my soule, as is the sword
Unto a wretch hath slaine his father: Come,
I'll beare thee hence,
And execute thy last will; that's deliver
Thy body to the reverend dispose

400 Of some good women: that the cruell tyrant
Shall not denie me: Then I'll poast to *Millaine*,
Where somewhat I will speedily enact
Worth my dejection.   *Exit* [*with the body*].

ACTUS V. SCENA I.

[*Milan*.]

[*Enter Antonio & Delio*.]

ANT. What thinke you of my hope of reconcilement
To the *Aragonian* brethren? DEL. I misdoubt it,
For though they have sent their letters of safe conduct
For your repaire to *Millaine*, they appeare
But Nets, to entrap you: The Marquis of *Pescara*
Under whom you hold certaine land in Cheit,
Much 'gainst his noble nature, hath bin mov'd
To ceize those lands, and some of his dependants
Are at this instant, making it their suit
10 To be invested in your Revenewes.
I cannot thinke, they meane well to your life,
That doe deprive you of your meanes of life,
Your living. ANT. You are still an heretique
To any safety, I can shape my selfe.
    DEL. Here comes the Marquis: I will make my selfe
Petitioner for some part of your land,
To know wh[i]ther it is flying. ANT. I pray doe.
                    [*Enter Pescara: Antonio withdrawes*.]
    DEL. Sir, I have a suit to you. PESC. To me?
    DEL. An easie one:
20 There is the Cittadell of St. *Bennet*,
With some demeasnes, of late in the possession
Of *Antonio Bologna*—please you bestow them on me?
    PESC. You are my friend: But this is such a suit,
Nor fit for me to give, nor you to take.
    DEL. No sir?
    PESC. I will give you ample reason for't,
Soone in private: Here's the Cardinalls Mistris.   [*Enter Julia*.]
    JUL. My Lord, I am growne your poore Petitioner,
And should be an ill begger, had I not

A Great mans letter here, (the Cardinalls)   30
To Court you in my favour.   [gives letter.]
    PESC. [reads] He entreates for you
The Cittadell of Saint *Bennet*, that belong'd
To the banish'd *Bologna*. JUL. Yes:
    PESC. I could not have thought of a friend I could
Rather pleasure with it: 'tis yours:
    JUL. Sir, I thanke you:
And he shall know how doubly I am engag'd
Both in your guift, and speedinesse of giving,
Which makes your graunt, the greater.   *Exit.* 40
    ANT. [aside] How they fortefie
Themselves with my ruine! DEL. Sir: I am
Litle bound to you: PESC. Why?
    DEL. Because you denide this suit, to me, and gav't
To such a creature.
    PESC. Doe you know what it was?
It was *Antonios* land: not forfeyted
By course of lawe; but ravish'd from his throate
By the Cardinals entreaty: it were not fit
I should bestow so maine a peece of wrong   50
Upon my friend: 'tis a gratification
Onely due to a Strumpet: for it is injustice;
Shall I sprinckle the pure blood of Innocents
To make those followers, I call my friends
Looke ruddier upon me? I am glad
This land, (ta'ne from the owner by such wrong)
Returnes againe unto so fowle an use,
As Salary for his Lust. Learne, (good *Delio*)
To aske noble things of me, and you shall find
I'll be a noble giver. DEL. You instruct me well: 60
    ANT. [aside] Why, here's a man, now, would fright im-
                pudence
From sawciest Beggers.
    PESC. Prince *Ferdinand's* come to *Millaine*
Sicke (as they give out) of an Appoplexie:
But some say, 'tis a frenzie; I am going
To visite him.   *Exit.*
    ANT. 'Tis a noble old fellow:
    DEL. What course doe you meane to take, *Antonio*?

ANT. This night, I meane to venture all my fortune
70 (Which is no more then a poore lingring life)
To the Cardinals worst of mallice: I have got
Private accesse to his chamber: and intend
To visit him, about the mid of night.
(As once his brother did our noble Dutchesse.)
It may be that the sudden apprehension
Of danger (for I'll goe in mine owne shape)
When he shall see it fraight with love, and dutie,
May draw the poyson out of him, and worke
A friendly reconcilement; if it faile...
80 Yet, it shall rid me of this infamous calling,
For better fall once, then be ever falling.
    DEL. I'll second you in all danger: and (how ere)
My life keepes rancke with yours.
    ANT. You are still my lov'd, and best friend.   *Exeunt.*

SCENA II.

[Milan. The Palace of the Cardinal and Ferdinand.]

[Enter Pescara and Doctor.]

PESC. Now Doctor; may I visit your Patient?
    DOCTOR. If't please your Lordship: but he's instantly
To take the ayre here in the Gallery,
By my direction.
    PESC. 'Pray-thee, what's his disease?
    DOC. A very pestilent disease (my Lord)
They call *Licanthropia*. PESC. What's that?
I need a Dictionary to't. DOC. I'll tell you:
In those that are possess'd with't there ore-flowes
10 Such mellencholy humour, they imagine
Themselves to be transformed into Woolves,
Steale forth to Church-yards in the dead of night,
And dig dead bodies up: as two nights since
One met the Duke, 'bout midnight in a lane
Behind St. *Markes* Church, with the leg of a man
Upon his shoulder; and he howl'd fearefully:
Said he was a Woolffe: onely the difference

Was, a Woolffes skinne was hairy on the out-side,
His on the In-side: bad them take their swords,
Rip up his flesh, and trie: straight I was sent for,   20
And having ministerd to him, found his Grace
Very well recovered. PESC. I am glad on't.

DOC. Yet not without some feare
Of a relaps: if he grow to his fit againe,
I'll goe a neerer way to worke with him
Then ever *Parac[el]sus* dream'd of: If
They'll give me leave, I'll buffet his madnesse out of him.
Stand aside: he comes.

[*Enter Ferdinand, Malateste, Cardinal & Bosola.*]

FERD. Leave me.
MAL. Why doth your Lordship love this solitarines?   30
FERD. Eagles commonly fly alone: They are Crowes, Dawes,
and Sterlings that flocke together: Looke, what's that, followes
me? MAL. Nothing (my Lord).
FERD. Yes: MAL. 'Tis your shadow.
FERD. Stay it, let it not haunt me.
MAL. Impossible; if you move, and the Sun shine:
FERD. I will throtle it.   [*Throws himself on the ground.*]
MAL. Oh, my Lord: you are angry with nothing.
FERD. You are a foole: How is't possible I should catch my
shadow unlesse I fall upon't? When I goe to Hell, I meane to 40
carry a bribe: for looke you good guifts ever-more make way,
for the worst persons.
PESC. Rise, good my Lord.
FERD. I am studying the Art of Patience.
PESC. 'Tis a noble Vertue;
FERD. To drive six Snailes before me, from this towne to
Mosco; neither use Goad, nor Whip to them, but let them take
their owne time: (the patientst man i'th' world match me for
an experiment) and I'll crawle after like a sheepe-biter.
CARD. Force him up.   50
FERD. Use me well, you were best:
What I have don, I have don: I'll confesse nothing.
DOCTOR. Now let me come to him: Are you mad (my Lord?)
Are you out of your Princely wits?
FERD. What's he? PESC. Your Doctor.

FERD. Let me have his beard saw'd off, and his eye-browes
Fil'd more civill.

DOCT. I must do mad trickes with him,
For that's the onely way on't. I have brought
60 Your grace a Salamanders skin, to keepe you
From sun-burning.

FERD. I have cruell sore eyes.

DOCT. The white of a Cockatrixes-egge is present remedy.

FERD. Let it be a new-layd one, you were best:
Hide me from him: Phisitians are like Kings,
They brooke no contradiction.

DOCT. Now he begins
To feare me, now let me alone with him.   [*takes off his gown.*]

CARD. How now, put off your gowne?

70   DOCT. Let me have some forty urinalls fill'd with Rose-
water: He, and I'll go pelt one another with them——now he
begins to feare me: Can you fetch a friske, sir? Let him go, let
him go, upon my perrill: I finde by his eye, he stands in awe of
me, I'll make him——as tame as a Dormouse.

FERD. Can you fetch your friskes, sir? I will stamp him into
a Cullice: Flea off his skin, to cover one of the An[a]tomies, this
rogue hath set i'th'cold yonder, in Barber-Chyrurgeons hall:
Hence, hence, you are all of you, like beasts for sacrifice, [*Throws
the doctor down & beats him*] there's nothing left of you, but
80 tongue, and belly, flattery, and leachery.   [*Exit.*]

PES. Doctor, he did not feare you throughly.

DOCT. True, I was somewhat to[o] forward.

BOS. Mercy upon me, what a fatall judgement
Hath falne upon this *Ferdinand*!

PES. Knowes your grace
What accident hath brought unto the Prince
This strange distraction?

CARD. [*aside*] I must faigne somewhat: Thus they say it
     grew.
You have heard it rumor'd for these many yeares,
90 None of our family dies, but there is seene
The shape of an old woman, which is given
By tradition, to us, to have bin murther'd
By her Nephewes, for her riches: Such a figure
One night (as the Prince sat up late at's booke)

Appear'd to him—when crying out for helpe,
The gentlemen of's chamber, found his grace
All on a cold sweate, alter'd much in face
And language: Since which apparition,
He hath growne worse, and worse, and I much feare
He cannot live.   100
    Bos. Sir, I would speake with you.
    Pes. We'll leave your grace,
Wishing to the sicke Prince, our noble Lord,
All health of minde, and body.
    Card. You are most welcome:
                        [*Exeunt. Manent Cardinal and Bosola.*]
Are you come? so: [*aside*] this fellow must not know
By any meanes I had intelligence
In our Duchesse death: For (though I counsell'd it,)
The full of all th'ingagement seem'd to grow
From *Ferdinand*: [*to Bosola*] Now sir, how fares our sister?   110
I do not thinke but sorrow makes her looke
Like to an oft-di'd garment: She shall now
Tast comfort from me: why do you looke so wildely?
Oh, the fortune of your master here, the Prince
Dejects you—but be you of happy comfort:
If you'll do on[e] thing for me I'll entreate,
Though he had a cold tombe-stone ore his bones,
[I'll] make you what you would be.
    Bos. Any thing—
Give it me in a breath, and let me flie to't: 120
They that thinke long, small expedition win,
For musing much o'th'end, cannot begin.   [*Enter Julia.*]
    Jul. Sir, will you come in to Supper?
    Card. I am busie, leave me.
    Jul. [*aside*] What an excellent shape hath that fellow!   *Exit.*
    Card. 'Tis thus: *Antonio* lurkes here in *Millaine*,
Enquire him out, and kill him: while he lives,
Our sister cannot marry, and I have thought
Of an excellent match for her: do this, and stile me
Thy advancement.   130
    Bos. But by what meanes shall I find him out?
    Card. There is a gentleman, call'd *Delio*
Here in the Campe, that hath bin long approv'd

His loyall friend: Set eie upon that fellow,
Follow him to Masse—may be *Antonio*,
Although he do account religion
But a Schoole-name, for fashion of the world,
May accompany him—or else go enquire out
Delio's Confessor, and see if you can bribe
140 Him to reveale it: there are a thousand wayes
A man might find to trace him: As to know,
What fellowes haunt the Jewes, for taking up
Great summes of money, for sure he's in want,
Or else to go to th'Picture-makers, and learne
Who [bought] her Picture lately—some of these
Happily may take——
    Bos. Well, I'll not freeze i'th'businesse,
I would see that wretched thing, *Antonio*
Above all sightes i'th'world.
150   Card. Do, and be happy.   *Exit.*
    Bos. This fellow doth breed Bazalisques in's eies,
He's nothing else, but murder: yet he seemes
Not to have notice of the Duchesse death:
'Tis his cunning: I must follow his example,
There cannot be a surer way to trace,
Then that of an old Fox. [*Enter Julia, pointing a pistol at him.*]
    Jul. So, sir, you are well met. Bos. How now?
    Jul. Nay, the doores are fast enough:
Now, Sir, I will make you confesse your treachery.
160   Bos. Treachery? Jul. Yes, confesse to me
Which of my women 'twas you hyr'd, to put
Love-powder into my drinke?
    Bos. Love-powder?
    Jul. Yes, when I was at *Malfy*—
Why should I fall in love with such a face else?
I have already suffer'd for thee so much paine,
The onely remedy to do me good,
Is to kill my longing.
    Bos. Sure your Pistoll holds
170 Nothing but perfumes, or kissing comfits: excellent Lady,
You have a pritty way on't to discover
Your longing: Come, come, I'll disarme you,
And arme you thus—yet this is wondrous strange. [*Embraces her.*]

JUL. Compare thy forme, and my eyes together,
You'll find my love no such great miracle:
Now you'll say,
I am wanton: This nice modesty, in Ladies
Is but a troublesome familiar,
That haunts them.

BOS. Know you me, I am a blunt souldier. JUL. The better, 180
Sure, there wants fire, where there are no lively sparkes
Of roughnes. BOS. And I want complement.

JUL. Why, ignorance in court-ship cannot make you do amisse,
If you have a heart to do well.

BOS. You are very faire.

JUL. Nay, if you lay beauty to my charge,
I must plead unguilty. BOS. Your bright eyes
Carry a Quiver of darts in them, sharper
Then Sun-beames.

JUL. You will mar me with commendation,   190
Put your selfe to the charge of courting me,
Whereas now I wo[o] you.

BOS. [aside] I have it, I will worke upon this Creature—
Let us grow most amorously familiar:
If the great Cardinall now should see me thus,
Would he not count me a villaine?

JUL. No, he might count me a wanton,
Not lay a scruple of offence on you:
For if I see, and steale a Diamond,
The fault is not i'th'stone, but in me the thiefe,   200
That purloines it: I am sudaine with you—
We that are great women of pleasure, use to cut off
These uncertaine wishes, and unquiet longings,
And in an instant joyne the sweete delight
And the pritty excuse together: had you bin in'th'streete,
Under my chamber window, even there
I should have courted you.

BOS. Oh, you are an excellent Lady.

JUL. Bid me do somewhat for you presently,
To expresse I love you.   210

BOS. I will, and if you love me,
Faile not to effect it:
The Cardinall is growne wondrous mellancholly,

Demand the cause, let him not put you off,
With faign'd excuse, discover the maine ground on't.
    J u l. Why would you know this?
    B o s. I have depended on him,
And I heare that he is falne in some disgrace
With the Emperour—if he be, like the mice
220 That forsake falling houses, I would shift
To other dependance.
    J u l. You shall not neede follow the warres,
I'll be your maintenance.
    B o s. And I your loyall servant,
But I cannot leave my calling.
    J u l. Not leave an
Ungratefull Generall, for the love of a sweete Lady?
You are like some, cannot sleepe in feather-beds,
But must have blockes for their pillowes.
230   B o s. Will you do this? J u l. Cunningly.
    B o s. To-morrow I'll expect th'intelligence.
    J u l. To-morrow! get you into my Cabinet,
You shall have it with you: do not delay me,
No more then I do you: I am like one
That is condemn'd: I have my pardon promis'd.
But I would see it seal'd: Go, get you in,
You shall see me winde my tongue about his heart,
Like a skeine of silke.
                [*Exit Bosola, into her cabinet. Enter Cardinal.*]
    C a r d. Where are you? [*Enter Servants.*] S e r v. Here.
240   C a r d. Let none, upon your lives,
Have conference with the Prince *Ferdinand*,
Unlesse I know it: [*aside*] In this distraction   [*Exeunt Serv.*]
He may reveale the murther:
Yond's my lingring consumption:
I am weary of her; and by any meanes
Would be quit off. J u l. How now, my Lord?
What ailes you? C a r d. Nothing.
    J u l. Oh, you are much alterd:
Come, I must be your Secretary, and remove
250 This lead from off your bosome, what's the matter?
    C a r d. I may not tell you.
    J u l. Are you so farre in love with sorrow,

You cannot part with part of it? or thinke you
I cannot love your grace, when you are sad,
As well as merry? or do you suspect
I, that have bin a secret to your heart,
These many winters, cannot be the same
Unto your tongue?
    CARD. Satisfie thy longing,
The onely way to make thee keepe my councell,   260
Is not to tell thee. JUL. Tell your eccho this,
Or flatterers, that (like ecchoes) still report
What they heare (though most imperfect), and not me:
For, if that you be true unto your selfe,
I'll know. CARD. Will you racke me?
    JUL. No, judgement shall
Draw it from you: It is an equall fault,
To tell ones secrets, unto all, or none.
    CARD. The first argues folly.
    JUL. But the last tyranny.   270
    CARD. Very well; why, imagine I have committed
Some secret deed, which I desire the world
May never heare of.
    JUL. Therefore may not I know it?
You have conceal'd for me, as great a sinne
As adultery: Sir, never was occasion
For perfect triall of my constancy
Till now: Sir, I beseech you.
    CARD. You'll repent it. JUL. Never.
    CARD. It hurries thee to ruine: I'll not tell thee——   280
Be well advis'd, and thinke what danger 'tis
To receive a Princes secrets: they that do,
Had neede have their breasts hoop'd with adamant
To containe them: I pray thee yet be satisfi'd,
Examine thine owne frailety, 'tis more easie
To tie knots, then unloose them: 'tis a secret
That (like a lingring poyson) may chance lie
Spread in thy vaines, and kill thee seaven yeare hence.
    JUL. Now you dally with me.
    CARD. No more——thou shalt know it.   290
By my appointment, the great Duchesse of *Malfy*,
And two of her yong children, foure nights since

Were strangled.

    JUL. Oh heaven! (sir) what have you done?

    CARD. How now? how setles this? thinke you your bosome
Will be a grave, darke and obscure enough
For such a secret?

    JUL. You have undone your selfe (sir.)

    CARD. Why? JUL. It lies not in me to conceale it. CARD. No?
300 Come, I will sweare you to't upon this booke.

    JUL. Most religiously. CARD. Kisse it.
Now you shall never utter it, thy curiosity
Hath undone thee: thou'rt poyson'd with that booke—
Because I knew thou couldst not keepe my councell,
I have bound the[e] to't by death.   [*Enter Bosola.*]

    BOS. For pitty sake, hold. CARD. Ha, *Bosola*?

    JUL. I forgive you
This equall peece of Justice you have done:
For I betraid your councell to that fellow,
310 He overheard it; that was the cause I said
It lay not in me, to conceale it.

    BOS. Oh foolish woman,
Couldst not thou have poyson'd him?

    JUL. 'Tis weakenesse,
Too much to thinke what should have bin done—I go,
I know not wh[i]ther.   [*Dies.*]

    CARD. Wherefore com'st thou hither?

    BOS. That I might finde a great man, (like your selfe,)
Not out of his wits (as the Lord *Ferdinand*)
320 To remember my service.

    CARD. I'll have thee hew'd in peeces.

    BOS. Make not your selfe such a promise of that life
Which is not yours, to dispose of.

    CAR. Who plac'd thee here?

    BOS. Her lust, as she intended.

    CARD. Very well,
Now you know me for your fellow murderer.

    BOS. And wherefore should you lay faire marble colours,
Upon your rotten purposes to me?
330 Unlesse you imitate some that do plot great Treasons,
And when they have done, go hide themselves i'th'graves
Of those were Actors in't? CARD. No more,

There is a fortune attends thee.

Bos. Shall I go sue to fortune any longer?
'Tis the fooles Pilgrimage.

Card. I have honors in store for thee.

Bos. There are a many wayes that conduct to seeming
Honor, and some of them very durty ones.

Card. Throw to the divell
Thy mellancholly—the fire burnes well,   340
What neede we keepe a-stirring of't, and make
A greater smoother? thou wilt kill *Antonio*?

Bos. Yes. Card. Take up that body.

Bos. I thinke I shall
Shortly grow the common B[ie]re, for Church-yards?

Card. I will allow thee some dozen of attendants,
To aide thee in the murther.

Bos. Oh, by no meanes—Phisitians that apply horse-leiches
to any rancke swelling, use to cut of[f] their tailes, that the
blood may run through them the faster: Let me have no traine, 350
when I goe to shed blood, least it make me have a greater, when
I ride to the Gallowes.

Card. Come to me
After midnight, to helpe to remove that body
To her owne Lodging: I'll give out she dide o'th' Plague;
'Twill breed the lesse enquiry after her death.

Bos. Where's *Castruchio*, her husband?

Card. He's rod[e] to *Naples* to take possession
Of *Antonio's* Cittadell.

Bos. Beleeve me, you have done a very happy turne.   360

Card. Faile not to come: There is the Master-key
Of our Lodgings: and by that you may conceive
What trust I plant in you.

Bos. You shall find me ready.   *Exit* [*Cardinal*].
Oh poore *Antonio*, though nothing be so needfull
To thy estate, as pitty, Yet I finde
Nothing so dangerous: I must looke to my footing;
In such slippery yce-pavements, men had neede
To be frost-nayld well: they may breake their neckes else.
The Pre[ce]dent's here afore me: how this man   370
Beares up in blood!—seemes feareles!—why, 'tis well:
Securitie some men call the Suburbs of Hell,

Onely a dead wall betweene. Well (good *Antonio*)
I'll seeke thee out; and all my care shall be
To put thee into safety from the reach
Of these most cruell biters, that have got
Some of thy blood already. It may be,
I'll joyne with thee, in a most just revenge.
The weakest Arme is strong enough, that strikes
380 With the sword of Justice: Still me thinkes the Dutchesse
Haunts me: there, there!. . .'tis nothing but my mellancholy.
O Penitence, let me truely tast thy Cup,
That throwes men downe, onely to raise them up.   *Exit.*

SCENA III.

[Milan. Part of the fortifications of the city.]

[Enter Antonio & Delio. There is an] Eccho, (from the
Dutchesse Grave.)

DEL. Yond's the Cardinall's window: This fortification
Grew from the ruines of an auncient Abbey:
And to yond side o'th' river, lies a wall
(Peece of a Cloyster) which in my opinion
Gives the best Eccho, that you ever heard;
So hollow, and so dismall, and withall
So plaine in the destinction of our words,
That many have supposde it is a Spirit
That answeres.
10   ANT. I doe love these auncient ruynes:
We never tread upon them, but we set
Our foote upon some reverend History.
And questionles, here in this open Court
(Which now lies naked to the injuries
Of stormy weather) some men lye Enterr'd
Lov'd the Church so well, and gave so largely to't,
They thought it should have canopide their Bones
Till Doombes-day: But all things have their end:
Churches, and Citties (which have diseases like to men)
20 Must have like death that we have.
ECCHO. *Like death that we have.*
DEL. Now the *Eccho* hath caught you:

ANT. It groan'd (me thought) and gave
A very deadly Accent?

ECCHO. *Deadly Accent.*

DEL. I told you 'twas a pretty one: You may make it
A Huntes-man, or a Faulconer, a Musitian,
Or a Thing of Sorrow.

ECCHO. *A Thing of Sorrow.*

ANT. I sure: that suites it best.   30

ECCHO. *That suites it best.*

ANT. 'Tis very like my wi[f]es voyce.

ECCHO. *I, wifes-voyce.*

DEL. Come: let's ∧ walke farther from't:
I would not have you go to th' *Cardinalls* to-night:
Doe not.

ECCHO. *Doe not.*

DEL. Wisdome doth not more moderate wasting Sorrow
Then time: take time for't: be mindfull of thy safety.

ECCHO. *Be mindfull of thy safety.*   40

ANT. Necessitie compells me:
Make scruteny throughout the pass[ag]es
Of your owne life; you'll find it impossible
To flye your fate.

[ECCHO.] *O flye your fate.*

DEL. Harke: the dead stones seeme to have pitty on you
And give you good counsell.

ANT. *Eccho*, I will not talke with thee;
For thou art a dead Thing.

ECCHO. *Thou art a dead Thing.*   50

ANT. My Dutchesse is asleepe now,
And her litle-Ones, I hope sweetly: oh Heaven
Shall I never see her more?

ECCHO. *Never see her more:*

ANT. I mark'd not one repetition of the *Eccho*
But that: and on the sudden, a cleare light
Presented me a face folded in sorrow.

DEL. Your fancy; meerely.

ANT. Come: I'll be out of this Ague;
For to live thus, is not indeed to live: 60
It is a mockery, and abuse of life—
I will not henceforth save my selfe by halves,

Loose all, or nothing.

DEL. Your owne vertue save you!
I'll fetch your eldest sonne; and second you:
It may be that the sight of his owne blood
Spred in so sweet a figure, may beget
The more compassion.

[ANT.] How ever, fare you well:
70 Though in our miseries, Fortune have a part,
Yet, in our noble suffrings, she hath none—
Contempt of paine, that we may call our owne.   *Exe.*

SCENA IIII.

[*Milan. The Palace of the Cardinal and Ferdinand.*]

[*Enter Cardinal, Pescara, Malateste, Roderigo, Grisolan.*]

CARD. You shall not watch to-night by the sicke Prince,
His Grace is very well recover'd.

MAL. Good my Lord suffer us.

CARD. Oh, by no meanes:
The noyce, and change of object in his eye,
Doth more distract him: I pray, all to bed,
And though you heare him in his violent fit,
Do not rise, I intreate you.

PES. So, sir; we shall not—

10 CARD. Nay, I must have you promise
Upon your honors, for I was enjoyn'd to't
By himselfe; and he seem'd to urge it sencibly.

PES. Let ou[r] honors bind this trifle.

CARD. Nor any of your followers.

MAL. Neither.

CARD. It may be, to make triall of your promise,
When he's asleepe, my selfe will rise, and faigne
Some of his mad trickes, and crie out for helpe,
And faigne my selfe in danger.

20 MAL. If your throate were cutting,
I'll'd not come at you, now I have protested against it.

CARD. Why, I thanke you.   [*withdraws a little.*]

GRIS. 'Twas a foule storme to-night.

ROD. The Lord *Ferdinand's* chamber shooke like an Ozier.

MAL. 'Twas nothing but pure kindnesse in the Divell,
To rocke his owne child.   *Exeunt, [except Cardinal.]*
    CARD. The reason why I would not suffer these
About my brother, is, because at midnight
I may with better privacy, convay
Julias body to her owne Lodging: O, my Conscience!   30
I would pray now: but the Divell takes away my heart
For having any confidence in Praier.
About this houre, I appointed *Bosola*
To fetch the body: when he hath serv'd my turne,
He dies.   *Exit. [Enter Bosola.]*
    BOS. Hah? 'twas the Cardinalls voyce: I heard him name,
Bosola, and my death: listen, I heare ones footing.   *[Enter*
    FERD. Strangling is a very quie[t] death.   *Ferdinand.]*
    BOS. Nay then I see, I must stand upon my Guard.
    FERD. What say' to that? whisper, softly: doe you agree to't? 40
So—it must be done i'th' darke: the Cardinall
Would not for a thousand pounds, the Doctor should see it. *Exit.*
    BOS. My death is plotted; here's the consequence of murther.
"We value not desert, nor Christian breath,
When we know blacke deedes must be cur'de with death.
                [Enter Antonio & Servant.]
    SER. Here stay Sir, and be confident, I pray:
I'll fetch you a darke Lanthorne.   *Exit.*
    ANT. Could I take him
At his prayers, there were hope of pardon.
    BOS. Fall right my sword: *[Strikes him.]* 50
I'll not give thee so much leysure, as to pray.
    ANT. Oh, I am gone: Thou hast ended a long suit,
In a mynut.
    BOS. What art thou?
    ANT. A most wretched thing,
That onely have thy benefit in death,
To appeare my selfe.   *[Re-enter Servant, with light.]*
    SER. Where are you Sir?
    ANT. Very neere my home: *Bosola*?
    SER. Oh misfortune!   60
    BOS. *[to the Servant]* Smother thy pitty, thou art dead else:
        Antonio?
The man I would have sav'de 'bove mine owne life!

We are meerely the Starres tennys-balls (strooke, and banded
Which way please them)—oh good *Antonio*,
I'll whisper one thing in thy dying eare,
Shall make thy heart breake quickly: Thy faire Dutchesse
And two sweet Children...
    A n t. Their very names
Kindle a litle life in me.
70   B o s. Are murderd!
    A n t. Some men have wish'd to die,
At the hearing of sad tydings: I am glad
That I shall do't in sadnes: I would not now
Wish my wounds balm'de, nor heal'd: for I have no use
To put my life to: In all our Quest of Greatnes...
(Like wanton Boyes, whose pastime is their care)
We follow after bubbles, blowne in th'ayre.
Pleasure of life, what is't? onely the good houres
Of an Ague: meerely a preparative to rest,
80 To endure vexation: I doe not aske
The processe of my death: onely commend me
To *Delio*.
    B o s. Breake heart!
    A n t. And let my Sonne, flie the Courts of Princes. [*Dies.*]
    B o s. Thou seem'st to have lov'd *Antonio*?
    S e r. I brought him hether,
To have reconcil'd him to the Cardinall.
    B o s. I doe not aske thee that:
Take him up, if thou tender thine owne life,
90 And beare him, where the Lady *Julia*
Was wont to lodge: Oh, my fate moves swift.
I have this Cardinall in the forge already,
Now I'll bring him to th'hammer: (O direfull misprision:)
I will not Imitate things glorious,
No more then base: I'll be mine owne example.
On, on: and looke thou represent, for silence,
The thing thou bear'st.   *Exeunt.*

SCENA V.

[The same.]

[Enter] Cardinall (with a Booke).

CARD. I am puzzell'd in a question about hell:
He saies, in hell, there's one materiall fire,
And yet it shall not burne all men alike.
Lay him by: How tedious is a guilty conscience!
When I looke into the Fish-ponds, in my Garden,
Me thinkes I see a thing, arm'd with a Rake
That seemes to strike at me:
         [Enter Bosola & Servant bearing Antonio's body.]
Now? art thou come? thou look'st ghastly:
There sits in thy face, some great determination,
Mix'd with some feare.   10
    BOS. Thus it lightens into Action:
I am come to kill thee.
    CARD. Hah? helpe! our Guard!
    BOS. Thou art deceiv'd:
They are out of thy howling.
    CARD. Hold: and I will faithfully devide
Revenewes with thee.
    BOS. Thy prayers, and proffers
Are both unseasonable.
    CARD. Raise the Watch: 20
We are betraid.
    BOS. I have confinde your flight:
I'll suffer your retreyt to *Julias* Chamber,
But no further.
    CARD. Helpe: we are betraid!   *[Enter Malateste, Roderigo,*
    MAL. Listen: *Pescara, Grisolan, above.]*
    CARD. My Dukedome, for rescew!
    ROD. Fye upon his counterfeyting!
    MAL. Why, 'tis not the Cardinall.
    ROD. Yes, yes, 'tis he: 30
But I'll see him hang'd, ere I'll goe downe to him.
    CARD. Here's a plot upon me, I am assaulted: I am lost,
Unlesse some rescew.
    GRIS. He doth this pretty well:

But it will not serve; to laugh me out of mine honour!

CARD. The sword's at my throat:

ROD. You would not bawle so lowd then.

MAL. Come, come: [let]'s goe to bed: he told us thus much
    aforehand.

PESC. He wish'd you should not come at him: but beleev't,

40 The accent of the voyce sounds not in jest.

I'll downe to him, howsoever, and with engines
Force ope the doores.   *[Exit above.]*

ROD. Let's follow him aloofe,
And note how the Cardinall will laugh at him.   *[Exeunt above.]*

BOS. There's for you first: 'cause you shall not unbarracade
The doore to let in rescew.   *He kills the Servant.*

CARD. What cause hast thou
To pursue my life?

BOS. Looke there:

50 CARD. *Antonio?*

BOS. Slaine by my hand unwittingly:
Pray, and be sudden: when thou kill'dst thy sister,
Thou tookst from Justice her most equall ballance,
And left her naught but her sword.

CARD. O mercy!

BOS. Now it seemes thy Greatnes was onely outward:
For thou fall'st faster of thy selfe, then calamitie
Can drive thee: I'll not wast longer time: There. *[Wounds him.]*

CARD. Thou hast hurt me:

60 BOS. Againe:

CARD. Shall I die like a Levoret
Without any resistance? helpe, helpe, helpe:
I am slaine.   *[Enter Ferdinand.]*

FERD. Th'allarum? give me a fresh horse:
Rally the vaunt-guard: or the day is lost:
Yeeld, yeeld: I give you the honour of Armes,
Shake my Sword over you—will you yeilde?

CARD. Helpe me, I am your brother.

FERD. The divell?

70 My brother fight upon the adverse party? *He wounds the Cardinall,*
There flies your ransome.   *and (in the scuffle) gives*

CARD. Oh Justice: *Bosola his death wound.*
I suffer now, for what hath former bin:

"Sorrow is held the eldest child of sin.

FERD. Now you're brave fellowes: *Cæsars* Fortune was
harder then *Pompeys*: *Cæsar* died in the armes of prosperity,
Pompey at the feete of disgrace: you both died in the field—
the paine's nothing: paine many times is taken away with the
apprehension of greater, (as the tooth-ache with the sight of a
Barbor, that comes to pull it out) there's Philosophy for you.   80

BOS. Now my revenge is perfect: sinke (thou maine cause
Of my undoing)—the last part of my life,
Hath done me best service.   *He kills Ferdinand.*

FERD. Give me some wet hay, I am broken-winded—
I do account this world but a dog-kennell:
I will vault credit, and affect high pleasures,
Beyond death.

BOS. He seemes to come to himselfe,
Now he's so neere the bottom.

FERD. My sister, oh! my sister, there's the cause on't.   90
"Whether we fall by ambition, blood, or lust,
"Like Diamonds, we are cut with our owne dust.   [*Dies.*]

CARD. Thou hast thy payment too.

BOS. Yes, I hold my weary soule in my teeth,
'Tis ready to part from me: I do glory
That thou, which stood'st like a huge Piramid
Begun upon a large, and ample base,
Shalt end in a little point, a kind of nothing.
     [*Enter Pescara, Malateste, Roderigo & Grisolan.*]

PES. How now (my Lord?)

MAL. Oh sad disastre!   100

ROD. How comes this?

BOS. Revenge, for the Duchesse of *Malfy*, murdered
By th'*Aragonian* brethren: for *Antonio*,
Slaine by [t]his hand: for lustfull *Julia*,
Poyson'd by this man: and lastly, for my selfe,
(That was an Actor in the maine of all,
Much 'gainst mine owne good nature, yet i'th'end
Neglected.)

PES. How now (my Lord?)

CARD. Looke to my brother: 110
He gave us these large wounds, as we were strugling
Here i'th' rushes: And now, I pray, let me

Be layd by, and never thought of.   [*Dies.*]

PES. How fatally (it seemes) he did withstand
His owne rescew!

MAL. Thou wretched thing of blood,
How came *Antonio* by his death?

BOS. In a mist: I know not how,
Such a mistake, as I have often seene
120 In a play: Oh, I am gone—
We are onely like dead wals, or vaulted graves,
That ruin'd, yeildes no eccho: Fare you well—
It may be paine: but no harme to me to die,
In so good a quarrell: Oh this gloomy world,
In what a shadow, or deepe pit of darknesse,
Doth (womanish, and fearefull) mankind live!
Let worthy mindes nere stagger in distrust
To suffer death, or shame, for what is just—
Mine is another voyage.   [*Dies.*]
130 PES. The noble *Delio*, as I came to th'Pallace,
Told me of *Antonio's* being here, and shew'd me
A pritty gentleman his sonne and heire.

    [*Enter Delio with Antonio's Son.*]

MAL. Oh Sir, you come to[o] late.

DEL. I heard so, and
Was arm'd for't ere I came: Let us make noble use
Of this great ruine; and joyne all our force
To establish this yong hopefull Gentleman
In's mothers right. These wretched eminent things
Leave no more fame behind 'em, then should one
140 Fall in a frost, and leave his print in snow—
As soone as the sun shines, it ever melts,
Both forme, and matter: I have ever thought
Nature doth nothing so great, for great men,
As when she's pleas'd to make them Lords of truth:
    "*Integrity of life, is fames best friend,*
    Which noblely (beyond Death) shall crowne the end.   Exeunt.

FINIS.

COMMENTARY

THE DUCHESS OF MALFI

C = Crawford, *Collectanea*.
H.D.S. = H. Dugdale Sykes.

TITLE-PAGE

priuatly, at the Black-Friers: not "privately" in any modern sense. It is merely that Blackfriars was a "private" house as contrasted with "public" theatres like The Globe. It has been suggested by W. J. Lawrence that a "private house" was originally one where payment was made in advance, not at the door, in order to evade restrictions like those of the Act of Common Council of Dec. 6th 1574, where an exception is made in favour of "any plays, interludes, comedies, tragedies, or shows to be played in the private house, dwelling, or lodgings of any nobleman, citizen, or gentleman...*without public or common collection of money of the auditory*". (Cf. the performances of the modern Stage Society and others.) But in any case, if this distinction about the method of payment ever existed, it had ceased by the time Dekker wrote, in his *Gull's Horn-Book* (1609), "whether therefore the gatherers of the public *or private* Playhouses stand to receive the afternoon's rent". And it seems more probable that the private theatres of Blackfriars, Whitefriars, and St Paul's really owed their name to the fiction that the performances of the boy-companies who first played there, were mere rehearsals of the plays they were to act before the Queen; to "*a private view*" of which a select audience was thus admitted, but without any flying of flags or beating of drums through the streets. (Cf. J. Q. Adams, *Shakespearian Playhouses*, 93–4.)

At all events after 1608, when the Blackfriars Theatre was taken over from the Children of the Revels by R. Burbage as a winter-house for the King's Men, the distinction between public and private theatres became very shadowy: though there remained the important structural difference between the public playhouse, derived from the inn-yard, which was open to the sky and lit by daylight; and the private house, in origin a large room, which was roofed and artificially illuminated.

Kings Maiesties Seruants: see Chambers, *Eliz. Stage*, II. 192 ff.
diuerse things Printed...not...in the Presentment. For "cuts" thus restored in the published text, cf. Jonson, *Ev. Man out of h. H.* (1600), advertised as "containing more than hath been publiquely spoken or acted"; Barnes, *Devil's Charter* (1607), "Corrected and

augmented". (See Chambers, *Eliz. Stage*, III. 192–3; where it is suggested that Q₂ of *Hamlet* was perhaps similarly enlarged.)

Hora: Horace, *Epistles*, I. 6. 67–8. The full sentence runs:

Si quid novisti rectius istis,
Candidus imperti: si non, his utere mecum.

"If you know wiser precepts than these of mine, be kind (*not* 'candid') and tell me them: if you know none, then practise mine with me."

As usual, Webster's application of his Latin tag is obscure in the extreme: the only possible meaning here seems to be—"If you know a better play, let's hear it; if not, hear mine". The inappropriateness of the quotation makes one suspect borrowing by Webster: and, sure enough, I have found the tag at the end of Dekker's *Lanthorn and Candle-light* (1609).

Nicholas Okes: see on *W.D.*, title-page.

John Waterson: bookseller 1620–? 1641: died 1656.

THE ACTORS NAMES

Where there are two names to a part, the first would appear to belong to the original performance. Ostler, at all events, died in Dec. 1614. We may suppose that there was a revival in 1617–8, to account for the topical allusion to the Concini murder, inserted in I. 1 (see on I. 1. 8 ff.); this might be the performance referred to, as if fairly recent, by Orazio Busino in Feb. 1618 (see p. 180). Certainly there seems to have been a revival after Burbage's replacement by Taylor in 1619; and it is probably to this last that the other names numbered "2", like Taylor, Robinson, and Benfeild belong. The same applies to Rice, who was one of the Lady Elizabeth's Men in 1611 and does not appear in any King's lists before 1619; and to Pollard (who appears there 1616–7), Tomson (apparently still acting women's parts in 1631), Pallant (b. 1605). See J. T. Murray, *Eng. Dram. Companies*, II. 147; Bentley, II.

J. Lowin (1576–1653), whose portrait is in the Ashmolean Museum at Oxford, is said to have acted Falstaff, Volpone, Sir Epicure Mammon, Melantius (in *The Maid's Tragedy*), and Hamlet(?); and as the first Henry VIII to have "had his instructions from Mr Shakespeare himself". He made money and became one of the two managers of the King's Men from 1630. But the Civil War brought him hard times. It was in vain that in 1648 he and J. Taylor attempted to revive acting at The Cockpit; after three or four days the players were seized by soldiers while acting *The Bloody Brother*, carried off to Hatton House, then a prison, and only released after being despoiled of their stage-clothes. In 1652 Fletcher's *Wild Goose Chase* was published in folio for his and Taylor's benefit. But the benefit was little or short-lived; for when the old man died as host of "The Three Pigeons" at Brentford, "his poverty was as great as his age".

R. Burbidge, son of James, the founder of the first Elizabethan public theatre, was born about 1573, and long before his death in 1619 had become the most distinguished actor of his day. An Elegy records some of his chief parts:

> No more young Hamlett, ould Heironymoe.
> Kind Leer, the greved Moore, and more beside
> That lived in him, have now for ever died.

Richard III and many of the chief parts in Jonson and Beaumont and Fletcher were also his: and a special link between him and Webster is perhaps to be found in the "Character of an Excellent Actor", printed in "Overbury's" *Characters*, 6th ed., 1615. For its allusion to his skill in painting makes it probable that Richard Burbage was the model; and its style, that Webster was the author. (See *Wks.* iv. 57.)

J. Taylor (? 1586–? 1652) appears to have left the Prince's company for the King's Men in 1619, as successor to Burbage. He is said to have played Hamlet "incomparably well"; also Iago, Mosca (*Volpone*), Face (*The Alchemist*), and Truewit (*Epicoene*). Later we find him one of the two managers, with Lowin, of the King's Men. In the lean years of the Commonwealth he was one of the ten actors who tried to raise a little money by publishing the First Folio of Beaumont and Fletcher in 1647.

H. Cundaile or *Condell* is best known as one of the editors (1623) of the First Folio of Shakespeare, who had bequeathed him 26s. 8d. to buy a ring. He seems to have ceased acting in 1619; and died in 1627.

R. Robinson (d. 1648). Praised by Jonson in *The Devil is an Ass*, ii. 3. for his skill in acting as a woman.

W. Ostler (d. 1614) began as one of the child-actors of Q. Elizabeth's Chapel in 1601, taking women's parts; then married Hemminge's daughter Thomasine and was admitted to partnership in the Globe in 1611–2. He may, then, have been about twenty-five in 1614; making perhaps, still, a rather feminine young Antonio.

J. Underwood (d. 1624–5): one of the Children of the Chapel in 1601.

N. Towley, *R. Sharpe* died respectively in 1623 and 1632.

J. Tomson (d. 1634) seems still acting female roles in 1631. In 1619-23 a very youthful Julia?

R. Pallant (b. 1605). A youthful Cariola, and still more youthful Doctor!

DEDICATION

George Harding, thirteenth Baron Berkeley, was now twenty-two and took his M.A. at Oxford in this year. He had a family connection with the stage and with the King's Men in particular; for his mother's grandfather and father, the first and second Lords Hunsdon, held the office of Lord Chamberlain and were patrons of the most famous of Elizabethan companies, the Lord Chamberlain's Men, whom James I made the King's Majesty's Servants. Indeed it has been suggested that *A Midsummer Night's Dream* was written for the wedding of George Harding's parents (Chambers, *Eliz. Stage*, II. 194). Two years before, in 1621, Burton had brought to this youthful patron the sombre offering of *The Anatomy of Melancholy*, and was rewarded in 1630 with the living of Segrave in Leicestershire; in which year Massinger in his turn dedicated *The Renegado* to "George Harding, Baron Barkeley".

Knight...to...Prince Charles: i.e. he had been made a Knight of the Bath at the creation of the Prince on Nov. 3rd 1616.

3–5. *Sea...River, to guide.* Cf. *W.D.* I. 2. 342–3.

10. *Nobility...rellique.* Cf. Overbury, *Wife*, xx. 3: "Gentry is but a relique of time past". (H.D.S.)

12. *which: i.e.* a practice which.

19–21. *scorners of the Muses...forgotten.* Cf. Sappho's famous expression of the same idea, addressed to a wealthy, but Philistine woman-friend. Bergk, *Poet. Lyr. Graeci* (1843), Fr. 73:

> κατθάνοισα δὲ κείσεαι οὐδέ ποτα μναμοσύνα σέθεν
> ἔσσετ' οὐδέποτ' εἰς ὕστερον· οὐ γὰρ πεδέχεις βρόδων
> τῶν ἐκ Πιερίας· ἀλλ' ἀφάνης κἠν Ἀίδα δόμοις
> φοιτάσεις πεδ' ἀμαύρων νεκύων ἐκπεποταμένα.

When thou art not, thou shalt lie forgot, all memories of thee
Shall be lost and dumb through the years to come. Since now from the Muses' Tree
Thou hast plucked no rose, a wraith none knows, that none remembereth,
Thou shalt drift 'mid the hosts of nameless ghosts that haunt the House of Death.

COMMENDATORY VERSES

MIDDLETON'S.

Middleton may have collaborated with Webster about two years before, in *A.Q.L.* (*c.* 1621); Rowley and Ford were to collaborate with him about a year later in *The Late Murder of the Son upon the Mother* (1624).

In Tragœdiam.
To Tragedy.
As light at the Thunderer's stroke from darkness springs,
   To the wicked, doom, to the poet, life she brings.

Chron: Londinensis. Middleton received this office of City Chronologer in 1620. For its duties see on III. 3. 24.

ROWLEY'S.

3–6. "However eloquently in her real life the Duchess may have defended that misalliance *which* her brothers' anger made so fatal, though she may have spoken more, she can never have spoken so well as in your play." Cf. Margaret, Duchess of Newcastle, *Sociable Letters*, CXXIII (of Shakespeare): "Certainly *Julius Caesar*, *Augustus Caesar*, and *Antonius* did never Really Act their parts Better, if so Well, as he hath Described them, and I believe that *Antonius* and *Brutus* did not Speak Better to the People, than he hath Feign'd them".

For *answer* = "justify" cf. Beveridge, *Sermons* (1729), I. 307: "How they will answer it. . . at the last day I know not".

FORD'S.

1–2. Perhaps ultimately modelled on Propertius' tribute to Virgil's *Aeneid* (II. 34. 65–6):

> Cedite Romani scriptores, cedite Grai:
> Nescio quid maius nascitur Iliade.

3. *whiles words and matter change*: seems to mean—"while things are put into words", "while literature lasts".

I. I.

Outer stage, probably, till 406; then whole stage.

1. The *W.D.* begins with "Banisht!" (cf. III. 5 below); this, Webster's next play, with a return from banishment—"You are wel-come to your country".

2. *long in France*. Antonio had followed the deposed Federico, the last Aragonese king of Naples, into his French exile, which lasted from 1501 to his death at Tours in Nov. 1504.

4 ff. Contrast the description of the French court at the opening of Chapman's *Bussy d'Ambois*.

8 ff. *Quits . . . Sicophants*. Vaughan first suggested that this, and indeed the whole speech, is an allusion to the assassination of the Maréchal d'Ancre on April 24th 1617.

Concino Concini, son of a Florentine notary, after spending a dissolute youth came to France in the train of Marie de' Medici, the queen of Henri IV; and there married her *femme de chambre*, Leonora Galigai. This woman had an extraordinary influence over her mistress, and when the Queen became Regent after Henry's murder, the Regent herself was still ruled by Leonora; while Concini, though not liked by the Queen and perpetually at feud with his wife, in some strange way contrived to use the two women to make himself the chief power in France. The greater his influence became, the greater he made it, by pretending that it was even greater than it was, so that a sycophantic court flocked to the feet of this supreme dispenser of favours. In his hands the boy Louis XIII, already crushed by an indifferent mother, became a mere *roi fainéant* at the mercy of his Mayor of the Palace; whole armies were maintained in the usurper's pay; and some sudden stroke, whether arrest or assassination, was the only weapon left to the young king. On the morning of April 24th 1617, Concini in the midst of his enormous suite was confronted by de Vitry, captain of the royal guard, and a few followers at the entrance to the Louvre; and, at the first sign of resistance to arrest, riddled with bullet and sword-thrust. The hated corpse was torn limb from limb in the streets of Paris; and throughout France, already partly in rebellion, the news roused wild enthusiasm. The old counsellors of Henri IV, Villeroi, Jeannin, du Vair, de Sillery were recalled (cf. 18–9), the Queen-Mother and Concini's tools disgraced or imprisoned (cf. 8–10). Marie de' Medici had been the friend of Spain; and accordingly there were great rejoicings throughout Protestant Europe, so that in England not to share the general joy was to brand oneself as "more than half Spanish". (Cf. *Cal. Venet. State-Papers*, 1615–7, 510 *n*.) A dozen or more pamphlets still testify to the popular interest.

This allusion, however, is questioned by J. R. Brown (see Introduction, "Date"). He also points out (*Phil. Quart.* xxxi. 360–2) that the plagiarizing Webster has based ll. 6–16 on the advice given by his mother Mammea (Mamaea) to the Emperor Alexander Severus in Sir Thomas Elyot's *Image of Governance* (printed 1541), ch. viii, sig. D 4v; and that I. I. 456–61 below has the same source (ch. xxvi, sig. P 1v): "onely take frome me the name of a father, or the dotynge pleasure to se my lytell sonne ryde on a cokhorse, or to here hym chatter and speake lyke a wanton".

10. *which he sweetely termes*, etc.: the antecedent to *which* has troubled editors. *Pallace* (Vaughan and Allen) makes little sense; *persons* (Sampson—"man being the chief work of the creator") makes even less; while *Order*, his other suggestion, is too far away. But there is no difficulty if *which* is taken to refer to *the whole previous sentence* (cf. Lat. *id quod*), *i.e.* his policy of cleansing his court. Then *Considering*, etc., in 12 follows quite naturally to explain *why* he terms his action a heavenly piece of work. For this use of *which* cf. the Dedication of the Play, 12.

11. *Masters Master-peece*: crowning master-piece. Krusius ingeniously sees an allusion to Christ's cleansing of the Temple: I am inclined to think, however, that if Webster had meant this, he would have made it clearer. No suspicion of it seems to have occurred to any of his editors.

14. *in generall*: *not* "as a rule", but "universally", "without exception". Cf. *Troil. and Cress.* iv. 5. 21: "'Twere better she were kiss'd in general" (*i.e.* by everyone).

17–23. Cf. Louis XIII's words to the Assembly of Notables at Rouen summoned in October, 1617: "que sans autres respect ni considération quelquonque, crainte ou désir de plaire ou complaire à personne, ils nous donnent en toutes franchise et sincérité les conseils qu'ils jugeront en leurs consciences les plus salutaires et convenables". (Stoll: from Isambert et Decrusy, *Recueil Général des Anciennes Lois Françaises* (1829), xvi. 108.)

24. *Court-Gall*: "gall" primarily in the sense of "sore place". So Spenser, *State of Ireland* (Globe ed. 654/1), speaks of the Irish as being "a gall and inconvenience". So Pericles called hostile Aegina "the eyesore of the Peiraeus", and Augustus described his degenerate posterity as his "sores and cancers" (Sueton. *Aug.* 65). The association with the *bitterness* of the gall-bladder is, however, doubtless meant to be present here as well.

33. *onely the reward*: *i.e.* the only reward. Cf. Caxton, *Golden Legend*, 333 b/₁: "Luke is only with me".

For the idea, cf. Montaigne II. 16 (a rendering of Seneca): "The reward of well-doing is the doing and the fruit of our duty is our duty". (C.)

37. *two Towells in stead of a shirt*. Cf. 1 *Hen. IV*, IV. 2. 47 (Vaughan).

39. *black-birds...hard weather*: a medieval idea, perhaps due to the birds fluffing out their feathers. Cf. *Hortus Sanitatis*, III. 74 (of the ousel): "and in the winter for fatness it can scarcely fly".

40. *dogge dayes*: evil days. See on *W.D.* III. 3. 67.

43–5. Cf. Montaigne I. 38: "It was told Socrates that one was no whit amended by his travell: I believe it wel (said he) for he carried himselfe with him". Similarly the famous tag of Horace (*Ep.* I. 11. 27):

Caelum, non animum mutant qui trans mare currunt.

So in the *Characters* the "Improvident Young Gallant" comes back from abroad "never the more mended in his conditions, cause he carried himselfe along with him".

51. *standing-pooles*: stagnant pools with green scum. Cf. *Lear*, III. 4. 137: "the green mantle of the standing pool".

58–9. *died...pardon*: we may recall Tourneur, *Revenger's Tragedy*, III. 3.

59. *rewards*: a technical hunting term. See on *W.D.* IV. 2. 193.

62–5. *Geometry...Crowtches*. "To hang by geometry" is a curious idiom used to describe clothes hanging awkwardly and angularly. *E.g.* Fletcher, *Span. Curate*, III. 2: "and the old Cut-worke Cope, that hangs by Gymitrie". So Swift, *Pol. Convers.* I. 85: "Lord! my Petticoat! how it hangs by Jommetry".

Here the obvious resemblance between a man on crutches and a pair of compasses must come in, as well as the idea of hanging stiffly and awkwardly. But it would no doubt be fanciful to press further the original meaning of "geometry"—"earth-measurement"—and to imagine the cripple, as he swings over the countryside, to be compared with a pair of dividers traversing a map (cf. Donne's likening of his mistress and himself to a pair of compasses). Webster's mind runs on such "mystical Mathematicks"; cf. *W.D.* I. 2. 93; *D.M.* I. 1. 137; II. 2. 19; IV. 2. 227; *D.L.* I. 1. 72.

73. *Gaston de Foux*: Gaston de Foix (1489–1512), "whose fame," says Guicciardini, "will last as long as the world", both made his name and lost his life in the space of those two months of 1512 which

culminated in the victory of Ravenna over the Spanish and Papal armies. There the young leader of twenty-four fell in the moment of his success, after having revealed to the world the marching power of French infantry and how to make full use of it. (He had, however, nothing to do with the taking of Naples in 1501, at which date he was, indeed, a mere child.)

The allusion was clearly suggested to Webster by Painter, who quite correctly uses the victory "of that notable Capitayne Gaston de Foix...at the Journey of Ravenna" to date the misfortunes of the Duchess.

80. *rust unto the soule.* Cf. *Characters*, "A Fayre and happy Milke-mayde", 9 ff. For the general idea H.D.S. quotes Burton, *Anat.* I. 2. 2. 7.

82–3. *Breeds all blacke male-contents, and their close rearing*
      (Like mothes in cloath) doe hurt for want of wearing.
Sampson explains—"*is* like moths *which* do hurt". But it is surely impossible to supply *is* and ignore the brackets in this way. Fortunately there is an exactly parallel construction in *D.L.* IV. 2. 131–3:

> a kind of sawcy *pride,*
> Which *like to Mushromes,* ever *grow* most ranke,
> When they do spring from dung-hills.

Here we have exactly the same confusion in the simile, which causes *grow* to be in the plural, though its subject *Which* is singular, owing to the attraction of the plural *Mushromes.* So here, we should expect *does hurt,* not *doe hurt,* since the subject is clearly *close rearing;* but the plural *mothes* led Webster to write *doe.* "The secret breeding of these discontents is so harmful (like moths in clothes) just for want of stirring up". Only *wearing* is much more appropriate to the clothes than the discontents; just as the *dung-hills* in the *D.L.* passage really belong to the *Mushromes* rather than to *pride.* Webster telescopes together his main sentence and his simile.

It has also to be remembered that plural verbs with singular subjects, and *vice versa,* were in any case less startling in the looser English of the Elizabethans. Cf. 2 *Hen. VI,* III. 1. 301:

> Men's *flesh* preserv'd so whole *do* seldom win.

I.e. "men whose flesh is preserv'd"; so here *their close rearing* = "they, closely reared". It is the exact opposite of the Latin idiom in which *Caesar occisus* = "Caesar's murder".

83–4. s.d. *Silvio*: the name was doubtless suggested by Silvio Savello (see Hist. Introd. p. 10).

Castruchio is similarly derived from the historic Petrucci, Cardinal of Siena, in Bandello, whose name Belleforest, followed by Painter, changes to "Castruccio".

90. *the Ring*: running at the ring (*i.e.* trying to carry off on the point of one's lance a ring suspended in the air) was tending under James I to replace the more dangerous jousting of the previous reign; though

James himself was a poor hand even at this and was much talked of for the inferiority he showed compared with his brother-in-law, Christian of Denmark, when the latter visited England in 1606.

95–6. *go to war, in person.* Cf. *W.D.* II. I. 119 ff.

107. *fighting*: probably with a *double entendre*.

112. *all in Tents*: Tents being used (1) in the ordinary sense; (2) = "rolls of lint", not so much, here, for "searching a wound" (Dyce), as for keeping it open, like the rubber tubes of modern surgery; they were left to plug the wound. Hence "*lie* in Tents".

For the pun, cf. Middleton, *More Dissemblers besides Women*, II. 3. 103:

lies you all in tents
Like your camp-vict'lers. (Dyce.)

H.D.S. quotes also *Troil. and Cress.* v. I. 11–3.

115–6. With a double sense.

118. *Spanish Gennit*: a light, but valuable, breed of horse. The Spanish *ginete* (perhaps from the Gk. γυμνήτης, light-armed soldier) meant originally a horse*man* riding *à la gineta*, i.e. "with the legs trussed up in short stirrups, with a target and a ginnet launce".

120. *Pliney's opinion*: Pliny VIII. 42 (Holland's transl.): "In Portugall, along the river Tagus, and about Lisbon, certaine it is, that when the West wind bloweth, the mares set up their tailes, and turn them full against it, and so conceive that genitall aire in steed of naturall seed: in such sort as they become great withall, and quicken in their time, and bring forth foles as swift as the wind, but they live not above three yeares". It was a widely spread idea. Cf. Aristotle, *Hist. Anim.* VI. 18; Varro, *Re Rust.* II. 1; Virg. *Georg.* III. 273; Sil. Ital. III. 381; Justin XLIV. 3; Augustine, *Civ. Dei.* XXI. 5. D. W. Thompson in his note on the Aristotle passage in the Oxford transl. (1910) suggests that the idea may be traced back to Homer, *Il.* XX. 223 ff., where we hear how Boreas loved the mares of Erichthonios, King of Troy, and begat on them colts so light of foot that they could run over the waves of the sea. But this is rather one instance, than the origin, of so common an idea; the transition is natural enough from "swift as the wind" to "son of the wind".

The notion recurs in Fletcher's *Woman's Prize*, II. 5:

They are a genealogy of jennets, gotten
And born thus, by the boisterous breath of husbands.

And among other "Vulgar Errors" Sir T. Browne duly discusses also (III. 21) these "subventaneous conceptions from the Western wind".

122. *reeles from the Tilt*. Such tilting phrases seem to be used in a metaphorical and wider sense in the current speech of the period. Thus Chamberlain writes to Carleton (Jan. 5th 1607–8), of a certain Fuller who has got into trouble in ecclesiastical controversy: "he hath...feigned himself sick in bed when he should come to the tilt"

—(*i.e.* "face the music" as we might say). It seems possible, then, that Silvio means here that the horse has a trick of jibbing and refusing in general.

138. *laugh out of compasse*: beyond bounds, out of measure. So Hall in his *Characters*, of the Unthrift: "He ranges beyond his pale, and lives without compasse". There is perhaps also the sense of "laughing *impertinently*". Cf. the story in Bacon's *Apophthegms* (6) (*Wks.* ed. Spedding, VII. 125): "Pace, the bitter Fool, was not suffered to come at the Queen, because of his bitter humour. Yet at one time some persuaded the Queen that he should come to her; undertaking for him that he should *keep compass* (*v.l.* within compass). So he was brought to her, and the Queen said: 'Come on, Pace; now we shall hear of our faults'. Saith Pace: 'I do not use to talk of that that all the town talks of'".

141–2. *excellent Riders in France*. Cf. *W.D.* IV. 3. 99; Ford, *Love's Sacrifice*, I. 2. The French were held the best horsemen in Europe. It is an interesting coincidence, at least, that a certain Monsieur St Anthoine was sent over by Henri IV in 1603 to be Prince Henry's riding-master and was known in England as "St Anthony the rider". On the prince's death in 1612 St Anthoine led a *cheval de deuil* in the funeral procession; and subsequently became equerry of Prince Charles, whose helmet he holds in the equestrian portrait by Vandyke. The Duchess of Newcastle speaks of him as accounted the best master of his art. (W. B. Rye, *England as seen by Foreigners*, 253.) So it is possible that Webster may have thought of St Anthoine here; though, independently of this, he had the authority of Painter for the horsemanship of Antonio—"for riding and manageing of greate horse, he had not his fellow in Italy".

144–5. *Grecian-horse... Princes*. Cf. Cicero's remark on the school of Isocrates (*De orat.* II. 22. 94): "From his school, as from the Trojan horse, came forth only men of sovereign rank".

155. *five thousand crownes, at Tennis*. Cf. *W.D.* II. 1. 185.

157. *flashes*: pieces of showy behaviour. Cf. Jonson's character, Sir Petronel Flash.

159–60. *Spring in his face... Toades*. Cf. Chapman, *Bussy d'Ambois*, III. 2. 452:

> That toad-pool that stands in thy complexion.

Camille Cé in his version (1922) renders *Spring* by *printemps*: but the parallel from Chapman is decisive. Cf., too, *Merch. of Ven.* I. I. 88–9:

> There are a sort of men whose visages
> Do cream and mantle like a standing-pond.

For the engendering of toads as a type of supreme loathsomeness, cf. *Troil. and Cress.* II. 3. 170–1: "I do hate a proud man, as I hate the engendering of toads"; and *Othello*, IV. 2. 56 ff.

179. *Rewards, by heare-say*: at random, without troubling to discover

the real deservers? Or does it mean: "Rewards with mere words, hearsay recompenses"? This makes good sense: but the first meaning is supported by Webster's seeming source, W. Alexander, *Alexandraean Tragedy*, 577–8.

180–1. *Law...cob-web...Spider*. Cf. Massinger and Fletcher, *Spanish Curate*, IV. 5:

> A lawyer that entangles all men's honesties,
> And lives like a spider in a cob-web lurking,
> And catching at all flies that pass his pit-falls.

The simile is more commonly used to illustrate the fact that there is one law for the strong, another for the weak; just as large flies break through the cobweb which holds the small ones. Dyce (p. xx) quotes examples of this from Field (*A Woman's a Weathercock*, 1612, sig. E), Braithwaite's *Honest Ghost* (1658), p. 79. (Cf. Tilley, L 116.)

185–6. Cf. *Char.* "An Intruder into favour", 20–1.

196–8. "You will wish that she was (even) less disposed to think it vain-glorious to talk much than you are disposed to think it wearisome to hear her." The whole passage 194–209 echoes Pettie's *Civile Conversation of M. Steeven Guazzo* (ed. Sullivan, 1925, Bk. II. p. 241); which is here far clearer: "you wyll ... wishe that shee woulde bee no more weary to speake, then you are to heare". See Textual Note; and *W.D.*, Appendix I.

200. *Galliard*: a particularly lively, capering dance. Cf. the description in Sir J. Davies, *Orchestra* (quoted in *Sh.'s Eng.* II. 448):

> A gallant dance that lively doth bewray
> A spirit and a virtue masculine;
> Impatient that her house on earth should stay,
> Since she herself is fiery and divine,
> Oft does she make her body upward fine,
> With lofty turns and capriols in the air
> Which with the lusty tunes accordeth fair.

202–3. *countenance...continence*: probably an intentional jingle.

206–7. Cf. Donne, *Of the Progress of the Soul* (1612), 463–4:

> Whose twilights were more cleare, then our mid-day;
> Who dreamt devoutlier, then most use to pray. (C.)

208–9. Cf. *Char.* "A vertuous Widdow", 20–2.

208. *flattring Glasses*. Cf. *Char.* "An Intruder", 22; and H. King, *Elegy on Gustavus Adolphus*:

> Here then break your false glasses, which present
> You greater than your Maker ever meant.
> Make Truth your Mirrour now.

So Burton curiously records (*Anat.* I. 2. 4. 7): "Acco, an old woman, seeing by chance her face in a true glass (for she used false flattering glasses belike at other times, as most gentlewomen do), *animi dolore in insaniam delapsa est*, ran mad".

211. *wire-drawer*: one who draws out and distorts the truth.

212. *case the picture up*: put it away. Cf. III. 2. 162. (H.D.S.)

214. Repeated in *Mon. Col.* 278.

Staines—not in the modern sense, but "deprives of lustre" (the oldest meaning being "to deprive of colour", *not* "to colour"). Cf. W. Alexander, *Alexandraean Tragedy*, 1319:

Staine of times past, and light of times to come.   (R. W. Dent.)

Hence "stain" comes to mean simply "surpass" and in the *Arcadia* we have: "O voice that doth the Thrush in shrilnesse staine".

230. *Leaguer*: camp (Germ. *Lager*).

244. *lur'd*: met. of hawking. See on *W.D.* IV. 1. 139.

257. H.D.S. quotes Chapman, *Bussy d'Ambois*, I. 1. 5–6:

As cedars beaten with continual storms,
So great men flourish.

260–2. From Montaigne III. 9: "*Multi fallere docuerunt, dum timent falli, et aliis jus peccandi suspicando fecerunt* (Cic.): Many have taught others to deceive, while themselves feare to be deceived, and have given them just cause to offend by suspecting them unjustly". (C.)

265–6. With reference to the legend of Jupiter's finding access to Danae in her brazen tower in the shape of a shower of gold. Cf. II. 2. 18 below.

278. *familiars*: a word with sinister associations for an Elizabethan; being applied not only to evil spirits, but to servants of the Pope or Roman bishops and to officers of the Holy Inquisition, charged with making arrests.

280. *quaint*: cunning (Lat. *comptus*). So Gavin Douglas (*Aen.* II. 1. 59) speaks of "quent Ulexes".

281. *An Intelligencer*: another word with hateful associations to Elizabethan ears. The name was given to the special correspondents employed by ambassadors or great men to keep them posted with regular intelligence in the absence of newspapers. Chamberlain's letters to Carleton are a very honest example. Naturally the methods by which their information was procured were not always above suspicion: and the *Camb. Hist. of Eng. Lit.* (VII. 193) quotes Francis Osborne's *Advice to a Son*: "It is an office unbecoming a Gentleman to be an Intelligencer, which in real Truth is no better than a Spie". Nash couples them with Judas.

286. *Angels*: the Angel-Noble, first coined by Edward IV, was so-called from having on it, like our sovereign, a design of St Michael killing the dragon.

300. *Candies...[o'er]*: sugars over. Cf. *W.D.* v. 6. 60–1.

301. *complementall*: *i.e.* a polite accomplishment.

307. *dormouse*. Cf. III. 1. 25.

308–13. Bosola, like an old blood-hound, kindles to excitement as the Duke brings back to his imagination the details of the hunt of intrigue.

315. *covet good fame*: *i.e.* good fame *only*, not those more material rewards which are the price of base services.

325. *luxurious*: wanton.

326. *wed twice*. Cf. Chapman's *Widow's Tears*, II. 4. 27 ff.: "open and often detestations of that incestuous life (as she termed it) of widows' marriages; as being but a kind of lawful adultery; like usury, permitted by the law, but not approved".

329. *Labans sheepe*: *Genesis* xxx. 31–42.

335–8. Cf. Chapman, *Widow's Tears*, I. 1. 106 ff.; *W.D.* v. 6. 155 ff.

336. *motion*: resolve.

341. *honney-dew*: a sweet, sticky substance found on plants and now supposed to be excreted by aphides.

345. *give the divell sucke*: one of the most recurrent details in witch-trials is the supposed suckling of animal familiars, either with the witch's blood or more often from a supernumerary nipple (one of the best established physical signs of a witch). See M. A. Murray, *Witchcult in Western Europe*, 90–6.

348. *Vulcans Engine*. Cf. Homer, *Od.* VIII. 266 ff., where Demodocus the minstrel tells how Hephaestus contrived an invisible engine to trap the guilty Ares in the arms of his wife Aphrodite.

353. *Under the E[a]ves of night*: a vivid phrase, doubtless helped by the similarity of "eve" in the sense of "evening". For hiding under eaves, cf. "to eavesdrop", which is "to lurk within the 'eaves-drop' of a house" (*i.e.* the space where fall the droppings from the eaves).

355. *Crab*. Cf. *Arcadia*, II. (*Wks.* 1. 164): "A Crab-fish which . . . lookes one way and goes another"; so *Hortus Sanitatis*: "The Crab goes backward, and has never known how to follow his nose".

359. *executed*, apart from its sinister associations with punishment, is a regular ecclesiastical word for performing a religious service.

366. *begins at the end*: considers the final view first. Cf. the Gk. saw, "σκόπει τέλος"—"Consider the end".

372. *chargeable*: "expensive", not "accusable", "compromising".

373. *whispering roomes*: privy closets for secret interviews.

375–6. *Lamprey . . . nev'r a bone*: so Sir T. Browne, *Pseudodoxia*, III. 19, speaks of its "defect of bones, whereof it hath not one".

379. *the Tongue*. Cf. Chambers and Sidgwick, *Early English Lyrics*, p. 191:

Wikked tungë breketh bone
Thow the tungës self have none.

380–1. Cf. "Overbury", *Characters*, "A Good Woman": "She leaves the neat youth, telling his lushious tales". For the bearing of this parallel (cf. v. 2. 244) on the date of the play, see p. 13. H.D.S. points out another borrowing by N. Richards, in "The Flesh" (*Poems Sacred and Satirical*, 1641):

As what cannot a spruce Queane with a smooth Tale
Make him believe?

384. *foote-steps*: *i.e.* not in our sense, but steps to tread on, or rungs of a ladder. Thus Latimer speaks (*6th Sermon before Edw. VI*) of "the footsteps of the ladder of heaven".

386. *apprehending danger*: not "fearing", but "grasping" it, taking the bull by the horns.

390. *wincked, and chose a husband*: not "gained a husband by bold encouragement" (Allen), but "shut my eyes and blindly chose". Thus Topsell says that female goats "never wink in their sleep". Cf. III. I. 8; *A.V.* IV. I. 312; Middleton, *Roaring Girl*, II. 2. 15:

> I know that man
> Ne'er truly loves—if he gainsay't, he lies—
> That winks and marries with his father's eyes.
> I'll keep mine own wide open.

H.D.S. quotes from Ray's *Proverbs* the expression "you may wink and choose". It recurs in Ford, *Lady's Trial*, II. I.

398. *ingenious*: "ingenuous", the two words being interchangeable in the English of the time.

404–6. *wildernesse...guide*: imitated by Shirley (*The Brothers*, II. I):

> Sir, with your pardon
> You lead me to a wilderness and take
> Yourself away, that should be guide.

406. S.D. *The Duchess draws the traverse*: the Quarto has no directions: *Enter Antonio* is usually supplied. The fact however that Antonio is not told to enter—"He attends", says Cariola, who then conceals herself behind the arras—makes my arrangement slightly easier. His sitting down to write implies the use of the inner stage with its properties; and there is something more dramatic in the idea of the Duchess taking the initiative in this also. With the cry "I am going into a wilderness" she turns and stepping to the curtain reveals the lover who is to be her ruin. The action then proceeds on the whole stage (there would be no lack of hangings round the stage, as far as one can gather, to hide Cariola). Then at the end of the scene the curtain is drawn again upon the lovers and the next act begins on the outer stage.

412. *triumphs*: festivities.

413. *husbands*: a significant and ambiguous word. Cf. the play on the double sense of "husbandry" in Chapman, *All Fools*, I. I. 141: Valerio seeing his wife Gratiana cries, weary of his household economies:

> And see, bright heaven, here comes my husbandry.

417. *I look yong for your sake*: (1) "thanks to you". Cf. Tindall, *Genesis* iii. 17: "Cursed be the erth for thy sake". (2) "For love of you".

435. *Over-seer*: a technical term, overseers being appointed to oversee and assist executors. However, as usual, *Quis custodes custodiet ipsos?* Judging, at least, by the fifteenth-century proverb "Too

secutours and an overseere make thre theves", overseers were only. too capable of oversights.

443. *In a winding sheete*: since her husband is dead.

444. *In a cople*: *i.e.* of sheets, with also the inevitable *double entendre.*

445. *St. Win[i]frid* lived in the seventh century and was the daughter of the Welsh Tenyth ap Eylud. She had her head struck off by Caradoc ap Alauc whose advances she had rejected; but was restored to life by St Bruno. From the spring which bubbled up where her blood was shed, the town of Holywell in Flint takes its name; and the stones in it are still streaked as with blood. (See Baring-Gould, *Lives of the Saints*, November, 1. 69–72.)

St Winfrid, on the other hand, in case that should be the right reading, is Boniface the missionary of Germany who was born, also in the seventh century, at Crediton in Devon.

449–51. It seems to me possible that these lines were suggested to Webster by a note on two lines of Tofte's Ariosto, *Satire IV* (from which he certainly copies a whole passage in II. 1), although the sense is exactly opposite. The note runs: "The Poet compareth marriage to Purgatory, where, as they say, they continue in paine but for a certaine time. But the Batchellors life he termeth hell, because he thinkes that none perhaps live honest untill they be married; & therefore in greater danger if they die not maides". (The lines of Ariosto are:

Yet better 'tis in Purgatory dwell
A little space than always live in hell.)

456–61. One of those general gnomic passages to which Webster, like Euripides (who was similarly much exercised about this particular question of children), is too prone to sacrifice strict dramatic relevance. Cf. II. 45 and Bosola's bald "Observe my meditation now"—followed by fifteen lines clearly based on Webster's commonplace-book; *D.L.* II. 3. 110, where Romelio similarly launches into a "meditation" in couplets; and again the obscurely apposite parables of the Crocodile in *W.D.*, of the Salmon and of Reputation later in this play. Too often Ariosto's comment in *The Devil's Law-Case* is justified of Webster in general: "Very fine words, I assure you, if they were to any purpose". These are from Sir Thomas Elyot. See on 8 above.

472. *in this circle*: the necromancer would, of course, be in extreme danger once the devil got *inside* his circle.

479. *roofe...low built.* Cf. Hall, *Characters*, "Humble Man": "a true temple of God built with a low roofe".

483 ff. Almost prophetic: cf. IV. 2. 44 ff.

498. *trades-men...i'th'City*: for this dishonest darkening of shops, a perpetual accusation in the writings of the time, cf. *W. Ho!* I. 1 (p. 73): "politic penthouses, which commonly make the shop of a mercer or a linen-draper as dark as a room in Bedlam"; *A.Q.L.* II. 2, 51–2; Beaum. and Fl., *Philaster*, v. 3: "May their false lights undo them,

and discover presses, holes, stains, and oldness in their stuffs ". In Middleton's *Michaelmas Term*, again, Quomodo the draper has a satellite pointedly named Falselight:

> Go, make my coarse commodities look sleek...
> Be near to my trap-window, cunning Falselight.

502. *progresse*: the word appropriate to a prince surveying his kingdom.

504–5. An echo, with a difference, of Bosola's words above, 33–4.

506. *paies it*: "repays it", "rewards your conduct" rather than "pays your wages", which would need *them*, not *it*.

507–8. Cf. Painter: "'Alas,' sayd shee, 'am I happed into so straunge misery, that with mine owne mouth I must make request to him, which with all humility ought to offer mee hys service!'"

514–5. Cf. *W.D.* IV. 2. 119–20.

520–1. *figure cut in Allablaster...husbands tombe*: an ominous comparison, with its suggestions both of death and her forgetfulness of the dead. Cf. *Merch. of Ven.* I. 1. 83–4:

> Why should a man, whose blood is warm within,
> Sit like his grandsire cut in alabaster?

(There too "Alablaster" in the original spelling.)

532. *Quietus est*: (medieval Lat.) = "he is quit, acquitted of his obligations". Cf. Massinger, *Gt. Duke of Flor.* v. 3. The phrase easily became applied (helped perhaps by its resemblance to "quiet") to "death", as being the final payment of nature's debt. Cf. *Haml.* III. 1. 75: *Mon. Col.* 220. And though that sense is not present here, the word may help to create that atmosphere of mortality which broods over all this love-scene.

533–4. Repeated in *A.V.* I. 1. 20–1. A similar phrase occurs in *Arcadia*, I. (*Wks.* I. 96): "*Zelmane's* eyes were (like children afore sweet meate) eager but fearefull of their ill-pleasing governors".

535, 541–3. Antonio's characteristic hesitancy (cf. above) is almost painfully lifelike. His gentle, uncertain character is never in danger of distracting our attention from the heroine his mistress.

548. *Per verba [de] presenti*. By the canon law *sponsalia de presenti*, in which the pair recognized each other as wife and husband at the time of speaking, were valid; as contrasted with *sponsalia de futuro*, which were only an undertaking to enter into that relationship at some future time and were not binding unless followed by intercourse. The Council of Trent (1563) insisted on all marriages taking place henceforward *in facie ecclesiae*; but in Protestant countries the canon law remained in force (it had been abolished in England by Henry VIII, but was restored under Edward VI) though such a union had to be consecrated subsequently by a religious service, under pain of certain penalties. Thus it was by *sponsalia de presenti* that the first Duke of Amalfi, our heroine's father-in-law, wedded Maria d'Aragona; the historic Bracciano, Vittoria; and Shakespeare's Claudio, his Juliet (*Meas. for Meas.* I. 2. 155 ff.).

549. *Gordian.* Gordius was a Phrygian peasant. One day as he was ploughing, an eagle alighted on the yoke of his oxen and sat there till evening; going to the Telmissians to ask the meaning of this portent, he met outside one of their villages a young prophetess who bade him sacrifice to Zeus βασιλεύς (the King). In return for this counsel he wedded her and so she became the mother of the notorious Midas. When her son grew up dissensions broke out in Phrygia; and an oracle bade the people take as king him whom a chariot should bring them. At this vital moment Gordius appeared in a chariot with his wife and son; and either he or Midas—accounts differ—was raised to the throne. In memory of this the car of Gordius and the yoke of his oxen were dedicated to Zeus at Gordium; and another oracle declared that whoever untied the cunning knot with which the yoke was fastened, would become lord of all Asia. Centuries later Alexander, after trying in vain to disentangle it, sundered it with his sword.

So here the phrase is again ominous, when we remember that final severance by the sword. Cf. *D.L.* II. 4, end:

> With Gordi[a]n knots, of such a strong threed spun,
> They cannot *without violence* be undone.

Similarly Chapman, *Bussy d'Ambois*, IV. I. 227:

> To cut a gordian when he could not loose it.

552. *still*: always.

555. *the loving Palmes.* Holland's Pliny (XIII. 4), has a charming passage: "The females be naturally barrein, and will not beare fruit without the company of the males among them to make them for to conceive;...and verily a man shall see many of the femals stand about one male, bending and leaning in the head full kindly toward him, yeelding their braunches that way as if they courted him for to win his love. But contrariwise he, a grim sir and a coy, carrieth his head aloft, beareth his bristled and rough arms upright on high, and yet what with his very lookes, what with his breathing and exhalations upon them, or else with a certain dust that passeth from him, he doth the part of an husband, insomuch as all the females about him, conceive and are fruitfull with his onely presence. It is said moreover, that if this male tree be cut downe, his wives will afterwards become barrein and beare no more Dates, as if they were widdowes". Dyce quotes a similar passage to Webster's from Glapthorne, *Argalus and Parthenia*; there is another in Du Bartas, *Oeuvres* (1593), II. 63, describing the loving palms embracing across a river. Cf. *Char.* "A Vertuous Widdow", I.

563–4. *the Church...must but eccho this. Sponsalia de presenti,* though valid by themselves, had to be completed ceremonially by a marriage *in facie ecclesiae*; and a refusal to obey the injunction of an ecclesiastical judge to do this was punishable with excommunication and imprisonment.

565. *I now am blinde*: like Love, as well as Fortune? Blind, also, to the consequences—there is surely here an intentional tragic irony.

570 ff. The sudden revulsion of the Duchess to womanly shame, which Fletcher, say, might easily have made hateful, is naturally and charmingly drawn.

571. *humorous*: full of humours, difficult-tempered.

572. *Alexander and Lodowicke.* There is a ballad on this subject from the Pepys collection (printed in Th. Evans, *Old Ballads*, 1810, 1. 77): "The Two Faithful Friends, the pleasant History of Alexander and Lodowicke, who were so like one another, that none could know them asunder; wherein is declared how Lodwicke married the Princesse of Hungaria, in Alexander's name, and how each night he layd a naked sword betweene him and the Princesse, because he would not wrong his friend". The ballad is poor enough doggerel, of the style—

> But every night between them twain
> His naked sword he'd lay,
> Such constant friendship at that time
> His heart and thoughts did sway.

Henslowe in his *Diary* (p. 79) mentions a play by Martin Slaughter on the subject. And there are references to the tale in Dekker's *Satiromastix* (*Wks.* 1873, 1. 235) and Cooke's *Greene's Tu Quoque* and a partial adaptation in Heywood's *A Challenge for Beauty*.

The commentators here have omitted however to point out that the tale is itself a variant of one of the most famous stories of the Middle Ages, which perhaps came from the East through Byzantium —*Amis and Amiloun*. The version of it, in which the friends are Alexandre and Loys (Louis, Lodowick), is to be found in *L'Ystoire des Sept Sages de Rome* (ed. by G. Paris, *Soc. des Anc. Textes Franç.*, 1876, pp. 167 ff. Also in Latin in Buchner, *Historia Septem Sapientium*, 1889, p. 71).

Alexandre persuaded Florentine, the daughter of the Emperor, to become the mistress of his friend Loys; after a time, however, the intrigue was suspected and Loys challenged to an ordeal by battle. Being weak in body and dreading defeat, he went in search of Alexandre and found him on the point of mounting the throne of Egypt. Now the two friends were exactly alike in appearance; and so Alexandre agreed to impersonate his friend in the lists. Since, however, Alexandre could not openly leave Egypt, they decided that Loys should at the same time impersonate Alexandre with the Egyptians and with the Queen his bride. So Alexandre departed and defeated the challenger; while Loys lay night after night with a sword between him and his friend's wife. When Alexandre returned, however, the woman, resenting her treatment, poisoned him so that he became a leper. Then followed the episode, famous in *Amis and Amiloun*, of the father (Loys) killing his own sons to cure his friend's leprosy; and the children's miraculous restoration to life. (See W. Pater, *Renaissance*, "Two Early French Stories".) The impersonation of one friend by another and the naked sword curiously recall Sigurd's winning of Brynhild for Gunnar in the *Volsunga Saga*.

574. *shrowd*: shelter. See on *W.D.* 1. 2. 33. H.D.S. quotes Middleton's *Changeling* (acted 1623), III. 4. 167:

Come, rise and shroud your blushes in my bosom.

576–8. These forebodings of Cariola's correspond to the gloomy anticipations expressed by the author in Belleforest-Painter at this point.

II. I.

Outer stage.

3. *maine*: not "main part", but "goal", "objective" ("perhaps originally a term of archery". *N.E.D.*). Cf. Jonson's *Tale of a Tub*, III. 4:   That was all the main I aimed at.

Similarly *Arcadia*, I. (*Wks.* I. 89): "I thought nothing could shoot righter at the *mark* of my desires".

5. *night-cap*: lawyer's coif. See on 21 below.

6. *strings of your band*: Elizabethan sergeants already wore the white bands or tabs familiar to-day.

7–9. Cf. *Char.* "A Fellow of an House", 12–3: "Hee hath learn't to cough, and spit, and blow his nose at every period, to recover his memory". And for the *hum*, cf. "Overbury's" Character of "An Hypocrite" with his "endless tongue", "the motion whereof, when matter and words faile, must be patched up . . . with long & fervent hummes".

9–12. For Webster's obvious and inveterate hatred of lawyers, cf. the trial-scenes in *W.D.*, *D.L.*, and *A.V.*

16. *roaring-boyes*: the regular Elizabethan slang-word for "bullies", "rowdies". See *Char.* "A Roaring Boy"; and there is a scene in a mock-school for training them in Middleton, *Fair Quarrel*, IV. I.

21. *night-caps*: "lawyers", not here "bullies", as *N.E.D.* suggests. Indeed it ignores the first sense altogether. But "lawyer" is certainly the meaning in a number of passages, including this one: cf. *D.L.* II. I. 43; IV. I. 73; *A.V.* IV. I. 121, where the Nurse calls the advocate "the fellow i'th' nightcap".

Vaughan first suggested that lawyers were meant here: but he missed the true explanation, in which however I later found I had been anticipated by Mr Sykes. The nickname "nightcap" is simply due to the white coif or skull-cap of lawn or silk worn by Sergeants at Law (who ceased to exist at the end of the nineteenth century, but corresponded to the modern Q.C.). It was of immemorial antiquity— seven centuries old, said Selden—and only disappeared with the coming of the large wig, at the end of the seventeenth century.

Even then a relic of it survived in the shape of a small hole cut in the top of the wig, as if to show the coif, but really filled up with a black patch edged with white. Cf. Pulling, *Order of the Coif* (1884), pp. 13 ff. and Plates I–IV and VII: *Sh.'s Eng.* I. 396. Jonson makes similar references to the "nightcap" in *Staple of News*, v. 1; *Magnetic Lady*, I. 1.

21. *Old Lady*: this personage appears to be the same as the midwife of 183.

25. *These...*: a word like "dimples" may have dropped out; or Bosola may simply point.

26. *sloughes*: (1) "bogs"; (2) "dead tissue" to be sloughed off.

27–30. *Lady in France.* Cf. Montaigne I. 40: "Who hath not heard of her at Paris who only to get a fresher hew of a new skin, endured to have her face flead all over?" (C.)

    The Secretes of Maister Alexis (transl. by W. Warde, 1558, p. 69) gives an actual recipe for a composition which, applied to the face for eight days, purports to fetch off the old skin and leave new.

32. *carreening*: *i.e. lit.* "turning a ship on one side to scrape the paint, etc."; hence "scraping clean". Cf. Fletcher, *A Wife for a Month*, II. 4: "a weather-beaten lady new-careen'd".

32. *morphew'd*: scurfy, tettered.

33. *disembogue*: "'empty', properly of a river, here figuratively" (Sampson). But what then is the meaning? "To disembogue" is *lit.* "to come out of the mouth of a river into the open sea". Hence, here, "to put to sea in search of fresh prizes after careening and re-fitting". The Old Lady is to be on the war-path again, in Massinger's words (*Guardian*, v. 4):

>   as the pirate
> Who, from a narrow creek, puts off for prey
> In a small pinnace.

For "disembogue" of ships, cf. Fletcher and Massinger, *Knight of Malta*, I. 3:

>   My ships ride in the bay
> Ready to disembogue.

And for the metaphor, cf. Massinger, *Old Law*, v. 1 (Gnotho, of his aged wife): "She's going to sea...; she has a strong wind with her, it stands full in her poop; when you please, let her disembogue"—(though here it is into another world that she is to sail).

    Similarly Jonson, *Magnetic Lady*, II. 1:

> And maidens are young ships that would be sailing
> When they be rigged; wherefore is all their trim else?

And we may recall the description of Dalila in *Samson Agonistes.*

33. *rough-cast*: a rough mixture of lime and gravel for cheap plastering of walls. Cf. Mabbe's transl. of Aleman's *Guzman d'Alfarache* (1622 ed.), I. 39: "The face of her looked like an old wall all to bedawbed with rough-cast". There is of course a play on this and the sense of harsh home-truths.

34. *plastique*: modelling.

37–9. Sampson quotes Tofte's version of Ariosto's *Satires* (1608) IV:

> Knew *Herculan* but where those lips of his
> He layeth when his *Lidia* he doth kisse,
> He would disdaine and loath himselfe as much
> As if the loathsom'st ordure he did touch.
> He knows not, did he know it he would spewe,
> That painting's made with spettle of a Jewe...
> Little thinks he that with the filthy doung
> Of their small circumcised children young,
> The fat of hideous serpents, spaune of snakes,
> Which slaves from out their poisonous bodies takes.

(*I.e.* that the paint is made with these.)

Similarly Lyly, *Euphues*, 116: "Looke in their closettes, and there shalt thou finde an Appoticaryes shop of sweete confections, a surgions boxe of sundry salves, a Pedlers packe of newe fangles"; cf. Massinger, *Bondman*, IV. 4, and B. Rich, *Irish Hubbub* (1619), sig. C3.

40–1. *dead pidgeon...plague*: a regular treatment, of which however there seem to be two forms. In one the birds are applied to the feet in order "to draw the vapors from the Head", as here; while in the other they are applied directly to the plague-sore with the idea of extracting its poisonous matter. This approaches the general treatment of devouring ulcers with flesh to feed them, as in *W.D.* v. 3. 55–6.

For the first method cf. *The English Huswife* (1615), quoted by Sampson, which recommends the application of hot bricks to the feet—"then to the same apply a live Pidgeon cut in two parts". Donne (*Devotions*, 12) characteristically compares such pigeons to the Dove of the Holy Spirit, which draws down the vapours of sin to be trodden under our feet. Cf. Congreve, *Love for Love*, IV. 3: "Ha! ha! ha! that a man should have a stomach to a wedding-supper when the pigeons ought rather to be laid to his feet, ha! ha! ha!"

For the second method, see T. Lodge, *Treatise of the Plague* (1603): "It is likewise very allowable, to draw out the venime from the sore, to take a chicken or cocke, and to pull the feathers from his taile, and to apply him to the soare, for by this meanes he drives out the venome, and when he is dead, apply another: Instead of this remedy, some use to take great pullets, and pigeons, and cutting them in two along the backe, apply them hote as they are upon the tumor or carbuncle".

Thus of Prince Henry's last illness (1612) we hear: "The extremity of his disease seemed to lie in his head, for remedy whereof they shaved him, and applied warm cocks, and pigeons newly killed, but with no success". See also *N.Q.*, CLI. 136 and 175.

41. *kisse one of you fasting*: *i.e.* when *you* are fasting and the offensiveness therefore at its worst. Cf. Massinger, *A Very Woman*, I. 1:

> strong perfumes to stifle
> The sourness of our breaths as we are fasting.

43. *foote-cloth*: housings of his horse or mule, and the regular mark of the eminent physician. Cf. *D.L.* III. 2. 155–6; Massinger, *Bondman*, II. 3:

> Your lord that feels no ache in his chine at twenty,
> Forfeits his privilege; how should their surgeons build else
> Or ride on their footcloths?

Nares (*s.v.* "footcloth") quotes Howell's *Parly of Beasts* (1660), 73: "Nor are the fees which belong to that profession anything considerable; where doctors of physic use to attend a patient, with their mules and foot-cloths, in a kind of state, yet they receive but two shillings for their fee, for all their gravity and pains".

45–6. *observe my meditation.* See on I. I. 456.

56. *Woolfe*: lupus, ulcer. See on *W.D.* v. 3. 55–6.

56. *Meazeall*: there is no real connection, only a confusion of popular etymology, between common human measles (O.H.G. *masala*, blood-blister) and the older English use of "mesel" to mean "leprosy" or "leprous" (O.F. *mesel*, Lat. *misellus*). It was on the analogy of the latter that "measle" or "measles" became applied to a skin-disease of swine, really caused by tape-worm.

64. *wels at Leuca*: warm springs in the Val di Lima, containing carbonic acid gas, unknown to the Romans, but frequented from the thirteenth century to the present day. They were visited by Montaigne, but he remained as sceptical about their value as about most other things. Cf. *W.Ho!* I. 2 (p. 79).

67. *fins of her eie-lids*: N.E.D. gives "fins" = "eye-lids". But "eyelids of her eyelids"? It must mean here "rims, edges". Dyce quotes Marston, *Malcontent*, I. I. 103: "Till the fin of his eyes look as blue as the welkin".

67. *teeming blue*: blue like those of a pregnant woman.

69–70. *contrary to our Italian fashion..loose-bodied Gowne*: on the other hand Sampson quotes from Montaigne's *Italian Journey* (Hazlitt's transl. p. 574): "but their (Roman women's) custom of having the waist exceeding loose gives them all the appearance of being with child". Such gowns in Elizabethan England were regularly associated with prostitutes. Cf. Middleton, *Michaelmas Term*, I. 2. 14.

71. *tricke*: for Bosola's trick with the Apricocks, cf. Donne, *Elegies* IV, where his mistress's "immortall mother", in her suspicion,

> To trie if thou long, doth name strange meates
> And notes thy palenesse, blushing, sighs, and sweats.

79 ff. After baiting Castruchio and the Old Lady, Bosola is now baited in his turn.

81–2. From Montaigne II. 12: "the opinion of wisdome is the plague of man". (C.)

81. *tettor*: skin-disease.

82–3. *if simplicity....happy being.* From Montaigne II. 12: "If simplicitie directeth us to have no evill, it also addresseth us according to our condition to a most happy estate". (C.)

83–4. *subtlest folly...subtlest wisedome*: from the same essay of
Montaigne as the previous borrowing, though separated by many
pages: "Whence proceeds the subtilest follie but from the subtilest
wisedome?" (C.)

92–3. From Montaigne 1. 42: "It is for Gods to mount winged horses,
and to feed on Ambrosia". (C.)

98. Repeated in *D.L.* v. 4. 222.

that rules i'th'aire. Cf. *Ephesians* ii. 2: "the prince of the power of the
air" (the air being supposed full of spirits, largely evil). Webster is
however certainly closer to the rendering of the Bishops' Bible (which
Shakespeare also used)—"the governour that ruleth in the ayre".

99. *Lord of the ascendant.* In astrology the heavens are divided into
twelve "houses" or sections (six above, six below, the horizon) by
imaginary lines drawn through the north and south points of the
horizon. The "first house" or "house of the ascendant" is that part
of the sky which is at the moment rising above the horizon, and
extends from 5° above the east horizon to 25° below. From it the other
houses were numbered in order eastwards. (There are, however, other
rival and more complicated methods of marking out the houses: see
Wilson, *Dict. of Astrology*, *s.v.* "Figure".) Each planet is associated
with some one or two signs of the zodiac; and the "lord of the first
house" or "of the ascendant" at a given moment is that planet whose
sign is entering the first house. Thus the sign Pisces is the mansion
of Jupiter: when Pisces are entering the "house of the ascendant",
Jupiter is "lord of the ascendant". And accordingly Pisces and
Jupiter will be dominating factors in the nativity of a child born at
that moment. For the first house is the "House of Life".

102–9. Again from Montaigne II. 12: "The soules of Emperours and
Coblers are all cast in one same mould. Considering the importance
of Princes actions, and their weight, wee perswade ourselves that they
are brought forth by some as weighty and important causes; wee are
deceived: They are moved, stirred and removed in their motions by
the same springs and wards that we are in ours. The same reason
that makes us chide and braule and fall out with any of our neighbours,
causeth a warre to follow betweene Princes; the same reason that
makes us whip or beat a lackey maketh a Prince (if hee apprehend
it) to spoyle and waste a whole Province". And later in the same
essay, speaking of laws, Montaigne says: "In rowling on they swell
and grow greater and greater, as doe our rivers: follow them upward
into their source, and you shall find them but a bubble of water". (C.)

It will be noticed that the picturesque "tithe-pig" (l. 107) is
Webster's addition; but for that cf. *Rom. and Jul.* 1. 4. 80 (Mercutio
of Q. Mab):

> And sometimes comes she with a tithe-pig's tail,
> Tickling a parson's nose as a' lies asleep,
> Then dreams he of another benefice.

117. *Lymmon pils*: Sampson doubts whether "pills" or "peels" is meant; by the spelling it might equally well be either. It is, however, certainly lemon-*peel* that is intended here. Cf. Wycherley, *Love in a Wood*, III. 2: "Warrant her breath with some Lemmon Peil"; L'Estrange, *Fables*, cxxxvi: "Never without Lemmon Pill in her Mouth to correct an unsavoury Vapour of her Own". Sampson supports "pills" by a passage from the *Secretes of Maister Alexis* mentioning "orenge pilles": but the context shows, on the contrary, that "peel" is meant even there, for it is a recipe for *candying* it.

118. *sound*: swoon.

118–9. *troubled With the mother*: *i.e.* with hysteria. Cf. *D.L.* III. 3. 256–7; *Lear*, II. 4. 56:

> O! how this mother swells up toward my heart;
> *Hysterica passio!* down, thou climbing sorrow.

On which W. J. Craig in the *Arden* edition quotes from E. Jordan's *A Brief Discourse of a Disease called the Suffocation of the Mother* (1605), where the commonest symptom is said to be a choking in the throat.

122. *hats on fore the King*: Grandees of Spain had this same privilege, and the ceremony of their creation consisted simply in the King saying "Cobrese por Grande"—"Cover yourself for a Grandee". (Howell, *Letters* (1890), I. 263.)

126. *Why should not we bring up that fashion?* This rash caprice of the Duchess is doubtless meant as another symptom of her hysterical condition.

132. *in colder countries then* (*than*) *in France*: clearly an allusion to English loyalty.

139. *to yeare*: this year; like "to-day".

144. *pare*: peel.

145. *muske*: an esteemed flavour in fruit. Cf. Parkinson, *Paradise* (1629 ed.), 583: "The Muske Nectorin... both smelleth and eateth as if the fruit were steeped in Muske".

148–50. It is hard to be sure whether this is mere Elizabethan nastiness for its own sake, or whether Bosola's mind is running on the dirty work connected with his provisorship of the horse (cf. I. I. 312: "say then my corruption Grew out of horse-doong"). Or is he testing the violence of the Duchess's craving by suggesting obstacles to it? Both of these last possibilities seem quite probable.

159. *this grafting*: editors and the *N.E.D.* have ignored the *double entendre* with which this word is sometimes used. Cf. the fuller phrase "graft the forked tree", copied from Montaigne (II. 12) by Marston (*Fawn*, IV. I. 104).

163. *-farthingalls*: a hooped petticoat, cf. the crinoline (O.F. *vertugall*, Span. *verdugado* from *verdugo*, a rod).

165. *apparently*: clearly, manifestly.

166. *spring-hall*: springal, stripling.

178 ff. It is just like Antonio to be "lost in amazement"; and like Delio to keep his head and think for both.

II. 2.

Outer stage: no break is needed.

1. *teatchines*: irritability. (Fr. *taché*, "spot"; and thence "bad habit, blemish of character".)

2. *apparant*: manifest.

6. *Glasse-house*: for this favourite topic of Webster's see on *W.D.* I. 2. 134.

13–4. *The Orrenge tree beare[s] ripe and greene fruit, and blossoms altogether.* The point is apparently that the race of women, like the orange-tree, produces all sorts together—women that love for love's sake, women that love for a price.

Cf. *Mon. Col.* 45–6; Bacon, *Sylva Sylvarum* (pub. 1627), VI. 581: "There be divers fruit trees in the hot countries, which have blossoms, and young fruit, and ripe fruit, almost all the year succeeding one another. And it is said the orange hath the like with us for a great part of summer, and so also hath the fig". (C.)

18. *Dan[a]es*: see on I. I. 265–6. This heroine, whose lover appeared in the shape of a shower of gold, had already in antiquity become the ironic type of mercenary love. Cf. the inscription in Buecheler's *Carmina Latina Epigraphica* (Teubner), No. 938:

> Pulveris aurati pluvia sit sparsa papyrus:
> Rescribet Danae sollicitata "Veni".

> Shower gold-dust on the note, when you address
> Your love; and Danaë will answer "Yes".

21–2. *lines meete in one center*: *double entendre*. Cf. Montaigne III. 5: "(love) is a matter everywhere infused, and a centre whereto all lines come, all things looke". Similarly Marston, *Dutch Courtezan*, II. I. 121: "love is the centre in which all lines close".

24. *false rusty watch.* Cf. Middleton, *Roaring Girl*, II. 2. 111–2:

> his watch ne'er goes right
> That sets his dial by a rusty clock.

32. *Forobosco*: the name recurs in Webster's part of *F.M.I.* and was perhaps suggested by Alphonso Ferrabosco or Ferabosco of Bologna (d. 1628), who like his father and his son served the gaieties of the English court, and provided airs for many of Jonson's Masques from 1606 to 1611. In 1605 he had been appointed musical instructor to Prince Henry. The name had however already been used by Marston for a character in *Antonio's Revenge*.

38. *Switzer*: Swiss mercenary soldiers were common then, as for centuries to come.

40. *Pistoll in his great cod-piece.* For the great cod-piece see on *W.D.*

v. 3. 101. The whole passage recalls Nashe's *Unfortunate Traveller*: "the molds of his buttons they turnd out, to see if they were not bullets covered over with thred, the cod-peece in his divels breeches (for they wer then in fashion) they said plainly was a case for a pistol". (Ed. Brett-Smith, p. 20.)

47. *Caniball*: blood-thirsty savage.

48. *French*: possibly with a play on the *morbus Gallicus*.

67. *Black-guard*: scullions and turnspits. See on *W.D.* 1. 2. 128.

73. *poast to Rome*: to keep watch on the Duchess's brothers there.

80. *mind*: pay heed to.

81 ff. Cf. Montaigne 11. 12: "A gust of contrarie winds, the croking of a flight of Ravens, the false pace of a Horse, the casual flight of an Eagle...are enough to overthrowe, sufficient to overwhelme and able to pull him (man) to the ground". (H.D.S.) Similarly Wither, *Abuses Stript and Whipt* (1613):

> For worthlesse matters some are wondrous sad
> Whom if I call vaine I must terme mad.
> If that their Noses bleede some certaine Drops,
> And then againe upon the suddaine stops,
> Or if the babling Foule we call the Jay,
> A Squirrell, or a Hare, but crosse their way,
> Or if the Salt fall toward them at the Table,
> Or any such like superstitious Bable,
> Their mirth is spoil'd, because they hold it true
> That some mischance must thereupon ensue.

There is an allusion to the title of this book, it may be noted, in *A.Q.L.* 11. 2. 181–2.

81. *throwing downe salt*: a superstition probably connected with the feeling that salt, with its preservative qualities, was the symbol of enduring friendship and faith.

81. *crossing of a Hare*. From S. Africa to Scotland this is held an evil omen; perhaps because the animal was a favourite disguise of witches, but more probably because it is a weak timorous creature, whereas the savage wolf has been regarded as lucky to meet (Grimm, *Teut. Mythology* (Eng. transl.), 111. 1126; Brand, *Pop. Antiq.* 689–90). The crossing of the hare was supposed also to disorder the senses. Cf. "Beaum. & Fl.", *Wit at Sev. Weapons*, 11. 3 (where a clown is behaving fantastically): "I'll lay my life some hare has crossed him".

82. *Bleeding at nose*: as Antonio fears when his bleeds in 11. 3. 58. Cf. *Merch. of Ven.* 11. 5. 24: and the alarm of Charles II's servants when his nose bled during his hiding at Boscobel House.

82. *stumbling of a horse*. Cf. *Rich. III*, 111. 4. 83:

> Three times to-day my foot-cloth horse did stumble.

Similarly in the *Ballad of Lord Derwentwater* (Child's *Engl. and Scott. Ballads*, iv. 120):

He set his foot in the level stirrup,
  And mounted his bonny grey steed;
The gold rings from his fingers did break
  And his nose began for to bleed.

He had not ridden past a mile or two,
  When his horse stumbled over a stone.
"There are tokens enough," said my Lord Derwentwater,
  "That I shall never return."

83. *Criket*: for this omen see on *W.D.* v. 4. 79.
84. *To daunt whole man in us*: all our manhood. Cf. *W.D.* i. 1. 44;
"Beaum. & Fl.", *Bonduca*, iv. 3:

'Tis loss of whole man in me.

Double Marriage, iii. 3:

For sure there is no taste of right man in it.

Middleton, *Fair Quarrel*, iv. 3. 111–2:

Being his soul's wish to depart absolute man,
In life a soldier, death a christian.

92. *a figure for's Nativitie*: a typical first step for Antonio to take immediately after a lecture from his friend against superstition (but see v. 2. 135-7). It is curiously ironic, whether intended by Webster or no, that though the infant turns out in the next scene to have the most appalling horoscope, it is eventually the one member of the family to survive.

II. 3.

Outer stage: Bosola's lantern would suffice to imply night to the audience in the public theatre.
15. *This Moale do's undermine me*: see on *D.L.* iv. 2. 322–4.
25. Cf. ii. 5. 97–9; iv. 2. 364.
27–8. For this recourse to astrology for the discovery of lost goods cf. Donne, *Elegies* xi, where the poet imagines going to "some dread Conjurer", who is in league with thief and murderer, to recover his mistress's lost bracelet; and the "Character of a Quack-Astrologer" (1673), quoted in Brand, *Pop. Antiq.* 623—"to help people to what they have lost, he picks their pockets afresh. Not a ring or spoon is nim'd away but pays him twelve pence toll". Cf. *F.M.I.* ii. 2. 85.
30. *radicall*: not, here, "going to the root of the matter", "conclusive" (Sampson): it is a technical term in astrology, meaning "fit to be judged or decided". Cf. Lilly, *Chr. Astrol.* (1647 ed.), 121: "The question then shall be taken for radicall, or fit to be judged, when as the Lord of the hour at the time of proposing the question...and the Lord of the Ascendant or First House, are of one Triplicity or be one". (The twelve signs of the zodiac were divided into four triplicities.) So Wilson (a fiery believer, who regards Newton with his gravitation as a superstitious bigot) in his *Dict. of Astrol.* (1819)

explains "radical" as "a term used of horary questions to signify that the question is fit and may be resolved".

37. *I came to say my prayers*: there is a disinterested sense of humour and irony about Bosola which helps to raise his villainy almost to an art.

43. *spanish figge*: there has been great confusion about the Elizabethan use of "fig". For the fruit is associated (1) with the poison often administered in it; (2) with an indecent gesture based on its appearance; (3) with contempt, on account of its cheapness.

For (1) cf. *W.D.* iv. 2. 63 and note.

(2) In several European languages the fig is associated with an offensive gesture as old, at least, as Rome itself (cf. Span. *dar una higa* (*higo*, fig); Ital. *far le fiche* (plural for both hands); Fr. *faire la figue*; Germ. *die Feigen zeigen*; Eng. "to give the fig" or "to fig" a person). The gesture consisted in thrusting the thumb between fore-finger and middle-finger (or into the mouth), with a phallic implication, from which the name is perhaps derived owing to the resemblance between the opening fig and the *vulva*. Both in ancient Rome and in Spain and Portugal up to the last century amulets resembling a hand in this position were hung on children and beasts of burden to avert the evil eye. Villani relates that the men of a neighbouring town set up a statue in the thirteenth century, making this gesture in the direction of Florence. The practice was prohibited altogether by Paul II on pain of a fine of 20 soldi: but clearly with little effect. (There is a ridiculous account of the origin of the name quoted in Littré's *French Dict. s.v. figue*—see *N.Q.* 9. 11. 185; Douce, *Illustrat. of Shakesp.* (1807), 1. 492.)

(3) There is, lastly, a second contemptuous use, perhaps really derived from (2) by misunderstanding or bowdlerization, in such phrases as "not worth a fig", figs being abundant in the south.

Here, at all events, Bosola doubtless makes the indecent gesture as he speaks.

52–3. *snake...warme...sting*: with allusion to the fable of the country-man and the snake. "Scarce warme" because of the newness of Bosola's provisorship of the horse. So Spenser in his *State of Ireland* says of an O'Neale favoured by the Queen: "now hee playeth like the frozen snake, who being for compassion releived of the husband-man, soone after he was warme began to hisse, and threaten danger even to him and his".

54–7. An obscure passage (see Text. Note) neglected by editors. Allen indeed suggests that Antonio hands Bosola the horoscope about the stolen jewels with the intention that he should copy it, "adding at the same time the propitiatory remark 'you libel well'". Bosola however refuses the paper and offers as proof of his innocence to sign a copy of the horoscope drawn up by Antonio. But it is ridiculous to suppose that Antonio had really written out also an astrological figure for the theft. That figure was merely invented as an excuse, on the spur of the moment: it did not actually exist. In any case why should it be copied, or signed, by Bosola? Sampson remarks: "Bosola's speech is tantamount to saying 'As I am innocent, I will sign a statement you have made concerning the jewels'". But what sort of statement? And why sign it? What would that prove?

It seems probable that a line has dropped out (the Quarto repeats "*Ant.*" as the speaker in 55, though no intervening speech appears), in which Bosola repeated some such charge as "You are a false steward" (cf. 49)—perhaps accused Antonio of being himself the thief. "You are a fine slanderer," replies Antonio. Now "to libell" can mean not only "to defame", but also "to bring a suit with a *libel, i.e. a formal charge in writing*". And so Bosola plays on this second sense and rejoins, "No, but write out yourself the charge (libel) I bring against you and I will sign it with pleasure". It is merely a rather pointless, quibbling thrust in their verbal fencing-match.

This seems a possible explanation; though it is not a very satisfactory one.

61. *Two letters*: initials worked in his handkerchief; *not*, as has been suggested, in the copy of the horoscope.

68–9. Cf. Lucan, v. 290: "Facinus quos inquinat, aequat".

71. *falce-friend*: the dark-lantern, a thing of sinister association for Webster's audience. For Barrington, *Observations on the Antient Statutes* (quoted in Brand, *Pop. Antiq.* 781), mentions a vulgar error that their use was unlawful,—a notion which may have arisen from Guy Fawkes's use of one a few years before this.

77–8. *Lord of the first house...ascendant*: see on II. 1. 99.

77. *combust*: lit. "burnt up", means within $8\frac{1}{2}°$ of the sun, whereby a planet's influence was supposed to be destroyed.

78. *human signe*: Aquarius, Gemini, Virgo, or Sagittarius.

79. *the Dragon*: the apparent path of the sun, or ecliptic, is intersected in two places by the path of the moon. (It is simplest to imagine the two lines drawn on the sky above one.) That part of the moon's path which lies to the south of the ecliptic was called "the Dragon". The Dragon's Head lay where the moon in its ascent crossed the ecliptic, the Tail where it re-crossed the ecliptic in its descent. The influence of the former was auspicious, that of the latter sinister. The names were due to the fact that these two points of intersection are the only places where eclipses occur; and eclipses all the world over have been associated with the efforts of a dragon to swallow the sun and moon. Cf. Chaucer, *Astrolabe*, II. 4: "a fortunat assendent clepen they whan that no wykkid planet, as Saturne or Mars, or elles the tail of the dragoun, is in the hous of the assendent". Thus Edmund in *King Lear* was begotten under it (I. 2. 144).

79. *the eight house*: regularly signifies the manner of death, just as the first is the "House of Life": *eight* is quite common for "eighth".

80. *Caete[r]a non scrutantur*: "the rest is not investigated". (*Scrutor*, a

deponent verb in classical Latin, is used as a passive in later writers.

74–80. This horrid horoscope is astrologically correct; but the stars were not so placed in any year round 1504. (J. Parr, *PMLA.* LX. 760–5.)

81. *precise*—puritanical: "Precisians" was another name for the Puritans.

II. 4.

Inner stage (cf. "Sit" in l. 1). With the drawing back of its curtain the audience would be prepared for a change of scene. The second line tells them whither—"to Rome".

7. *witty*: note this echo of the warning last line of the previous scene.

21. *glasse male-able*: malleable. It is conceivable that a pun on "male" is intended. At all events this idea of malleability was doubtless suggested by the well-known story of the inventor who came to Tiberius with an actual specimen of malleable glass he had made: and was put to death for his pains because the Emperor was jealous, says Dio (LVII. 21). Pliny, more plausibly, suggests economic reasons, *i.e.* consideration for the glass-makers. Albertus Magnus in his *Of the Virtues of Animals* actually gives a recipe: "If Goat's blood be taken warm, with vinegar and the juice of hay, and the like be boiled with glass, it makes the glass soft like paste, and it may be thrown against a wall, and will not break". Sir T. Browne (*Pseud.* II. 5. 2) is eloquently sceptical of the possibility of such a thing: our age has however at last really invented it.

24–5. *fantastique glasse . . . Galileo.* The first practical telescope (though the idea seems to occur in Roger Bacon) was constructed by the Dutch spectacle-maker Nippershey about 1608. In 1609 Galileo, hearing in Venice that some such instrument had been devised, solved the problem independently and with considerable improvements. This anachronism of Webster's worried the precise Theobald. In his preface to *The Fatal Secret* (1735) he complains of our poet: "Nor has he been less licentious in another respect (*i.e.* in addition to infringing the Unities): he makes mention of Galileo and Tasso, neither of whom were born till near half a century after the Dutchess of Malfy was murthered". These lines of Webster will recall to many those of a greater poet on the same theme:

the Moon whose Orb
Through Optic Glass the Tuscan Artist views
At Ev'ning, from the top of Fesole
Or in Valdarno, to descry new Lands,
Rivers or Mountains in her spotty Globe.

26–7. *Moone . . . constant woman*: this can hardly be a reminiscence of Lyly's *Woman in the Moon*, for *she* is placed in that sphere because her inconstancy and its changeableness go well together:

Forgetfull, foolish, fickle, franticke, madde;
These be the humors that content me best
And therefore will I stay with Cynthia.

34. *since*: either the Cardinal is being paradoxical, or "though" would be more natural: for the fact that he is not Julia's husband and so cannot be cuckolded by her, is a reason for *not* being jealous.

42–3. *watch'd Like a tame Ellephant.* Does this mean "watched like an Elephant being tamed by being kept awake"? Cf. *A.Q.L.* i. i. 158–60: "she rail'd upon me when I should sleep, And that's, you know, intollerable; for indeed 'Twill tame an Elephant". This parallel is, I think, strong evidence: hawks also were regularly tamed in this way (*Sh.'s Eng.* ii. 357), and the idea may have come into Webster's mind by association with the hawking metaphors of the previous lines. Cf., too, *A.V.* v. i. 146–51, of taming lions by sleeplessness. Or does *watch'd* refer to the staring of a crowd of spectators at the animal? There was a famous exhibition of an Elephant in London (*c.* 1594), alluded to in literature for years after—cf. Basse (d. 1653?), *Metam. of the Walnut Tree*, "in our youth we saw the Elephant". It is sometimes coupled with Banks's horse (see on *W.D.* ii. 2. 14). Cf. Jonson, *Ev. Man out of his H.* iv. 4: "He keeps more ado with this monster than ever Banks did with his horse, or the fellow with the elephant". Grierson in a note on the date of Donne's *Satires* quotes Sir J. Davies, "In Titum" (about 1594—whence the date given above):

> Titus the brave and valorous young gallant
> Three years together in the town hath beene,
> Yet my Lo. Chancellors tombe he hath not seene,
> Nor the new water-worke, nor the Elephant.
> I cannot tell the cause without a smile:
> He hath been in the Counter all the while.

On the whole, however, though an allusion to this elephant would be quite possible, the passages from *A.Q.L.* and *A.V.* seem to me stronger evidence.

46–7. *a little fingring on the Lute, Yet cannot tune it.* Cf. *Haml.* iii. 2. 387–94; Chapman, *Seven Penitential Psalms* (1612), "To Young Imaginaries" (quoted on ii. 5. 50–1).

The sense seems to demand that *tune* should here mean "play". *N.E.D.* quotes no example of this sense before 1701: but *N.E.D.* is not at all reliable for fixing earliest dates (for instance, it gives no example before 1675 of "intelligency" as used in ii. 3. 83; nor before 1810 of "Alastor", which appears in *F.M.I.* iii. 1. 68). At all events "tuner" = "singer", "player" is found as early as *c.* 1580.

53. *Lightning mooves slow to't*: in comparison with it. Lightning is a dubious symbol for a constant affection; as perhaps the Cardinal is well aware. It is certainly a formidable, almost menacing one. For the image cf. Donne, *Of the Progress of the Soul*, "Harbinger to the Progresse" (1612), 11–2:

> Thy flight which doth our thoughts outgoe
> So fast, that now the lightning moves but slow.

72. *if he had had a good backe*: with a *double entendre*. Cf. II. 5. 94. Castruchio belongs to the same type of impotent nincompoop as Camillo in *The White Devil*.

80. *allowance* seems almost to mean "income", "revenue". Cf. J. Ward, *Diary* (1662: publ. 1839), 183: "Mr Shakespeare...had an allowance so large that he spent at the rate of 1,000 l. a-year". Otherwise the phrase must mean "('The gold is) allowed you by me".

86. *Cassia*: a coarser kind of cinnamon.

87. *phisicall*: good for the health, restorative. Cf. *W.D.* v. 4. 23–4 and note.

88. *Cullisses*: strengthening broths. See on *W.D.* v. 4. 23–4.

89. *Creature bred by*——: Julia was doubtless going to add "unnatural means" (cf. *Char.* "A Divellish Usurer", 6: "unnaturall Act of generation"), with allusion to the time-worn comparison of usury to an unnatural breeding of gold, which is older than Aristotle himself (*Politics* I. 10—cf. the Greek word for "interest", τόκος, *lit.* "offspring"; and *Merch. of Ven.* I. 3. 135, "breed of barren metal").

98. *my mistris*. It would seem, though it is far from clear and no one appears to have suggested it, that Delio means to use Julia as a means of extracting information about the Cardinal's intentions, just as Bosola actually does use her, and as Francisco uses Zanche in *W.D.* This would make the present scene somewhat less irrelevant: but it looks almost as if Webster, after starting with this idea, had then failed to develop it.

107–8. Cf. the Cardinal's similar maxim in I. I. 366. And for the inverted commas, used merely to mark a striking saying, see on *W.D.* II. I. 278–9.

II. 5.

Inner stage as before, though the Outer, of course, may have been used as well.

1. *dig'd up a man-drake*: for the madness supposed to ensue see on *W.D.* III. I. 54.

5. *loose i'th' hilts*: unchaste. Cf. Fletcher, *The Chances*, II. 4. The phrase appears simply a metaphor of an untrustworthy weapon: cf. variant forms such as "not sure in the haft" or "false in the haft" (see Tilley, H 472). But it seems possible, too, that there was a general sexual association with the screwing of hilt into blade: this would explain the applicability of the phrase to venereal disease in Fletcher's *Maid of the Mill*, I. 3:

> And this is a 'pothecary's: I have lain here many times
> For a looseness in my hilts.

11. *covetuous*: because hoping for hush-money.

15. *Service*: sexual indulgence? See *N.E.D. s.v.* "service[1]" 6 c and 36; "serve" *v*[1]. 52.

18–9. *rubarbe...choller*: see on *W.D.* v. 1. 193–4.

19. *here's the cursed day*: presumably, the horoscope, giving the date, which Bosola had picked up in II. 3 and has now forwarded to Rome.

20. *here'it shall sticke*. With these words the Duke must be imagined to thrust back the paper into his bosom, next his heart, whence he had taken it in the preceding line. Perhaps if he makes this gesture, the emphasis should be laid on "*her* bleeding heart" in the next line. *here'it*: the apostrophe, if correct, merely signifies that the preceding syllable is spoken shortly.

35. *cupping-glasse*: see on *W.D.* v. 6. 105.

44–5. *womens hearts...left-side*. Vaughan refers to Browne, *Pseudo-doxia*, IV. 2, which in turn quotes *Ecclesiastes* x. 2: "A wise man's heart is at his right hand; but a fool's heart at his left" (the Hebrew really means "A wise man's will is *for the right*; but a fool's desire is *for the left*, *i.e.* tends in the wrong direction"). Here too, as in *Ecclesiastes*, *left* is really figurative. Cf. "sinister" and "*gauche*"; and III. 1. 33–4 below:

> I grow to infinite purchase
> The leaft-hand way.

For the general sentiment cf. Painter, where, in the corresponding passage, the Duchess's brother exclaims of women: "they seem to be procreated and borne againste all order of Nature, and to live withoute Lawe, whych governeth al other things indued with some reason and understanding".

46–9. Cf. the sentiment of Bandello's preface to his narrative of the Duchess: "E nel vero grave sciocchezza quella degli uomini mi pare che vogliono che l' onor loro e di tutta la casata consista ne l' appetito d' una donna".

I do not see anything equivalent in Painter: and it suggests the possibility that Webster had also read Bandello. He had, we know, at all events enough Italian to quote Tasso.

50. *purchas'd*: obtained (Fr. *pour-chasser*). The meaning "pay for" is only secondary: the original sense being of violent or wrongful acquisition, as in hunting or theft or war. Thence it came to mean "acquire" in general. It might seem, none the less, thàt the meaning here was "bought", with a reference to the sale of honours. But cf. Otway, *Orphan*, I. 1:

> The honours he has gain'd are justly his;
> He *purchas'd* them in war.

There is a neat combination of the old sense and the new in Shirley, *Bird in a Cage*, IV. 2:

> Rol. And when I have put a girdle 'bout the world,
>   This purchase will reward me. (*I.e.* the *gain* of Eugenia's love.)
> Eug. Purchase! I am not bought
>   And sold, I hope.

50–1. Cf. Chapman, *Seven Penitential Psalms* (1612), "To Young Imaginaries":

> Terms, tongues, reading, all
> That can within a man, call'd learned, fall,
> Whose life is led yet like an ignorant man's,
> Are but as tools to gouty artisans
> That cannot use them. (C.)

58. *quoit the sledge*: throw the hammer. Cf. Nash, *Have with you to Saffron Walden* (Grosart), p. 52 (he is laughing at the ponderousness of a pamphlet of Gabriel Harvey's): "Credibly it was once rumord about the Court, that the Guard meant to trie masteries with it before the Queene, and, in stead of throwing the sledge or the hammer, to hurle it foorth at the armes ende for a wager".

77–9. One of Webster's deepest themes (cf. the knell of *W.D.* v. 6. 273–4). Cf. also W. Alexander, *Julius Caesar*, 1013–4.

87–91. This might seem a reminiscence of the Neronian *tunica molesta* or shirt smeared with combustibles in which condemned criminals were burned as illuminants. Cf. Juvenal VIII. 235—and J. B. Mayor's note.

It was, however, clearly suggested to Webster by a hitherto unnoticed passage in Painter's story of the Duchess (*Palace of Pleasure*, ed. Jacobs, III. 38): "We may confesse also these brutall brethren to be more butcherly than ever Otho Erle of Monferrato, and prince of Urbin was, who caused a yeoman of his chamber to be wrapped in a sheete poudred with sulpher and brimstone, and afterwards kindled with a Candle,...bicause he waked not at an hour by him appointed".

97–9. Cf. *W.D.* II. 1. 252–3.

101. *Scorpions*: see on *W.D.* II. 1. 247.

102. *generall ecclipse*: total.

III. I.

Outer stage.

18. *eare;*—if the semi-colon is right, we must suppose it to imply an awed hush before pronouncing the Cardinal's name.

25. *Dormise*. Cf. I. 1. 307.

33. *purchase*: aggrandisement. See on II. 5. 50 above.

33–42. An agreeable piece of irony at the expense of club-politicians with their profoundly subtle explanations of non-existent facts.

51. *sticke of sugar-candy*: *i.e.* cheap, sugary, and easily seen-through? Cf. *D.L.* II. 1. 153–5: "You are a foole, a precious one—you are a meere sticke of Sugar Candy, a man may looke quite thorow you". Similarly *Much Ado*, IV. 1. 322: "a goodly Count Comfect; a sweet gallant, surely".

59. *Pasquils paper-bullets*. Pasquino or Pasquillo was a sharp-tongued Roman schoolmaster or cobbler of the fifteenth century, whose name was subsequently given to a mutilated statue excavated in 1501 (close

to his shop, says one account) and set up opposite the palace of Cardinal Caraffa. Under the Cardinal's patronage the statue used to be dressed up every St Mark's Day and Latin verses affixed to it by students of the New Learning. Naturally these *pasquinate* tended to become satirical; and the "pasquinade" spread to France and across the Channel, so that Nash, for instance, took to signing himself "Pasquil of England".

These satires generally took the form of dialogues between Pasquillo and another statue from the Forum called Marforio. Thus under Sixtus V Pasquillo appeared in a dirty shirt. "Why?" asked Marforio. "I have no laundress," replied Pasquillo, "since the Pope's sister became a princess". Then Pasquillo took to hastily turning and returning the shirt. "Why such haste?"—"Before they start a tax on sunlight!" Sixtus wanted to throw Pasquillo into the Tiber; but Tasso wrote on his behalf: "Do not drown him or on the bank of the river there will spring up from his dust innumerable frogs that will croak in derision night and day".

paper-bullets: Sampson quotes *Much Ado*, II. 3. 249: "paper bullets of the brain".

64. *apparant*: evident.

67. *This deadly aire is purg'd*: referring to the *pestilent ayre* of l. 60 above. Cf. Montaigne II. 3: "And God be thanked, since this good advertisement, our ayre is infinitely purged of them". (Not in C.)

69. *burning cultures*: coulters. The coulter is the iron blade in front of the plough-share which makes the vertical cut in the soil. The ordeal by red-hot plough-shares is familiar in old English and German law, nine shares being the usual number. Emma, mother of Edward the Confessor, for instance, is related to have passed through it successfully when accused of an intrigue with the Bishop of Winchester (Freeman, *Norman Conq.* II. Append. Note H); similarly St Cunigund, consort of the Emperor Henry II. Burton (*Anat.* III. 3. 2) has a characteristically recondite list of such cases.

73. *go read i'th' Starres*: an ironic reminiscence of Antonio's horoscope?

82–4. Perhaps an echo of *Othello*, I. I. 172:

> Is there not charms
> By which the property of youth and maidhood
> May be abused?

91. *lenative*: "soothing, but insidious" (Allen). Other editors have not even turned in their sleep over this strange epithet. But if *lenative* = "lenitive", it must mean simply "soothing"; and it is odd to be driven mad with soothing-syrup. It looks as if Webster's learning might have led him into either a false etymology or a new coinage of his own. "Lenitive" comes from "*lenire*, to soothe"; might not "lenative" be derived from "*lenare*, to prostitute" (cf. *lena*, bawd; *lenocinium*, meretricious attraction)? Then "lenative poisons" would be some such violent aphrodisiac as is said to have driven Lucretius

mad, when administered by his wife as a love-philtre. Cf. Ovid, *Ars Amat.* II. 105–6:

> Nec data profuerint pallentia philtra puellis:
> Philtra nocent animis vimque furoris habent.

If Webster really did mean "lenitive" ("lenatively" is certainly used in its normal sense in *A.Q.L.* I. I. 91; and "primitive" spelt "primative" elsewhere in *D.M.*) we can only explain—"poisons purporting to soothe the passion of the lover who administers the philtre". But this is very forced. Or simply "slow poisons"?

93. *by equivocation*: by some quibble, *e.g.* that love is a madness.

105. *girdle 'bout the world*: a favourite Elizabethan metaphor, usually to describe a literal journey round the world, like Drake's (cf. *Mids. Night's Dream*, II. I. 175; Chapman, *Bussy d'Ambois*, I. I. 23; Massinger, *Maid of Honour*, I. 1; Middleton, *Sun in Aries* (Bullen), p. 342, etc.); but it is used sometimes to express having done and seen everything, encompassed all knowledge, as here and in the character of "A noble and retir'd Housekeeper", 19–20: "he hath as it were, put a gird about the whole world and sounded all her *quicksandes*".

Parrott, on the Chapman passage, suggests that the phrase may have been suggested by a device in Whitney's *Choice of Emblems* (Leyden, 1586, p. 203) celebrating Drake's circumnavigation of 1577–80, in which the hand of Providence emerges from a cloud and holds the globe by a girdle. But it is unlikely that we can give so precise an origin to so general an idea. Indeed the print might equally well be based on the current phrase.

111. *your owne Chronicle*. Cf. *W.D.* V. I. 100–1.

III. 2.

Inner stage: the curtain may well have been drawn and disclosed the Duchess already untiring herself. In the latter part of the scene doubtless the whole stage was brought into use.

6. *with cap, and knee*: a regular phrase for "with cap in hand and bended knee". Cf. Marbeck, *Book of Notes*, 1189 (1581): "they shall have cappe and knee, and many gaye goodmorrowes in this lyfe".

9. *Lord of Misse-rule*: an unusual spelling. It *may*, one fears, be intended to suggest a play on "Misse" = "kept mistress" (cf. Evelyn, *Diary*, June 1645: "The com'on misses...go abroad bare-fac'd"). The Lord of Mis-rule, perhaps a survival of the old Fertility King, used to be appointed to reign over the Christian revels at Court, the Universities, the Inns of Court, and in the houses of the great. (See Frazer, *Golden Bough*, IX. 331 ff.; Chambers, *Medieval Stage*, I. 403 ff.)

31 ff. Antonio's panegyric of marriage is a charmingly ironic contrast to his very different view of it in I. I. 456 ff.

32. *Daphne*: wooed by Apollo (Ovid, *Met*. 1. 452).

32. *peevish*: not "foolish" (Dyce), but "froward", "perverse". Cf. *Ralph Roister Doister*, III. 3:

> These women be all such mad peevish elves
> They will not be won, except to please themselves.

33. *Siri[n]x*: a nymph vainly beloved by Pan, who made his Pan-pipe of the whispering reed into which she was changed (Ovid, *Met*. 1. 689).

34. *Anaxar[e]te*. Her rejected lover Iphis hanged himself at his stony mistress's door. As she was watching, still unmoved, his body on its journey to the grave, Venus in just anger changed her to a stone figure, which was thenceforth preserved in the goddess's temple at Salamis in Cyprus (Ovid, *Met*. XIV. 698).

38. *The Oliffe* was the gift to Athens of the virgin-goddess Athene; and so not a very happy instance from Antonio's point of view.

38. *Pomgranet*: I do not know of any woman turned into a pomegranate, though Robert Browning was to turn the pomegranate flower (βαλαύστιον) into a woman.

38. *Mulbery*: this tree changed the colour of its fruit to red from the blood of Pyramus, when he slew himself, thinking Thisbe dead (Ovid, *Met*. IV. 55).

39. *Flowres*: such as Clytie who loved Apollo and became a sunflower.

39. *eminent Starres*: *e.g.* Callisto, a nymph of Diana, loved by Jupiter and changed by the jealous Juno into the Great Bear (Ovid, *Met*. II. 409); Andromeda the bride of Perseus; the Pleiades, the seven daughters of Atlas, of whom one, Sterope, was fabled to shine faintly and almost invisibly because she alone gave herself to a mortal lover.

43–7. Suggested by W. Alexander, *Julius Caesar*, 59–60.

47. *Motion*: show, spectacle (often of puppets). Cf. Jonson, *Ev. Man out of his H.* II. 1: "They say there's a new Motion of the city of Nineveh, with Jonas, and the whale, to be seen at Fleet-bridge"; Marston, *Dutch Courtezan*, III. 1. 134: "A motion, sister".— "Nineveh, Julius Caesar, Jonas, or the destruction of Jerusalem?"

48–9. Cf. Archilochus' description of his love:

> ἐσμυρισμένας κόμας
> καὶ στῆθος, ὡς ἂν καὶ γέρων ἠράσσατο

(so that even an old man would have fallen in love with her); and J. M. Synge's rendering of Villon's "Regrets de la belle Heaulmière": "Where is the round forehead I had, and the two eyebrows, and the eyes with a big gay look out of them would bring folly from a great scholar?"

57. *Painter*: with, of course, an allusion to the painting of faces as well as of portraits.

61. *When were we so merry?* Cf. the "feyness" often supposed to

precede disaster: as when the suitors in the *Odyssey* laugh on the eve of their slaying "with alien lips". So Romeo says (*Romeo and Juliet*, v. 3. 88):

> How oft when men are at the point of death
> Have they been merry! which their keepers call
> A lightning before death.

The phrase was proverbial. Sir T. More, again, in Holinshed, describing the mood of Lord Hastings just before his sudden execution by Richard III, says: "he was never merier, nor never so full of good hope in his life; which selfe thing is oft seene a signe of change".

68. *Arras*: powdered orris- (iris-) root, a white powder with a smell of violets. Cf. *W.D.* v. 3. 118. The reader may perhaps recall this passage later on, at IV. 2. 134, 192.

69–70. *entred you into my heart...keyes.* From *Arcadia*, I. (*Wks.* I. 69): "His fame had so framed the way to my mind that his presence...had entred there before he vouchsafed to call for the keyes". (C.)

76. *Ghossips*: god-parents to your children.

77–9. A typical utterance of Webster's cardinal virtue of courage in despair. (Cf. *D.L.* I. 2. 259–60; *Char.* "Housekeeper", 22–3.) Equally typically, he borrowed it, from the *Arcadia*, I. (*Wks.* I. 25): "Lastly, whether your time call you to live or die, doo both like a prince".

It is a curious coincidence to find these words again in some of the verses written by Frederick the Great amid the disasters of the Seven Years War, which are better than his poetry usually is:

> Pour moi, menacé du naufrage,
> Je dois, en affrontant l'orage,
> Penser, vivre, et mourir en roi.

The situation may remind us of the first of the *Sonnets from the Portuguese*. There the poetess feels a presence behind her—Death it seems; but it proves to be Love. Here the Duchess looks round for Love, and sees Death standing before her.

81–5. *Vertue...a bare name, And no essentiall thing.* From *Arcadia*, II. (*Wks.* I. 146): "O Vertue, where doost thou hide thy selfe? or what hideous thing is this which doth eclips thee? or is it true that thou weart never but a vaine name, and no essentiall thing?" (C.) Cf. too Chapman, *Byron's Tragedy*, v. 3. 199 ff.; Massinger, *Bashful Lover*, IV. 1: "Virtue's but a word, Fortune makes all.—We are her tennis-balls".

But the ultimate source of all these in their turn has not, I think, been pointed out; it is the account in Dio Cassius (XLVII. 49) of the last utterance of Brutus at Philippi, which consists of two iambic lines (they might well be from some lost play of Euripides):

ὦ τλῆμον ἀρετή, λόγος ἄρ᾽ ἦσθ᾽ ἐγὼ δέ σε
ὡς ἔργον ἤσκουν· σὺ δ᾽ ἄρ᾽ ἐδούλευες τύχῃ.

Poor Virtue, so thou wast but a mere word!
I held thee real, that art but Fortune's slave.

Whence also Lord Chesterfield's acid summary of Henry Fox—"He lived, as Brutus died, calling virtue a name".

90–4. *reason...foresee...prevent...shame.* From *Arcadia*, II. (*Wks.* I. 146): "O imperfect proportion of reason which can too much forsee, and too little prevent!...In shame there is no comfort but to be beyond all bounds of shame". (C.)

98–9. *sheeres...flowne.* From *Arcadia*, II. (*Wks.* I. 177): "Alas, thought *Philoclea* to her selfe, your sheeres come to[o] late to clip the birds wings that already is flowne away". (C.)

102. *Basilisque*: the same as the cockatrice, a fabulous king of the serpents, with the body of a cock, the tail of a viper, and a crown-like crest on its head whence its name (βασιλισκός, royal). "The Basilisk," says the *Hortus Sanitatis*, III. 13, "is sometimes gendered from a cock; for towards the end of the summer the cock lays an egg from which the Basilisk is hatched. Also the opinion of some is that a viper or toad sits on that cock's egg—but this is doubtful." Its breath, even the sight of it, was fatal (Pliny VIII. 21); hence Topsell's story of the man who caused a great mortality among cockatrices by going about enclosed in mirrors so that they saw their own faces; Topsell, however, judiciously questions the truth of this, on the ground that the man would assuredly have been killed by their breath. Their only successful enemy was the weasel, which fortified itself against their poisonous exhalations by eating rue. For the repartee cf. *Rich. III*, I. 2. 150:

> *Glouc.* Thine eyes, sweet lady, have infected mine.
> *Anne.* Would they were basilisks, to strike thee dead!

106. *musicke to the[e]*: *i.e.* compared to thee.

119–20. *Such a roome...as our Anchorites*: *i.e.* walled up in a cell with only a small aperture, like Thais, for instance, after her conversion in Hroswitha's play; or, only a little before Webster wrote, the nun Virginia Maria de Leyva who was sentenced for unchastity to be "inclosed within a little dungeon, the door of which shall be walled up with stones and mortar, so that the said Virginia Maria shall abide there for the term of her natural life, immured both day and night, never to issue thence, but shall receive food and other necessaries through a small hole in the wall of the said chamber, and light and air through an aperture". (J. A. Symonds, *The Catholic Reaction* (1886), I. 353.) Crawford quotes Donne, *Of the Progress of the Soul*, 169:

> Thinke that no stubborne sullen Anchorit,
> Which fixt to a pillar, or a grave, doth sit
> Bedded, and bathed in all his ordures, dwels
> So fowly as our Soules in their first-built Cels.

There is an interesting likeness and difference between the two writers. Both dwell lovingly on the physically loathsome; but at least Webster never put it on an altar and grovelled before it like the Dean of St Paul's.

124. *Paraqueto.* Cf. the popinjay (or pyet) who betrays the murder in some versions of the Ballad of "Young Hunting" and the hawk who reveals the wife's infidelity in "The Bonny Birdy".

131–3. *sheete of lead...my heart.* Cf. *W.D.* III. 2. 343; H. King, *Poems*, "The Departure":

> Might all your crosses in that sheet of lead
> Which folds my heavy heart lie buried.

136. *hollow bullet*: *i.e.* cannon-ball, Fr. *boulet.* The explosive shell, as an improvement on the solid cannon-ball, was first introduced about the middle of the sixteenth century.

145 ff. *Reputation, Love, and Death.* This fable is the basis of a poem "Love, Death, and Reputation", generally (and, no doubt, rightly) assigned to Charles Lamb, in *Poetry for Children*, a joint-volume written by him and his sister Mary (1809):

> Once on a time, Love, Death, and Reputation,
> Three travellers, a tour together went;
> And, after many a long perambulation,
> Agreed to part by mutual consent.

> Death said: "My fellow tourists, I am going
> To seek for harvests in the embattled plain;
> Where drums are beating, and loud trumpets blowing,
> There you'll be sure to meet with me again.

> Love said: "My friends, I mean to spend my leisure
> With some young couple, fresh in Hymen's bands;
> Or 'mongst relations, who in equal measure
> Have had bequeathéd to them house or lands."

> But Reputation said: "If once we sever,
> Our chance of future meeting is but vain:
> Who parts from me, must look to part for ever,
> For *Reputation lost comes not again.*"

The third verse is the most altered from Webster and very much for the worse: we can ill exchange the shepherds for Hymen or the utter absence of legacies for that dubious source of affection, their equal division.

Here, as in III. 2. 278–80, III. 3. 50–2, III. 5. 17–24, Webster's source was doubtless P. Matthieu's *Histoire de la Mort de Henry IV* (tr. Grimeston, 1612). See R. W. Dent in *HLQ.* XVII. 75–82. Mr Robin Flower has kindly pointed out to me a recurrence of the essential idea in T. D. MacDonald's *Gaelic Proverbs*, p. 42:

> "She asked of the wind—'If I lost you where could I find you?'
> The wind—'On the top of the cairns.'
> She asked of the mist—'If I lost you where could I find you?'
> The mist—'On the top of the mountains.'

> She asked of fame—'If I lost you where could I find you?'
> Fame—'Lose me once, and you will never find me again'".

149–50. *Love...unambitiouِ shepheards.* Cf. Wordsworth's "Love had he found in huts where poor men lie". Note the irony of the contrast between the Duke's idyllic vision of an Arcadia with no dowries and no heirlooms, and that avarice which, as much as wounded pride, is at this very moment driving him to destroy the sister he preaches at and the family whose honour he upholds.

157. *shooke hands with.* Cf. the Greek χαίρειν λέγειν to a thing: Lyly, *Euphues*, p. 75: "Were I not over charie of mine honestie, you woulde inveigle me to shake handes with chastitie".

165. *Witches*: note that these form a perpetual subject of allusion with the Duke and his brother. Cf. I. I. 344; II. 5. 66; III. I. 92. Later it is on wolves that the Duke's mind runs, until he ends by believing himself one.

173. *That Gallery*: does this mean that the Duke is meant to be visible to the audience while crossing the upper stage, before he actually appears in the Duchess's room about 69?

174. *I would this terrible thing would come againe.* One almost wishes that Webster had spared his Antonio at all events this bluster of courage after the event, this *esprit d'escalier*.

186–8. Cf. *W.D.* IV. 2. 141.

201 ff. There is a certain lack of invention in Webster's repetition of this expedient of distracting suspicion by a pretence of theft, exactly as in II. 2 above.

203–9. *My brother stood engag'd...protested Against*: *i.e.* the Duke had become security for money borrowed (ta'ne up) by the Duchess from Jews in Naples. Antonio, by failing to make some payment that had fallen due, had "let the bonds be forfeyt". Accordingly the Jews "protested", *i.e.* made a written declaration that the bills backed by the Duke had not been met, as a preliminary to legal action for recovery of the debt. Cf. Massinger, *City Madam*, I. 3:

> I must and will have my money,
> Or I'll protest you first and, that done, have
> The statute made for bankrupts served upon you.

214. *Runnes upon engenous wheeles.* "To run on wheels" is "to move swiftly or uninterruptedly". Cf. Breton, *Pasquil's Passe (Wks.* (Grosart), I. 8/2): "A madding witte that runnes on wheeles". It is because of this *rapidity* that "short sillables, Must stand for periods".

Engenous seems to supplement the idea of swiftness with that of intricacy, as of "wheels within wheels". Dyce quotes Dekker, *Whore of Babylon* (1607), sig. C 2.

> For that one act gives, like an enginous wheel,
> Motion to all.

217. *Magnanima Mensogna*: from Tasso, *Gerus. Lib.* II. 22. An image of the Virgin, seized by the infidel tyrant of Jerusalem and placed

in the temple of Mahomet, mysteriously vanishes. In revenge the tyrant begins a wholesale persecution of the Christians; the *magnanima menzogna* is the pious fraud of a Christian maiden called Sofronia, who, to save her fellows, falsely takes the blame upon herself. Tasso's phrase was, of course, based in its turn on the famous *splendide mendax* applied by Horace (*Odes*, III. 11. 35) to Hypermnestra, who alone of the fifty daughters of Danaus broke her word to her father and saved her husband Lynceus, instead of slaying him on their marriage-night.

For Tasso, see also Hist. Introd. p. 26.

224. *Quietus*: see on I. 1. 532. The word must carry for the Duchess and her husband (and for the audience) a poignant association with that earlier, happier scene where she had signed his *Quietus* on Antonio's lips. And in the lines that follow, playing though she is for the life and honour of both, she cannot resist playing also with such double-edged hints at their secret love as—"that cur'de you Without helpe of a Doctor"—"I would have this man be an example to you all, So shall you hold my favour"—"h'as done that you would not thinke of". And with the same ambiguity Antonio answers "I am all yours".

227. *let him*: "let him go". The phrase is ambiguous; and might mean the exact opposite—"stop him": as in *Haml.* I. 4. 85: "I'll make a ghost of him that lets me". In *Winter's Tale*, I. 2. 40–2, there is the same doubt:

> I'll give him my commission
> To let him there a month behind the gest (time)
> Prefix'd for's parting.

Schmidt (*Lexicon*) and *N.E.D.* explain this—"so as to let him remain"; Malone—"to keep himself" ("him" for "himself"). Still the latter is much less plausible; and here, since the Duchess "intends to be rid of him", "let" probably means "let go", cf. 230. On the stage a gesture would make all clear. Cf. "Beaum. & Fl.", *Spanish Curate*, v. 2:

> Good sir, intend this business
> And let (*i.e.* let alone) this bawling fool.

Besides there is probably a play on "pray let him be an example".

249–51. Cf. Suetonius, *Vespasian*, (16) where that emperor is described as adopting this policy with his officials—"so that the common talk was he used them as sponges, letting them soak when they were dry and squeezing them out again when they were wet". The idea reappears in *Hamlet*, IV. 2. 16–23.

254. *abide to see a Pigges head gaping*. Dyce quotes *Merch. of Ven.* IV. 1. 54:

> Why he cannot abide a gaping pig.

(Though there the cause is hysteria, not Judaism.)

256. *I would you had bin his Officer*: *i.e.* you would have found it more profitable than being his mistress. Cf. Bacon. *Apophthegms* (1624), 10

(*Wks.* ed. Spedding VII. 126): "Bishop Latimer said, in a sermon at court; *That he heard great speech that the King was poor and many ways were propounded to make him rich: For his part he had thought of one way, which was, that they should help the King to some good office, for all his officers were rich*".

259. *blacke wooll*: H.D.S. explains the colour by a quotation from certain *Depositions from York Castle* in *The Denham Tracts* (ed. Hardy for the Folk-Lore Society, 1892), II. 294; in which a witness mentions how he went to a wise woman for ear-ache and "shee told him that blacke wool was good for itt". See *N.Q.* 11. XI. 118, 247.

266. *gold Chaine*: the steward's regular badge. Cf. *Twelfth Night*, II. 3. 129 (to Malvolio): "Go, Sir, rub your chain with crumbs" (Vaughan). Allen suggests that *fly* in the previous line is indicative; but it is clearly imperative, as a malediction.

277. *a sort of flattring rogues*: *i.e.* a set, company of them. Cf. Jonson, *Ev. Man in his H.*, I. 4: "I was requested to supper, last night, by a sort of gallants". It is not necessarily contemptuous, as has been suggested: cf. the compassionate cry of one of the judges of Babington's Conspiracy: "O Ballard, Ballard, what hast thou done! A sort of brave youths, otherwise endued with good gifts, by thy inducements hast thou brought to their utter destruction and confusion".

278–80. *Princes ... lies.* Almost word for word from P. Matthieu's *Mort de Henry IV* (tr. Grimeston, 1612), p. 188.

283. *Pluto the god of riches.* This fable occurs, as Vaughan points out, in Bacon's "Of Riches" (1625 ed.). Pluto should, of course, more strictly be Plutus. In origin Πλούτων is indeed merely a by-form of Πλοῦτος, Wealth; and this name was transferred to Hades, the god of the underworld, by a propitiatory euphemism, just as the name of the Black Sea was changed from Ἄξεινος (friendless) to Εὔξεινος (friendly). The link of association may have been that wealth came from underground (cf. Plato, *Crat.* 403 A; Cicero, *De Nat. Deor.* II. 66). Ultimately, however, the two deities became quite distinct, though we still find Plutus occasionally called Pluto—see Aristophanes, *Plutus*, 727 and Pearson's note on Sophocles, *Fragm.* 273; and cf. *Jul. Caes.* IV. 3. 101, *Troil. and Cress.* III. 3. 198 (where *Pluto* is wrongly emended to *Plutus* in some editions).

287. *by scuttles*: with a quick, hurried run.

292–3. Cf. Aristotle's ideal μεγαλόψυχος or "magnanimous man", who values himself neither too much nor yet too little (*Ethics*, IV. 3).

294. From Jonson's Dedication of his *Masque of Queens* (1609) to Prince Henry: "both your virtue and form did deserve your fortune". The passage is more extensively borrowed from in *Mon. Col.* 23–30. (C.)

295. From *Arcadia*, I. (*Wks.* I. 32): "A wit which delighted more to judge it selfe, then to showe it selfe." (C.)

297. Cf. *Mon. Col.* 78–9.

300–1. From *Arcadia*, I. (*Wks*. I. 15): "I am no herald to enquire of mens pedegrees, it sufficeth me if I know their vertues". (C.)

307. *the Bermootha's*: the Bermudas, famous for storms ("still-vexed"). Special interest in them had been excited by the wreck there in 1609 of Sir George Somers, to accounts of which *The Tempest* is indebted (see the edition of that play in the new *Cambridge Shakespeare*). Cf. *A.Q.L.* v. 1. 350 ff.; and Fulke Greville's *Caelica*, LIX:

> Whoever sailes neere to Bermuda coast
> Goes hard aboord the monarchie of Feare,
> Where all desires but life's desire are lost,
> For wealth and fame put off their glories there.

312–4. The idea recurs in *Arcadia*, I : "It can never be said that evil happeneth to him who falls accompanied with vertue".

317, 322. This sudden confiding in Bosola seems rather improbable.

325. *Seminary*: seed-plot, nursing-ground.

341. *Heralds…coates, to sell.* The sale of honours, then as now, was a perpetual subject of bitter allusion. The climax was reached when in 1616 Ralph Brooke, York Herald, tricked Segar, Garter King, into granting a coat of arms to Gregory Brandon, the London hangman. Cf. Jonson's supposed gibe at Shakespeare's new-bought coat with its motto *Non sanz droict*, when in *Ev. Man out of his Humour* Puntarvolo suggests for Sogliardo's "boar without a head, rampant" the legend "Not without mustard". (See *Sh.'s Eng.* II. 74–90.)

345. Cf. *Haml*. III. 2. 78: "I will wear him in my heart's core". (Dyce.)

353–4. *faigne a Pilgrimage To our Lady of Loretto.* In Belleforest-Painter this suggestion comes from the Duchess's woman. Why should Bosola make it here, thus furthering his victim's escape for the time being? Perhaps the best answer is to be found in the parallel situation in *W.D.*, where (IV. 1) Florence himself engineers Vittoria's flight with Brachiano and, when they escape to Padua, explains his motive (IV. 3. 55 ff.):

> How fortunate are my wishes! Why! 'twas this
> I onely laboured…Thy fame, fond Duke,
> I first have poison'd.

Similarly it would seem here that Bosola intends the Duchess to discredit herself with the world and her own subjects: the only alternative is to suppose that he really wants her to escape. That I can hardly believe, though it is certainly clear that he has at times a good deal of feeling for his victim.

354. *Loretto*: fifteen miles S.E. of Ancona. Its chief relic is the Holy House, supposed to be that of Mary at Nazareth. When threatened by the Turks in Palestine, this was carried through the air by angels to Tersatto in Dalmatia (A.D. 1291). Three years later it flew across the Adriatic to a wood (*lauretum—Loreto?*) near Recanati; and thence in 1295 to the hill where it has since remained. It contains a black image of Virgin and Child, attributed to St Luke; and is still visited by tens of thousands of pilgrims every year. (See *Encycl. Brit.* "Loreto".)

362. *Leuca*: see on II. 1. 64 above.

363–4. *Spaw In Germany*: Spa in Belgium, famous for its waters (the inhabitants of the Low Countries being included by the Elizabethans under the name "Dutch" or "Germans"). It seems to have escaped the lynx-eyes of both C. and H.D.S. that this combination of places was probably suggested to Webster by a passage in Montaigne II. 15: "Those of Marca d'Ancona, in Italy, make their vowes, and goe on pilgrimage, rather unto James in Galicia, and those of Galicia rather unto our Lady of Loreto. In the country of Liege they make more account of the Bathes of Luca; and they of Tuscany esteeme the Baths of Spaw more than their owne".

371. *Polititian...quilted anvell.* Cf. Chapman, *Byron's Tragedy* (pub. 1608), I. 2. 53–4:   great affairs will not be forged
         But upon anvils that are lined with wool.

373. Cf. *Char.* "A Jesuite", 18–9.

III. 3.

Outer stage.

s.d. Webster may conceivably have derived the name Malateste or Mallateste, though nothing more, from Malatesta Baglioni, one of a noble family of Perugia, who was a famous *condottiere* of this time and insisted on surrendering Florence to the Imperialists in 1530. But the name was in any case well-known as that of the ruling family of Rimini, to which Francesca's Paolo belonged.

2. *The Emperour*: Charles V.

2–6. The Cardinal, before entering the Sacred College, had been Marquis of Gerace and a tried soldier in his youth. (See Hist. Introd. p. 17.)

5. *the Marquis of Pescara*: Ferdinando Francesco d'Avalos (1489–1525), was in history the brother of the Duke Ferdinand's wife, Ippolita d'Avalos. He was born at Naples, of Spanish origin, and became the husband of the famous Vittoria Colonna. Webster makes him old. In reality he died, worn out and disappointed though only thirty-six, in the very year of his brilliant victory over Francis I at Pavia.

6. *Lanoy* (*c.* 1487–1527). Charles de Lannoy, Viceroy of Naples, was born at Valenciennes and became a favourite of Charles V. To him alone would Francis I·give up his sword at Pavia.

10. *plot*: plan.

18. *gun-powder, in's hollow tooth*: doubtless because of the anodyne effect of the nitre in it. Cf. Pliny XXXI. 10 (of nitre): "A collution made thereof, sodden in wine with pepper, easeth the tooth-ache". Cf. *Char.* "A Roaring Boy", 18–21.

22. *sent*: *i.e.* the smell of garlic.

23. *service*: military operations.

24. *City Chronicle.* Sampson suggests that this means Stowe's *Annales* (1592—new edit. 1605) or Grafton's *Chronicle at Large* (1568— new edit. 1611). But "all the *late* service" suggests something much more up-to-date in the way of news, some current periodical rather than a whole history. And it seems to me more likely that the City Chronicle compiled by the official City Chronologer (an office held by Middleton, Jonson, and Quarles) is here intended. Sampson objects that the City Records were not public enough. But we can hardly imagine that distinguished literary men were salaried by the City to compile some dry summary of events only to be locked away in a drawer. By the terms of Middleton's appointment he is for-bidden to *print* anything except with the permission of the Court of Aldermen; presumably, therefore, such records were of a sufficient topical interest for them to be worth printing. This impression is borne out by the numerous extra payments made to Middleton, and by Oldys's story of two MSS. of his sold by auction about 1735 and since lost: (1) *Annales*, dealing with strictly civic events. (2) *Middleton's Farrago*—social, political, and miscellaneous. The latter might well mention military events on the Continent. The most serious difficulty is the uncertainty whether the office of Chronologer existed before Middleton's appointment in 1620: it came to an end in 1669.

25–6. *Painters...Battailes in modell*: *model* was the regular word for "plan", of a house or the like; cf. 2 *Hen. IV*, I. 3. 41–2: "When we mean to build We first survey the plot, then draw the model". With the reading *Pewterers* (see Text. Note) *model* might be explained as referring to leaden soldiers. Cf. Jonson, *The Devil is an Ass*, III. 1:

> Get him the posture-book, and's leaden men
> To set upon a table, 'gainst his mistress
> Chance to come by, that he may draw her in
> And shew her Finsbury battles.

27. *fight by the booke*: Sampson explains *the booke* as "Vincentio Saviolo his Practise" (1595), a work in two parts: (1) On the use of the rapier and dagger; (2) On honour and honourable quarrels. It is the source of Orlando's wrestling-match and Touchstone's dis-quisition on Lies; but I doubt if it is meant here. *By the booke* simply means with all the preciseness of a book, whether in a good sense or a bad. Cf. *Rom. and Jul.* I. 5. 114: "You kiss by the book"; and a letter of Donne's quoted in E. Simpson's *Study of the Prose Works of J. Donne* (p. 295): "To know how to live by the booke is a pedantery" (*i.e.* a merely *theoretical* knowledge of life, as here of fighting). Cf. too the similar phrase *without booke*, *e.g.* in *W.D.* v. 3. 22 (see note), where there can be no question of any particular book.

32. *taffita*: "a plain-wove glossy silk", *N.E.D.*

38. *pot-gun*: *lit.* "pop-gun", thence "one who is charged with wind", "a braggart". Cf. Congreve, *Old Bachelor*, III. 3 (of a *miles gloriosus*): "that sign of a man there, that pot-gun charged with wind".

41–2. He is a mere ornamental appendage of the Court on its progress from place to place: *guarded*, (1) trimmed, (2) protected. Cf. *F.M.I.* v. 3. 319.

46. *Foxes*: an allusion to the jackals which Samson tied tail to tail (cf. *heads...devided*) to fire the corn of the Philistines. (*Judges* xv. 4.) Cf. *Char.* "Petifogger", 1.

50 ff. For this description of pedantry, cf. Montaigne's description (I. 38) of the scholar who ruins his life "to teach posteritie the measure of Plautus verses and the true orthography of a Latine word" (copied, as C. points out, by Marston, *Fawn*, IV. 1. 218–28; and Donne, *Progr. of the Soul*, 281–9). But in its concentration on *mythology* in particular, Webster's passage recalls rather the account of Tiberius in Suetonius (ch. 70): "Maxime tamen curavit notitiam historiae fabularis usque ad ineptias atque derisum"—asking the learned absurd questions about the name of Hecuba's mother, what Achilles was called as a girl, and what the Sirens sang. Ll. 51–2 are from Grimeston's P. Matthieu, see Appendix I.

61. *oppression*: stress of emotion.

63. *He lifts up's nose.* Cf. Massinger, *Roman Actor*, IV. 1 (of an informer):

> Here he comes
> His nose held up; he hath something in the wind.
>
> (T. S. Eliot.)

63–4. *Por-pisse...storme*: *Por-pisse—porcus, piscis*—porpoise (cf. Germ. *Meerschwein*). For its boding of storms cf. Dryden, *All for Love*, IV. 1: "That porc'pisce bodes ill-weather" (where Saintsbury in the *Mermaid* ed. gives the explanation "porcupine"!). Similarly in *Volpone*, II. 1, three porpoises appear "above the bridge"; and one at London Bridge ("always the messenger of tempests") in *Eastward Ho!* III. 3. Cf. Brand, *Pop. Antiq.* p. 711.

70–1. *deformed silence...charmes.* Cf. *Char.* "Usurer" 17–9.

75–6. *like leaprosie—The whiter, the fowler*: from Chapman, *Seven Penitential Psalms*, "A Great Man":

> th' embroidery
> Wrought on his state, is like a leprosy,
> The whiter, still the fouler. (C.)

82–3. The only mention of the Duchess's son by her first marriage, whose existence is rather hard to reconcile with the Duke's hope to inherit a mass of treasure by his sister's death. See Hist. Introd. p.18.

III. 4.

Whole stage: doubtless the pilgrims on the outer stage watched the ceremony going on in the inner, which would represent the shrine.

This scene appears to be described in a contemporary Italian account, the *Anglopotrida* of Orazio Busino (Feb. 7th 1618—quoted by Stoll, p. 29): "Prendono giuoco gli Inglesi della nostra religione come di cosa detestabile, et superstitiosa, nè mai rappresentano qualsivoglia attione pubblica, sia pura Tragisatiricomica, che non inserischino dentro vitii, et scelleragini di qualche religioso catolico, facendone risate, et molti scherni, con lor gusto, et ramarico de' buoni; fu appunto veduto dai nostri, in una Commedia introdur' un frate franciscano, astuto, et repieno di varie impietà, così d' avaritia come di libidine: et il tutto poi riuscì in una Tragedia, facendoli mozzar la vista in scena. Un' altra volta rappresentarono la grandezza d' un cardinale, con li habiti formali, et proprii molto[1] belli, et ricchi, con la sua Corte, facendo in scena erger un Altare, dove finse di far oratione, ordinando una processione: et poi lo ridussero in pubblico con una Meretrice in seno. Dimostrò di dar il Velleno ad una sua sorella,[2] per interesse d' honore: et d' andar in oltre alla guerra, con depponer prima l' abito cardinalitio sopra l' altare col mezzo de' suoi Cappellani, con gravità, et finalmente si fece cingere la spada, metter la serpa (sciarpa, scarf), con tanto garbo, che niente più: et tutto ciò fanno in sprezzo delle grandezze ecclesiastice vilipese, et odiate a morte in questo Regno.

Di Londra a' 7 feb[aio] 1618".

In quite another way also this scene, though not particularly striking in itself, gains a certain extraneous interest when we find it chosen to provide the opening of Mr Waley's charming transposition of *The Duchess of Malfi* into the form of a Nō play. His object was to help the readers of Nō plays; but I do not see why the readers of *The Duches of Malfi* should not also have the benefit; and by Mr Waley's kindness I am enabled to quote his adaptation here.

"The persons need not be more than two—the Pilgrim, who will act the part of *waki*, and the Duchess, who will be *shite* or Protagonist. The chorus takes no part in the action, but speaks for the *shite* while she is miming the more engrossing parts of her rôle.

The Pilgrim comes on to the stage and first pronounces, in his *Jidai* or preliminary couplet, some Buddhist aphorism appropriate to the subject of the play. He then names himself to the audience thus (in prose):

'I am a pilgrim from Rome. I have visited all the other shrines of Italy, but have never been to Loretto. I will journey once to the shrine of Loretto.'

---

[1] *molti* as quoted by Stoll and Chambers (III. 511).

[2] This seems a confusion of the deaths of Julia and the Duchess.

Then follows (in verse) the *Song of Travel* in which the Pilgrim describes the scenes through which he passes on his way to the shrine. While he is kneeling at the shrine, *Shite* (the Protagonist) comes on to the stage. She is a young woman dressed, 'contrary to the Italian fashion', in a loose-bodied gown. She carries in her hand an unripe apricot. She calls to the Pilgrim and engages him in conversation. He asks her if it were not at this shrine that the Duchess of Malfi took refuge. The young woman answers with a kind of eager exaltation, her words gradually rising from prose to poetry. She tells the story of the Duchess's flight, adding certain intimate touches which force the priest to ask abruptly, 'Who is it that is speaking to me?'

And the girl shuddering (for it is hateful to a ghost to name itself) answers: '*Hazukashi ya!* I am the soul of the Duke Ferdinand's sister, she that was once called Duchess of Malfi. Love still ties my soul to the earth. *Toburai tabi-tamaye!* Pray for me, oh, pray for my release!'

Here closes the first part of the play. In the second the young ghost, her memory quickened by the Pilgrim's prayers (and this is part of the medicine of salvation), endures again the memory of her final hours. She mimes the action of kissing the hand (*vide* Act IV. Scene I), finds it very cold:

> I fear you are not well after your travel.
> Oh! horrible!
> What witchcraft doth he practise, that he hath left
> A dead man's hand here?

And each successive scene of the torture is so vividly mimed that though it exists only in the Protagonist's brain, it is as real to the audience as if the figure of dead Antonio lay propped upon the stage, or as if the madmen were actually leaping and screaming before them.

Finally she acts the scene of her own execution:

> Heaven-gates are not so highly arched
> As princes' palaces; they that enter there
> Must go upon their knees. (*She kneels.*)
> Come, violent death,
> Serve for mandragora to make me sleep!
> Go tell my brothers, when I am laid out,
> They then may feed in quiet.
> > (*She sinks her head and folds her hands.*)

The chorus, taking up the word 'quiet', chant a phrase from the Hokkekyō: *Sangai Mu-an*, 'In the Three Worlds there is no quietness or rest'.

But the Pilgrim's prayers have been answered. Her soul has broken its bonds: is free to depart. The ghost recedes, grows dimmer and dimmer, till at last

> *use-ni-keri*
> *use-ni-keri*

it vanishes from sight." (From *The Nō Plays of Japan*. By Arthur Waley. 1921.)

9 ff. The authorship of this Ditty which Webster disclaims (as well he might), is unknown.

11–2. *flie-thee, nigh-thee*: note this use of hyphen (as again in the next stanza) to throw the stress on the syllable before it. Cf. II. 5. 68.

31. *determine of*: "This usage of the word, 'limiting the freedom of' a person, is apparently not recorded" (Sampson, followed by Allen). But why should it not mean simply "make decisions about", "adjudicate upon"? Thus H.D.S. quotes Massinger, *Renegado*, IV. 2:

> I claim the law and sue for
> A speedy trial; if I fail, you may
> Determine of me as you please.

45 ff. Cf. Montaigne II. 31: "The mischiefe is that after you are once falne into the pits it is no matter who thrusts you in, you never cease till you come to the bottome. The fall presseth, hasteneth, mooveth, and furthereth it selfe". (C.)

III. 5.

Outer stage.

1. *Banish'd Ancona!* A weaker echo of the thunder-crash which opens *The White Devil*, I. I. I.

8. *buntings*: a bird akin to the lark, but without its song. For the idea cf. *Timon* (first printed, as far as we know, in the First Folio of 1623), III. 6. 32:

> *Sec. Lord.* The swallow follows not summer more willingly than we your lordship.
> *Tim.* (*aside*). Nor more willingly leaves winter; such summer birds are men.

11–3. Cf. *Timon*, III. 3. 11:

> His friends, like physicians,
> Thrice give him over.

On which commentators quote this passage of Webster to support the reading *like physicians Thrive.* (Dyce.)

21–4. *Pearles...teares*: this interpretation of the dream is oneiro-critically quite correct (cf. Smedley, *Occult Sciences* (1855), p. 249). P. Matthieu's *Henry IV* (tr. Grimeston, 1612), p. 53, relates that Marie de' Medici dreamed of pearls before the assassination of her husband Henri IV, and was told it betokened tears. (Not that she appears in the upshot to have shed many: for she was not, in the words of le président Hénault, "assez surprise ni assez affligée de la mort funeste d'un de nos plus grands rois".)

25–6. *Birds...wilde benefit of Nature.* Cf. *Arcadia*, IV. (*Wks.* II. 119): "to have for foode the wilde benefites of nature". (H.D.S.) Repeated in *A.Q.L.* IV. 1. 81–2. Cf. *Macbeth*, IV. 2. 31, where little Macduff says he will live, now that he is fatherless, "As birds do, mother"

38. *equivocation*: using words in double senses to deceive. It became a byword owing to the use of it by Henry Garnet, superior of the Jesuits in England, during his trial for complicity in the Gunpowder Plot. Cf. *Macbeth*, II. 3. 10 (a supposed allusion to Garnet).

Here, *want his head in a busines* recalls Louis XI's ambiguous letter (Commynes, IV. xi.; also in Guicciardini) to the Constable of France (Mario Praz.) For *have his heart* cf. Sophocles, *Electra*, 1451, of the slayers of Clytemnestra, "They have touched their hostess to the heart" (φίλης γὰρ προξένου κατήνυσαν). Cf. too the stabbing of Vittoria Accoramboni, Hist. Introd. to *W.D.* ("Do I touch your heart?")

53–5. *league...politick Kings*: was this suggested to Webster by the infamous treaty of 1501 between Ferdinand the Catholic and Louis XII, by which the Spaniard sold his ally Federico of Naples (Antonio's master) to the invading French, in return for a share of the spoils? As the Spanish troops were unsuspectingly allowed to occupy the strong points of the Neapolitan Kingdom, Ferdinand easily made himself "of strength and powre To be the after-ruine" of the unfortunate Federico.

58. *this*: the letter. But should 61-2 follow 57?   (T. W. Craik.)

66. *Adamant*: loadstone. See on *W.D.* I. 2. 163.

70. *flye towards Millaine*: for Webster's departure here from the original story, see Hist. Introd. p. 20.

72. *bottom*: "hold" and so "ship". Proverbial; see Tilley, A 209.

75–8. Cf. Donne, *Anatomy of the World, A Funeral Elegy*, 37–46:

> But must wee say she's dead? may't not be said
> That as a sundred clocke is peecemeale laid,
> Not to be lost, but by the maker's hand
> Repollish'd, without errour then to stand...?

Similarly *Mon. Col.* 241–4.

81 ff. *Thou art happy...not understanding.* Cf. Sophocles, *Ajax*, 552–4:

> καίτοι σε καὶ νῦν τοῦτό γε ζηλοῦν ἔχω,
> ὁθούνεκ' οὐδὲν τῶνδ' ἐπαισθάνει κακῶν.
> ἐν τῷ φρονεῖν γὰρ μηδὲν ἥδιστος βίος.   (Vaughan.)

82–4. *wit...sorrow.* Cf. *Ecclesiastes* i. 18: "For in much wisdom is much grief: and he that increaseth knowledge, increaseth sorrow".

84–5. From *Arcadia*, II. (*Wks.* I. 233): "she sought all meanes...to send her soule, at least, to be married in the eternall church with him". (C.) Cf. H. King, "The Departure":

> 'Tis onely the Triumphant Church where we
> Shall in unsever'd Neighbourhood agree.

The *eternall Church* is the congregation of the saved in Heaven.

89. *Man (like to Cassia)...*: see on *W.D.* I. 1. 47–8.

90–1. *slave-borne Russian...tyranny*: from Sidney, *Astrophel and Stella*, II:

> And now like slave-borne Muscovite
> I call it praise to suffer tyrannie.

Cf. *F.M.I.* v. 3. 74: *Selimus*, 479. We have to remember that Ivan the Terrible had died as recently as 1584. Accounts of Sir Jerome Bowes's embassy in 1583 give a vivid impression of the contrast felt between the two nations. For Sir Jerome's benefit Ivan bade one of his courtiers leap out of a window, so that he was killed: to which the ambassador replied with some contempt that "his mistress did set more store by, and make better use of, the necks of her subjects". He also refused, it is said, to doff his cap before the Czar, though the French Ambassador had had his hat nailed to his head for similar boldness. (See "Sir J. Bowes" in *D.N.B.*) On another occasion Ivan is related to have addressed one of his boyars—"God save thee, my dear Boris, thou deservest a proof of my favour"; and so saying he struck the man's ear off. The boyar returned thanks for this graciousness and wished him a long reign. (Bell's *Hist. of Russia*, 1. 265.)

92. *Heaven...heavy*: doubtless intentional word-play.

93–5. *top...scourge-sticke*: from *Arcadia*, II. (*Wks.* I. 227—one of the few occasions when Webster borrows from Sidney's *verse*):

> Griefe onely makes his wretched state to see
> (Even like a toppe which nought but whipping moves)
> This man, this talking beast, this walking tree...
> But still our dazeled eyes their way do misse,
> While that we do at his sweete scourge repine,
> The kindly way to beate us to our blisse. (Not in C.)

95. *scourge-sticke*: whip for the top.

97–8. Cf. Donne, *Anat. of the World, First Anniversary*, 155–7:

> Wee seeme ambitious, Gods whole worke t' undoe;
> Of nothing hee made us, and we strive too,
> To bring our selves to nothing backe. (C.)

104. *an holy Anchorite*: we may be reminded here that it was as a holy Anchorite in a close cell that Ferdinand bade the Duchess keep her lover (III. 2. 119).

108. *Laurell...withered*: perhaps an echo of Cleopatra's parting cry (*Ant. and Cleop.* IV. 13. 64):

> O, wither'd is the garland of the war.

It must be remembered, however, that the withering of the naturally evergreen bay was an evil omen. Cf. *Rich. II*, II. 4. 7–8:

> 'Tis thought the king is dead: we will not stay.
> The bay-trees in our country are all wither'd.

So Evelyn, *Sylva*, II. 5: "In the year 1629 at Padua, preceding a great pestilence, almost all the Bay-trees about that famous University grew sick and died".

112. *Fortunes wheele...Princes*. Cf. Boethius II. Prose I. 2; Metre I (Vaughan).

114. *adventure*: quarry. H.D.S. quotes Marmion, *Holland's Leaguer*, I. 5:

> I have a bird i'th' wind, I'll fly thee on him:
> He shall be thy adventure, thy first quarry.

122. *flye in peeces.* Cf. *D.L.* III. 3. 297; and Donne, *Of the Progress of the Soul*, 181 (of a soul passing from the body at death):

> Thinke that a rustie Peece, discharg'd, is flowne
> In peeces.

130–2. From *Arcadia*, III. (*Wks.* I. 488): "with the same pittie as folkes keepe foule, when they are not fatte inough for their eating". (C.)

140. *base, low-fellow.* Bosola lightly sheds his democratic sentiments of a few pages before.

142. *counterfeit face*: Bosola is masked.

153. *high state of floods.* Cf. *2 Hen. IV*, v. 2. 132:

> Where it shall mingle with the state of floods. (Dyce.)

As R. P. Cowl points out, this parallel in Webster makes even more improbable Hanmer's emendation of the Shakespeare passage to *floods of state.*

169. Cf. *W.D.* IV. I. 26–7. The meaning is apparently—"Misery and greatness go together".

IV. I.

If the wax-figures are revealed in the "study", this scene must begin on the outer stage, the curtains of the study being closed again, to permit the removal of the wax-works, after l. 133. But it is hard to be sure.

It is generally assumed that the supposed scene is again Amalfi. Certainly Bosola said in the last scene that the Duchess was being carried "to your pallace". And yet four days after her murder here, we find her grave to be in Milan (v. 3). We can best reconcile the discrepancy by supposing that Bosola was lying and the Duchess was really cast into some castle of the Duke's near Milan, where the present Act would then take place. But the real answer is, I think, that neither Webster nor his audience cared for such precision: for them it was merely "Somewhere in Prison".

4–6. From *Arcadia*, II. (*Wks.* I. 332): "But *Erona* sadde indeede, yet like one rather used, than new fallen to sadnesse...seemed rather to welcome then to shunne that ende of miserie". (C.)

6–7. From *Arcadia*, I. (*Wks.* I. 16): "behaviour so noble, as gave a majestie to adversitie". Elsewhere Sidney says of Erona that one could "perceive the shape of loveliness more perfectly in woe than in joyfulness". (C.)

15. *Like English Mastiffes...tying.* Cf. *Arcadia*, i. (*Wks.* i. 25): "Leave women's minds, the most untamed that way of any; see whether any cage can please a bird? or whether a dogge grow not fiercer with tying". (C.)

23-4. Cf. *W.D.* iii. 2. 198-9.

35 ff. This scene with the dead hand and the mock corpses recalls, as C. points out, the pretended executions of Philoclea and Pamela in the sight of those dearest to them in *Arcadia*, iii.—with the difference however that Sidney's attempts to be terrifying are painfully ineffective. For the dead hand cf. Herodotus, ii. 121 (tale of Rhampsinitus).

40. *Cubbs*: the first touch of the Duke's future lycanthropia? His mind runs again more openly on wolves at the end of the next scene.

42-4. Almost repeated in *D.L.* iv. 2. 278-80.

50. *too much i'th' light*: too publicly conspicuous. Cf. *D.L.* i. 2. 52; *Hamlet*, i. 2. 67: "too much i' the sun" seems a different image.

66-7. S.D. How *many* wax children? I suspect, one. See Textual Note.

68-71. Cf. David when his son was dead (2 *Sam.* xii. 22-3).

74-6. *picture...dung-hill*: from Chapman, *Seven Penitential Psalms*, "A Fragment":

> like prick'd pictures charm'd,
> And hid in dung hills. (C.)

This familiar form of sympathetic magic is too common from N. America to Australia, from ancient Egypt to the Scotland of the last century even, to need much illustration. (See Frazer, *Golden Bough*, i. 55-70.)
The point of the dunghill was doubtless that its heat slowly melted the figure. Jonson in a Note on his *Masque of Queens* (1609: copied by Webster elsewhere) mentions "a relation of a French Ambassador's, out of England, of certain pictures of wax, found in a dunghill near Islington, of our late queen's: which rumour I myself (being then very young) can yet remember to have been current". Similarly in the room of the wife of the Maréchal d'Ancre there was said to have been found a wax image of the young Louis XIII, with one leg melted away (1617).

79. *bind...truncke*: the idea comes originally from Virgil, *Aeneid*, viii. 485-8, where this form of torture is ascribed to the Etruscan Mezentius. Cf. Marston, *Fawn*, i. 2. 203 ff.: "O Mezentius, a tyranny equal if not above thy torturing: thou didst bind the living and dead bodies together, and forced them so to pine and rot...".

84. *Portia.* Cf. Plutarch (North's transl.), *Brutus*, ch. 53: "As for Porcia, Brutus's wife, Nicolaus the Philosopher and Valerius Maximus do write, that she determining to kill herself (her parents and friends carefully looking to her to keep her from it), took hot burning coals and cast them into her mouth, and kept her mouth so close that she choked herself" (after her husband's fall at Philippi. Cf. *Jul. Caes.* iv. 3. 154).

90. *starve my selfe*: for a discussion of the legitimacy of this particular form of self-murder, with the same plea that fasting is legitimate, see Donne, *Biathanatos*, ii. 6. 5.

99–106. From *Arcadia*, ii. (*Wks.* i. 333): "But she (as if he had spoken of a small matter, when he mencioned her life, to which she had not leisure to attend) desired him if he loved her, to shew it, in finding some way to save *Antiphilus*. For her, she found the world but a wearisom stage unto her, where she played a part against her will: and therefore besought him, not to cast his love in so unfruitfull a place, as could not love it selfe". (C.)

109. *Ser.* Sampson suggests that this servant is perhaps *Cariola*. But in that case why should she not be called by her real name? It is simpler and better to suppose that the Duchess suddenly turns in her agony on some menial assistant of Bosola's. In any case Webster's main concern here was, clearly, to work in the retort he had admired in *Arcadia*, iii. (*Wks.* i. 485): "and he with an angry voice asked, Who was there? A poore Gentlewoman (answered the partie) that wish long life unto you. And I soone death to you (said he) for the horrible curse you have given me". (C.)

It is imitated by Shirley (*Love's Cruelty*, iii. 4):

> *Bel.* Do I live still?
> *Ser.* And shall, I hope, long.
> *Bel.* Thou'rt most uncharitable.

120. *the Starres shine still.* In this climax Bosola's cynicism rises to the sublime, as in four monosyllables he expresses the insignificance of human agony before the impassive Universe.

122. *make lanes...families*: from Chapman, *Seven Penitential Psalms*, "A Fragment": "Wars that make lanes thro whole posterities". Cf. *Bussy d'Ambois*, iii. 2. 469 ("a murthering piece, making lanes in armies") where the cannon-metaphor is clearer.

133. *It is some mercy, when men kill with speed.* An echo of Sidney's *Astrophel and Stella*, xlviii:

> A kind of grace it is to slay with speed. (G. K. Hunter.)

135. Wax images of the dead were much more familiar to Webster's audience than to us. A year or two before this play was acted, the citizens had watched a wax effigy of the dead Prince Henry borne through the London streets. "On the evening of that Sunday (Dec. 6th 1612) was brought a representation of the Prince, made at short notice, though extremely resembling him, and apparelled with clothes ...in short everything he wore at the time of his creation. This figure was laid on its back on the coffin, and fast bound to it; the head being supported by two cushions, just as it was to be drawn along the streets in the funeral chariot with eight black horses" (Birch, *Life of Prince Henry*, 1760, p. 362). The figure subsequently took its place among the other wax-works in Westminster Abbey.

Long search has failed to throw any light on Vincentio Lauriola.

The nearest approach to the name that I can find is the Cardinal Vincentio Laureo mentioned as having letters from Mary Queen of Scots just before her execution, in de Thou's *History* (1626 edit.), LXXXVI. 167 b (an account of Vittoria Accoramboni which Webster might have read, occurs in the same work, LXXXII. 42–3). But this is very remote indeed. Vincentio Saviolo who wrote a book on duelling well-known to the Elizabethans (1595; see on III. 3. 27) might just conceivably have suggested this name, *if* invented.

146–8. This, to me, suggests a physical passion for his sister.

155. Cf. Donne, *Satyres*, "Upon Mr Thomas Coryat's Crudities": "When wilt thou be at full, great Lunatique?"

162. *my intelligence*: my acting as intelligencer or spy in her court.

170. Cf. Publilius Syrus: "Crudelem medicum intemperans aeger facit". (G. K. Hunter.) And see Tilley, P 270.

IV. 2.

Whole stage. The Duchess may have sat in the inner stage, as in her cell. But she appears to be strangled on the outer stage since Bosola bears off her body at the end, though this point cannot be pressed.

2. *consort*: company.

15–6. *Robin...cages.* Cf. Tofte's Ariosto (1608), *Sat.* III:

> The cage is to the Nightingale a hell,
> The Thrush and Black-bird both do love it well;
> The Robin red-brest rob'd of libertie,
> Growes sad and dies with inward melancholy. (Sampson.)

19. *mad-man...eyes open*: an idea perhaps suggested by some kinds of somnambulism where the sleeper's eyes remain open.

22–3. Cf. Tennyson, *Maud*:

> Ah Christ, that it were possible
> For one short hour to see
> The souls we loved, that they might tell us
> What and where they be!

27–8. From *Deuteronomy*, XXVIII. 23. (Bradbrook.)

29–30. Cf. *Mon. Col.* 162–3; Marston, *Malcontent*, III. 1. 162–3:

> The galley-slave, that all the toilsome day
> Tugs at his oar against the stubborn wave.

There is a curious resemblance in a fine passage of D'Annunzio's *Paolo e Francesca*:

> *Paolo.*   Come debbo io morire?
> *Francesca.* Come lo schiavo al remo
>   nella galea che ha nome Disperata,
>   così dovete voi morire.

33–4. So in *Arcadia*, I. Pyrocles, entranced at the sight of Philoclea, stands "like a well wrought image, with some life in shew, but none in practise".

35–6. See on v. 3. 10 ff.

37. *Fortune...eie-sight.* The Duchess spoke only too truly when she offered herself to Antonio as his blind Fortune (i. 1. 565–7): now the bandage has fallen.

45–6. Cf. Donne, *Of the Progress of the Soul,* 477–9:

> When no Physitian of redresse can speake,
> A joyfull casuall violence may breake,
> The dangerous Apostem in thy breâst. (C.)

But the idea of such accidental cures is an old one.

46. *impost-hume*: ulcer.

49 ff. The modern reader has to remember in the scene that follows that to the audiences of the Globe madness was primarily funny. (Cf. the Bedlam-scenes of *Northward Ho!* iv. 3–4: Dekker, *Honest Whore*, Pt. i. v. 2.) Even the marriage-festival of the Princess Elizabeth was cheered with a masque of lunatics. It was therefore a refinement on this convention, far more novel to the Elizabethans than to us, when, as in *Hamlet* and *The White Devil* and here, what had been a mere matter of horseplay was used to deepen tragic pity and terror.

49. *secular Priest*: the "secular" clergy were those who lived in the world as contrasted with the monastic orders.

53. *day of doome.* Thus the astrologer Stoeffler predicted, owing to a conjunction of three planets in Pisces, a universal deluge for February 1524—a month, as it turned out, of unusual drought. A certain notable of Toulouse was, according to Voltaire, so convinced as to build himself an Ark, like the carpenter in Chaucer's *Miller's Tale.*

54–5. Webster, though born free of the Merchant Taylors, does not spare the trade. For jests on the English craze for new-fangled fashions, cf. *Merch. of Ven.* i. 2. 76 ff.; *F.M.I.* iv. 2. 125 ff. So Fynes Moryson: "No people in the world is so curious of new fangles as they of England be". Coryat in his *Crudities* describes the Italians as depicting the Englishman naked with a pair of shears "making his fashion of attire according to the vaine invention of his braine-sicke head". Cf. Lyly, *Euphues*, p. 437: and the lines on this subject in A. Borde's *Introduction of Knowledge*, beneath a print of a similar naked Englishman (*temp.* Henry VIII):

> I am an Englishman and naked I stand here,
> Musing in my mind what raiment I shall wear:
> For now I will wear this and now I will wear that
> And now I will wear what? I cannot tell what.

Similarly Harrison, in his *Description of England*, ii. 7 (in Holinshed), indulges in a long lament on the same subject, rising to the climax: "except it were a dog in a doublet, you shall not see anie so disguised as my countrymen of England".

58. *"how do you"*; I know no other instance of this plural without the "s" which is normally added, as in G. Harvey, *Letterbook*

(Camden), 90: "To requite your gallonde of godbwyes, I regive you a pottle of howedyes".

59. *knave in graine*: (1) in dye, *i.e.* fast-dyed, incorrigible; (2) in the grain-trade. Cf. "Beaum. & Fl.", *Maid in the Mill*, v. 2: "a miller, a thief in grain, for he steals corn".

Cf., for the idea, the farmer in *Macbeth*, II. 3, who "hang'd himself on th' expectation of plenty".

60. *transportation*: export. By 1 Jac. I, c. 25 (1603–4), grain is allowed to be exported, when wheat costs not more than 26*s.* 8*d.* per qr., rye not more than 15*s.*, barley not more than 14*s.*; with the proviso that the king can prohibit export either from the realm as a whole, or from the ports of any particular county. This regulation is modelled on previous enactments of the same nature, of which the first is a statute of Henry VI (1436). The average prices given by Rogers, *Hist. of Agric. and Prices in Engl.* vol. v, do not in fact ever fall below the legal limit which would have permitted export, between 1603 and 1619–20. But it is interesting to note that on Jan. 18th 1613 there was issued a special proclamation against the transportation of corn and grain on account of its high price and an apprehended scarcity (*Cal. State Papers, Dom.* (1611–8), p. 168). On Nov. 28th 1614, however, the Earl of Suffolk writes to the Customs Officers at London that the Eastland Merchants are to be allowed to re-transport their corn without export-duties, in case of its not finding sale in England (*ibid.* p. 261). The first date fits in quite well with the date assigned to the play.

61. *Broaker*: pawnbroker.

70. *b[e]ll*: bellow.

71. *yerk-some*: irksome.

72. *corasiv'd*: corroded. The *a* is due to confusion between *corrōdere*, to corrode, and *corrādere*, to scrape. Writers of the time sometimes try to distinguish the two, *e.g.* T. Adams, *Exp. 2 Peter*, II. 9 (1633): "They are our corrosives, corrasives, used only to pare off our excrements".

77 ff. 1. *Mad-man*, 2. *Mad.*, etc. I have sought to introduce a little method into this madness, by trying to identify their professions on the basis of the Servant's description above and their own remarks.

78. *perspective*: not here "magic-glass" (Sampson), but "telescope". Cf. Brereton, *Trav.* (1634–5: pub. 1844), 60: "perspectives which shew the new-found motion of the stars about Jupiter".

79–80. *pillow...stuff't...Porcupines.* Cf. *W.D.* 1. 2. 77–8; H. King, "Elegy occasioned by sickness": "His Pillow quilted with a Porcupine".

81. *glasse-house*: glass-factory. See on *W.D.* 1. 2. 134.

88–9. *sore throates*: *i.e.* with perpetual preaching.

92–3. *wood-cockes head, with the Braines pickt out*: the woodcock being a proverbially stupid fowl.

93. *ancient*: ironically—another jest at the mushroom nobility and gentry of the day.

94. *Greeke is turn'd Turke*: *i.e.* the Greek text of the Bible has been enlisted in the service of infidelity. The priest is satirized as a Puritan and so disapproves of all other translations except the Genevan; and he is here perhaps thinking of the Douay version of 1609–10 and the recent Authorized Version (1611). "To turn Turk" means ordinarily "to turn Moslem"—and so "become infidel"; and W. J. Craig's explanation "turn cruel" lacks either authority or meaning in this context.

95. *the Helvetian translation*. This is certainly not Coverdale's Bible of 1535 (Vaughan), but the Genevan or "Breeches" Bible of 1560. The whole point of this passage has been missed through commentators failing to see that it is a satire on Puritans.

The Genevan Bible, the work of a band of Puritan exiles, including Coverdale and Knox, had marginal notes of such a Calvinistic and anti-monarchist tendency that its printing was prohibited in England till Archbishop Parker's death in 1576. For instance, it observed on 2 *Chron.* xv. 16, that Asa after deposing his mother ought also to have put her to death; on *Rev.* ix. 3, it remarks: "Locustes are false teachers, heretikes, and worldlie suttil Prelates, with Monkes, Freres, Cardinals, Patriarches, Archbishops, Bishops, Doctors, Baschelers, and masters which forsake Christ to maintaine false doctrine". The 1569 edition also contained Calvin's Catechism; and shows a characteristic Puritan trait in recommending to parents a list of names for their offspring which includes such portents as Artashaste, Kerentrappuch, Mahazioth, Retrabeam, Tanhumeth, and Vopsi.

Accordingly it is little wonder that James I said at the Hampton Court Conference that "he thought the Geneva translation was the worst, and many of the notes very partial, untrue, seditious, and savouring too much of dangerous and traitorous conceits"; or that Laud should have tried to suppress it (one of the charges brought against him at his trial in 1637).

The Genevan version was, on the other hand, exceedingly popular (it was the first to introduce Roman type and the verse division of chapters) and went through some two hundred editions. The last Quarto of it was printed in England in 1615, the last Folio in 1616; but even then copies continued to flow in from Holland up to the middle of the century. (See Dore, *Old Bibles*, 1888.)

96. *lay the law*: expound it.

98. *drinkes but to satisfie nature*: for this suggestion of clerical tipsiness cf. *W.D.* v. 3. 121–2.

99. *If I had my glasse here*: it is suggested that this is some crystal or divining glass. But the sense remains obscure. Perhaps some kind of "perspective" glass is meant which produced an indecent illusion when looked through.

101. *rope-maker*: *i.e.* confederate of the hangman. Nash constantly
gibes at Gabriel Harvey for being the son of one. Cf. *Char.* "Sexton",
16.

102. *snufling knave*: with allusion to the notorious nasal whine of the
Puritans.

102–3. *shewes the tombes...placket*: *i.e.* he is a sort of Tartuffe,
pointing with a *memento mori* at the tokens of mortality, while at-
tempting seduction.

107. *paired the divells nayles.* Vaughan quotes *Twelfth Night*, IV. 2.
140 ff., where the Vice calls to the Devil to pare his nails. Malone
explains that this is an insult to that personage, because he likes to
keep his nails long. For nail-parings in popular superstition, cf.
Frazer, *Golden Bough*, IX. 57–8.

109. *possets*: made of hot *milk*, curdled with ale or wine, to which
sugar and spice were added.

111. *Colledge...caps.* Cf. *Char.* "A Quacksalver", 10: "All the
learned doctors may cast their Caps at him". But what is the meaning?
N.E.D. renders the phrase as "show indifference to, give up for lost".
But this makes no sense here; the idea seems rather—"they may do
their utmost against me, but it will be in vain". So in Dekker's *Dead
Term* (Grosart, p. 82) we have—"if he went away with it cleare
(*i.e.* brought off his trick), all the fresh men in Cambridge should
throw up their cappes at him, and not mend the devise". From this
the transition is not difficult to the meaning: "to give up a person or
a thing in despair, since doing one's utmost is in vain"; thus Chamberlain writes to Carleton on July 5th 1617 that Lord Hay is vainly
trying to appease the Earl of Northumberland whose daughter he is
marrying: "But he (Hay) may cast his cap at that, seeing him (the
Earl) so incensed". Equally decisive is *Timon*, III. 4. 103–4: "our
masters may throw their caps at their money; these debts may well
be called desperate ones". Mr Hayward points out a similar usage
of this gesture of despair in La Fontaine, *Fables*, II. 18:

> L'affaire est consultée: et tous les avocats
> Après avoir tourné le cas
> En cent et cent mille manières
> Y jettent leur bonnet, se confessent vaincus.

112. *Soape-boyler costive*: a peculiarly difficult feat, soap being used for
suppositories.

123. *salvatory*: ointment-box.

124. *greene mummey*: for mummey see on *W.D.* I. I. 16.
greene: undried (of any kind of flesh, *e.g.* "greene beefe").

124. *cruded milke*: curdled. Cf. Donne, *Of the Progress of the Soul*,
165–6:

> This curded milke, this poor unlittered whelpe,
> My body. (C.)

Only Krusius however has noted the echo of *Job* x. 9–10:

Remember, I beseech thee, that thou hast made me as the clay;
And wilt thou bring me into dust again?
Hast thou not poured me out as *milk*,
And *curdled* me like cheese?

Here again the Bishops' Bible is even nearer than the A.V. to Webster, reading:

Hast thou not poured me as it were milke, and turned me to cruddes like cheese?

125. *puffe-paste*: a light and flimsy sort of pastry. Applied to flimsy, worthless persons. Cf. "Beaum. & Fl.", *Wit at Several Weapons, Dram. Personae*: "Pompey Doodle, a Clown, Sir Gregory's Man, a piece of puff-paste".

127–8. *Larke in a cage.* Cf. *W.D.* IV. 2. 67.

135. *merry milkemaydes.* Cf. *Char.* "A fayre and happy Milke-mayd".

135–6. *mouse...cats eare.* The earliest instance of the phrase given by *N.E.D.* is in Lydgate, *Minor Poems* (Percy Society, p. 167), "The Order of Fools":

An hardy mowse, that is bold to breede
In cattis eeris, that breede shall never the (*i.e.* thrive).

Cf. Lyly, *Gallathea*, IV. I. 45–6.

138. *unquiet bed-fellow*: a poignant echo to our ears of the playful mirth of III. 2. 17.

141–2. Cf. *W.D.* v. I. 38–9 and note.

153 ff. This change to sepulchral-figures recumbent on their elbows makes its appearance in the sixteenth century—perhaps owing to the Renaissance influence of Etruscan tombs with their effigies lying as at table.

173. *Bell-man.* The bellman's bell, like the passing-bell in churches, was probably meant in origin to drive away the evil spirits that lie in wait for the departing soul; later, to invite also the prayers of the faithful. According to Douce (quoted in Brand, *Pop. Antiq.* p. 428) down to the middle of the eighteenth century a bellman of the dead used to walk the streets of Paris in a dress ornamented with death's-heads, bones, and tears, crying out: "Awake, you that sleep, and pray to God for the dead".

There is however both here and in the parallel passage in *Macbeth*, II. 2. 4 ("It was the owl, the fatal bellman, Which gives the stern'st good-night"), a possible allusion to a recently established London custom. Mr Robert Dowe, a Merchant Taylor like Webster himself, who died just before this, in 1612, had in 1605 (the probable date of *Macbeth* is 1606) given an endowment of £50 (26s. 8d. *per annum* for ever) to the parish of St Sepulchre's, to pay the clerk of that church for tolling the church-bell and going himself as bellman to exhort condemned criminals in the neighbouring Newgate on the night before their execution. He was to stand before their cell-window at midnight and give "12 solemn towles by double strokes" on a hand-bell provided by Mr Dowe's munificence. He was then to exhort them as follows:

> "You Prisoners that are within
> Who for your Wickedness and Sin,

after many Mercies shew'd you, are now appointed to be Executed to Death to-morrow in the Forenoon, give ear and understand that to-morrow morning the greatest Bell of St Sepulchre's Parish shall toll for you from six till ten in order and manner of a Passing Bell, which used to be toll'd for those who lie at the point of Death, to the end, that all godly People, hearing that Bell, and knowing it is for you going to your Deaths, may be stirr'd up to hearty prayer to God to bestow his Grace and Mercy on you whilst you yet live, etc." Not content with these consolations Mr Dowe ordained that the bellman should again exhort his victims in the early morning and deliver from the wall of St Sepulchre's churchyard another "pious and aweful admonition" to them in the cart on their way to Tyburn.

The Beadle of the Merchant Taylors' Hall was also paid from this endowment to see that the bellman did his business properly. So that the ceremony must have been doubly familiar to Webster; and his audience at this point must certainly have been reminded of the last nights of the condemned in Newgate. (See Wheatley, *London Past and Present*, III. 229–30. F. P. Wilson (*Elizabethan and Jacobean*, p. 141) points out that among the signatories to Dowe's benefaction was a John Webster, member of the Common Council.

181. *whistler*. Cf. Spenser, *F.Q.* II. 12. 36: "The Whistler shrill, that whoso hears doth die" (Dyce). This name is sometimes applied to the wigeon, the ring-ouzel, and the golden-eye (*Clangula glaucion*). But the superstition is attached rather to the cry of the so-called "Seven Whistlers", voices heard flying overhead in the darkness of the night. This cry was always regarded as an evil omen; and it is said that Leicestershire colliers would not go underground on a day when the Whistlers were heard. Sometimes the voices were supposed to be the wandering souls of Jews who took part in the Crucifixion; sometimes they were imagined as the hounds of a ghostly hunt and, near Sheffield for instance, called the Gabriel hounds, in Devonshire the Wish hounds. Cf. Wordsworth:

> The poor old man is greater than he seems.
> He the seven birds hath seen that never part,
> Seen the seven whistlers on their nightly rounds
> And counted them: and oftentimes will start,
> For overhead are sweeping Gabriel's hounds.
> (*Miscell. Sonnets*, XXIX; i. 457 in Nowell Smith's edit.)

What bird is the source of the cry and the legend, remains disputed; it has been identified as the golden plover, the curlew, or the migrant bean-goose. Mr H. W. Richmond, however, has pointed out to me yet another candidate, the whimbrel, a small relation of the curlew, which has the habit of whistling *seven times*. Cf. Yarrell's *British Birds* (1884), III. 510: "Whimbrels are often spoken of in the South and West as 'the seven Whistlers', the rippling whistle being repeated seven times". This certainly provides an explanation of the number— if indeed the mystic "seven" needs one. (See Swainson, *Folk-lore of British Birds*, pp. 180, 200; *N.Q.* 4. VIII. 134, 268.)

185. *competent*: sufficient.

190. *mist of error*: the essence of the greatest tragedy, the ἁμαρτία or Tragic Error of Aristotle's *Poetics*. Cf. the dying words of Flamineo and of Bosola (*W.D.* v. 6. 260; *D.M.* v. 5. 118).

192. *haire, with powders sweete*: a pathetic echo of the Duchess' laughing prediction (III. 2. 68).

201. *Remoove that noyse*: it has been suggested that this refers to the musicians (if there are any) to whose accompaniment the dirge is sung, if sung it is. "Noise" was indeed a regular word for a band of musicians; cf. Jonson, *Tale of a Tub*, I. 2: "Press all noises of Finsbury". But here only a commentator would apply the word to anything but the screams of Cariola, who is obviously meant.

213. *cathar*: "catarrh"—used to mean not only "a cold in the head" but, as here, "cerebral haemorrhage", which was once (wrongly) supposed regularly to accompany apoplexy.

215. *Doth not death fright you?* Cf. *W.D.* v. 6. 223.

217. *such excellent company*: the same consolation as Socrates gives himself, when he faces death and his judges in Plato, *Apology*, XXXII.

222 ff. Cf. Donne, *Fifty Sermons* (1649 ed.), p. 235: "This whisperer wounds thee, and with a stilletta of gold, he strangles thee with scarfes of silk, he smothers thee with the down of phoenixes, he stifles thee with a perfume of Ambar". (Cf. *whispering* in 229; was Donne thinking of this passage?)

227-8. *hinges...both wayes*: the meaning is apparently that Death can open the door out of life from his side, or man can open it from his: our exit may be by act of God or of man. This is unsatisfactory: but I see no alternative.

228-9. *any way...whispering*. Cf. *Rich. II*, IV. I. 315 (the deposition-scene): "Whither you will, so I were from your sights".

235. *Dispose my breath, how please you*: irony to the end? Cf. Socrates' jesting answer to Crito's question how they should bury him (*Phaedo*, 115 c): "As it pleases you, if you can catch me".

239-41. *heaven gates are not so highly arch'd...knees*. Cf. *Cymbeline*, III. 3. 2 (Dyce):

> Boys, this gate
> Instructs you how to adore the Heavens; and bows you
> To a morning's holy office; the gates of monarchs
> Are arch'd so high, that giants may jet through
> And keep their impious turbans on, without
> Good morrow to the sun.

It seems to me possible that this passage in its turn was suggested by the legend of Mahomet's first miracle (cf. *impious turbans*) in Mandeville XVI, where we are told how the Prophet was a humble camel-driver in his youth. "And at the desertes of Arabye he wente in to a chapell where a Eremyte duelte, And whan he entred in to the chapell that was but a lytill and a low thing and had but a lytil dore and a low, than the entree began to wexe so gret and so large and so high as though it had ben of a gret mynstre or the gate of a paleys."

241–2. *death, Serve for Mandragora.* Cf. Donne, *Anat. of the World, A Funeral Elegy,* 79–80:

> And the worlds busie noyse to overcome,
> Tooke so much death, as serv'd for *opium.* (C.)

259. *your wedding Ring.* Cf. Painter (p. 37): "and instead of a Carcanet placed a rope about her neck" (Stoll).

266. *This two yeeres. This* for *these* (of which it is an old variant-form found from the twelfth to the seventeenth century) is, naturally, commoner with plurals which, as here, may be thought of as a single whole; cf. "within this three hours" (*Rom. and Jul.*); "by this means"; and even "against this fearful odds" (Southey).

266. *When!*: exclamation of impatience.

267. *quicke with child.* Cf. the similar plea of Joan of Arc in 1 *Hen. VI,* v. 4 (based on a calumny of Holinshed's).

272. Here Bosola, if the children have been strangled off the stage (see Text. Note on 246–7), must "discover" their bodies by drawing back the curtain of the inner stage.

275. *young Wolffes.* Note that the Duke's mind, as though to lead up to his lycanthropic mania, is already running on wolves, cf. IV. I. 40; 332 below.

279–80. Craig points out a parallel in Nash, *Unfortunate Traveller* (ed. Brett-Smith), 115: "water powred forth sinkes downe quietly into the earth, but bloud spilt on the ground sprinkles up to the firmament".

281. *dazell*: the intransitive sense as here (= "are dazzled") is the original one.

This well-known line needs no comment; but, as a curiosity, it is perhaps worth preserving William Archer's contemptuous dismissal of it: "It is not difficult to hit upon sayings which shall pass for highly dramatic simply because they are unforeseen and unlikely".

282–3. The just fame of the preceding line has overshadowed the quieter beauty of these two that follow.

304. *infinite masse of Treasure.* See on III. 3. 82–3.

308–9. *good Actor...villaines part.* We have to remember that these lines were originally spoken by Burbage, the most famous of all Elizabethan actors.

310. Cf. *W.Ho!* I. I (p. 71).

332. *The Wolfe...*: see on *W.D.* v. 4. 97.

347. *Like two chain'd bullets.* Cf. Heywood, *Challenge for Beauty*, II. (*Wks.* v. 26):

> My friend and I
> Like two chaine-bullets, side by side, will fly
> Thorow the jawes of death. (Dyce.)

Similarly Chapman, *Rev. of Bussy*, v. 1. 7 (of divine justice):

> who in th' act itself
> Includes th' infliction, which like chained shot
> Batter together still.

349. *take...in a blood*: goes by families. *Take* = "take effect", as we speak of vaccination "taking".

352–3. Cf. *K. John*, IV. 2. 242, where John cries to his tool Hubert on the news of Arthur's murder:

> Out of my sight, and never see me more. (Dyce.)

360. *hunt the Badger, by Owle-light.* Cf. Topsell, *Four-Footed Beasts*: "These Badgers are very sleepy, especially in the daytime, and stir not abroad but in the night, for which cause they are called *Lucifugae*; that is *avoiders of the light*". Turberville says in his *Noble Art of Venerie* (1611 ed., ch. 69): "He that would hunt the Badgerd, must seeke the earths and burrows where they lie, and in a faire mooneshine night" (the whole passage is well worth reading).

Owle-light: dusk.

362. *my painted honour*: generally taken to mean his disguise (Sampson, Allen). But what *honour* there is in being disguised as an old bell-man, I cannot imagine. Surely *painted* here means, as so often in Webster, "deceptive"; and *honour* refers to his advancement in the world. He had received the provisorship of the Duchess's horse; he had hoped for further promotion—in vain. Cf. III. 2. 321: "wealth and painted honors"; v. 2. 336: "honors in store for thee".

367. *She stirres.* Dyce compares *Othello*, v. 2. 115, where Desdemona revives in the same way. Had the commentators on that scene remembered this passage, they might have saved all those medical disquisitions, which fill pages of Furness's *Variorum* edition, on the question whether a person once suffocated can first revive and then die, or whether we must suppose Othello to have used his dagger also. Whether or no it is actually possible to revive and then expire after suffocation, matters little; Webster's words prove decisively that to Elizabethans it *seemed* possible; and that is all we need to know.

373. *pitty would destroy pitty*: *i.e.* calling for help to save her life would only seal her death, by bringing back Ferdinand.

380. *attonement*: reconciliation (at-one-ment).

381. *Mercy!*: "she is probably acknowledging the mercy of God" (Allen). This is an edifying conception; but it seems to me much more likely to be a last half-conscious appeal to her murderers to spare her.

382. *the cords of life broake.* Cf. *Eccles.* xii. 6: "Or ever the silver cord be loosed, or the golden bowl be broken" (Krusius); (the met. is of a golden lamp hung from the ceiling by a silver cord: the cord gives way and the lamp is smashed in sudden darkness). Here the Bishops' Bible is quite unlike—"Or ever the sylver lase be taken away, and or the golden wel be broken".

389. *manly sorrow*: of course, ironic.

390–1. Cf. iv. 1. 166.

391–2. *below The degree of feare*: *i.e.* past fearing for, as being utterly desperate. Cf. *Arcadia*, ii. (*Wks.* i. 208): "our state is soncke below the degree of feare". (C.)

V. 1.

Outer stage.

6. *hold...in Cheit*: *i.e.* "subject to escheat"; "escheat" (*lit.* chance, accident) signifies the reversion of land held "in fee" to the lord of the fee, on the death of the tenant intestate and without heirs, or when he had committed treason or other felony. Doubtless Antonio was held to have committed a felony.

20. *St. Bennet*: St Benedict.

51–2. From Montaigne 1. 29 (which probably suggested the whole episode); there it is related how Epaminondas, having refused the freedom of a youth in prison to his friend Pelopidas, yet granted it to the youth's mistress, "saying it was a gratification due unto a Courtizan, and not to a Captaine". (C.)

67. *noble old fellow*: Pescara (who was actually only thirty-six at his death in 1525).

77. *fraight*: fraught.

81. *fall once...ever falling*: from Montaigne 1. 32: "there is no man so base minded that loveth not rather to fall once than ever to remaine in feare of falling". (C.)

V. 2.

Whole stage: it seems impossible that Ferdinand should appear literally in the "gallery" or upper stage (cf. l. 3); for he could not there be seen throwing himself on the ground to catch his own shadow.

7. *Licanthropia*: the mania of one who believes himself a were-wolf. Webster's source is Goulart's *Histoires Admirables* (1600), translated by Grimeston (1607), pp. 386–7 (the section containing the story of the *D.M.* ends on p. 368): "For there be *Licanthropes* in whom the melancholike humor doth so rule, as they imagine themselves to be transformed into Wolves...and all night doe nothing but runne into Church-yardes, and about graves...one of these melancholike *Licanthropes*...carried then upon his shoulders the whole thigh and the legge of a dead man....A Countri-man neere

unto Pavia, in the yeare 1541 ... did constantlye affirme that he was
a Wolfe, and that there was no other difference, but that Wolves
were commonlie hayrie without, and hee was betwixt the skinne and
the flesh. Some (too barbarous and cruell Wolves in effect) desiring
to trie the truth thereof, gave him manie wounds upon the armes and
legges"—(as the result of which the man died).

So Bishop Hall saw a man executed at Limburgh, "who confessed
on the wheel (where indeed most of us would have confessed anything) to have devoured two and forty children in that form"; and
Peucer (1525–1602) states that the sorcerers of Livonia, whom the
devil changed annually into wolves, were only to be identified by
their having wolf's hair under their skins.

The disease is, however, despite these fables, a real one. Morel
(*Études Cliniques*, 1852, II. 58) describes a patient who was so
convinced he was a wolf, that he demanded raw meat and rejected
it as not rotten enough. "See this mouth," he exclaimed, separating
his lips with his fingers, "it is the mouth of a wolf; these are the teeth
of a wolf; I have cloven feet; see the long hairs which cover my body;
let me run into the woods and you shall shoot me." (See Hack Tuke,
Dict. of Psycholog. Medicine, 1892, II. 754.)

A Lycanthropic Madman appears also in the "Masque of Melancholy" in Ford's *Lover's Melancholy* (III. 3), crying: "Bow-wow!
wow-wow! the moon's eclipsed; I'll to the church-yard and sup, etc."

26. *Parac[el]sus* (*c.* 1490–1541) was the Swiss-born son of a German
physician. It is hard to separate clearly the scientist in him from the
quack; or the bold advocate of a return to nature and the use of one's
own eyes in medicine in place of the formulas of Galen and Avicenna,
whose volumes he burnt as lecturer at Bâle, from the mystery-monger
who kept a familiar spirit in his sword-hilt and captured the imagination of posterity with his fantastic dreams.

31. *Eagles ... alone.* From *Arcadia*, I. (*Wks.* I. 56): "Eagles we
see fly alone, and they are but sheepe which alwaies heard together".
(H.D.S.) Cf. Sir Philip Francis on the hated Pitt, whom he yet
admired for his splendid isolation: "The lion walks alone. The jackals
herd together"; *Troil. and Cress.* I. 2. 263; Tilley, E 7.

49. *sheepe-biter*: "a dog that worries sheep" thence "a sheep-stealer";
and so "any sneaking thief". Cf. *W.Ho!* IV. I. (p. 133): "Master
Justiniano here hath layed lurking, like a sheep-biter".

Sampson suggests that Ferdinand's idea of himself as a wolf is still
influencing him; but this is not very convincing.

51–2. Cf. *Othello*, v. 2. 302–3 (Dyce), where Iago says:

Demand me nothing: what you know, you know:
From this time forth I never will speak word.

56–7. *beard saw'd off ... eye-browes Fil'd*: perhaps the doctor is meant
to add point to this remark by standing with a stiff, statuesque dignity
which suggests to Ferdinand the idea of improving his appearance

with file and saw, as if he really were a graven image. Stoll quotes *Lear*, III. 6. 84, where the mad King says to Edgar: "Only I do not like the fashion of your garments: you will say they are Persian attire: but let them be changed". Still the resemblance is not very striking.

57. *more civill*: (1) "more decent"; (2) with allusion, I think, to the lack of civility in the doctor's hectoring attitude, "more polite".

69. *put off your gowne?* The Q. of 1708 has the stage-direction, doubtless traditional, "puts off his four cloaks, one after another". Dyce mentions that the Grave-digger in *Hamlet* used as late as 1830 to go through a similar piece of buffoonery.

76. *Cullice*: strengthening broth, made partly by *bruising* the flesh and bones of a fowl or the like. See on *W.D.* v. 4. 23–4.

76. *An[a]tomies*: skeletons.

77. *Barber-Chyrurgeons hall.* The Barber Surgeons were granted a charter as a Company by Henry VIII in 1541—a scene represented in a famous picture, partly by Holbein, which Pepys once thought of buying. Their Hall was in Monkswell St; and they were granted the bodies of four executed felons a year.

80. *tongue, and belly*: the tongue and the entrails being often among the parts left for the gods in ancient sacrifices.

89 ff. It is noticeable that even when the Cardinal lies about his family, it is the curse of avarice that runs in his mind; and indeed it is possible that we are meant to believe in the vision of the old woman (to which the Cardinal appeals as if a matter of common knowledge) as an actual superstition of the house of Aragon (like the white bird of the Oxenhams); perhaps symbolic of the family avarice. M. Summers (*N.Q.* CLXIII. 424) found this same story, told of the Torelli family at Parma, in Cardan, *De Rerum Varietate* (1557), XVI. ch. xciii.

109. *th'ingagement*: the employment of Bosola.

112. *oft-di'd garment.* Cf. Donne, *Anat. of the World, First Anniversary*, 355–6:

> summer's robe growes
> Duskie, and like an oft dyed garment showes. (C.)

121–2. Cf. *Arcadia* I. (*Wks.* I. 60): "too much thinking doth consume the spirits: & oft it falles out, that while one thinkes too much of his doing, he leaves to doe the effect of his thinking". (H.D.S.)

136–7. *religion But a Schoole-name*: it seems strange that this intellectual boldness should be attributed to the mild and superstitious Antonio.

168. One of Webster's beloved equivocations.

170. *kissing comfits*: sweetmeats to scent the breath.

173. *arme*: embrace.

174–5. *Compare...miracle*: from *Arcadia*, v. (*Wks.* II. 186): "Let her beawtie be compared to my yeares, and such effectes will be found no miracles". (Not in C.)

183–4. With a *double entendre*. From *Arcadia*, I. (*Wks.* I. 106): "doing all things with so pretie grace, that it seemed ignorance could not make him do amisse, because he had a hart to do well". (C.) Cf. *Char.* "Milke-mayd", 21–3.

219–20. *mice...falling houses.* Cf. Pliny VIII. 28 (H.D.S.): "When an house is readie to tumble downe, the mice goe out of it before; and first of all the spiders with their webs fall down". So Lupton, *A Thousand Notable Things*, II. 87: "It is found by observation that Rats and Dormice will forsake old and ruinous houses, three months before they fall".

228–9. *feather-beds...blockes*: from *Arcadia*, III. (*Wks.* I. 419): "she was like them that could not sleepe, when they were softly layed".

237–8. Cf. Chapman, *Gentleman Usher*, III. 2. 372–3:

> For he that cannot turn and wind a woman
> Like silk about his finger is no man.

238–9. s.d. She hides him in "the study" and draws the curtain.

244. *lingring consumption.* Cf. "Overbury's" "A Very Woman": "She is Solomon's cruell creature and a man's Walking-consumption".

249. *Secretary*: confidant, repository of secrets (the original sense of the word).

260–1. Cf. 1 *Hen. IV*, II. 3. 114:

> for secrecy
> No lady closer; for I well believe
> Thou wilt not utter what thou dost not know. (Dyce.)

277. *triall of my constancy.* Cf. Brutus and Portia in *Jul. Caes.* II. 1 (Sampson), esp. l. 299:

> I have made strong proof of my constancy.

283. *breasts hoop'd with adamant*: a phrase ultimately derived from the famous Horatian—

> Illi robur et aes triplex
> Circa pectus erat. (*Odes*, I. 3. 9.)

Cf. Chapman, *Bussy d'Ambois*, III. 2. 224; Marston, *Antonio's Revenge*, IV. 1. 66.

294 ff. From Julia's agitation as she realizes that she has put the Cardinal's vital secret in Bosola's hands, it is clear that, however wanton, she still cares for her old lover.

295. *how setles this?* It seems to be a metaphor of a turbid liquid subsiding and clearing (Sampson). Less probably it might mean: "Is this sinking down into the secrecy of your heart?"

314–5. *weakenesse...done*: from *Arcadia*, I. (*Wks.* I. 24): "But since it is weakenes too much to remember what should have beene done". (H.D.S.)

315–6. Cf. *W.D.* v. 6. 248–9.

328–9. *marble colours...rotten purposes*: i.e. like one painting rotten wood to resemble marble. Cf. *Arcadia*, II. (*Wks.* I. 260): "Shall I labour to lay marble coulours over my ruinous thoughts?" (H.D.S.)

330–2. *great Treasons . . . Actors in't*: from Chapman, *Seven Penitential Psalms*, "A Great Man":

> Plots treason and lies hid in th' actor's grave. (C.)

345. *the common B[ie]re, for Church-yards*. Cf. Swinburne's humorous self-criticism in one of his letters (ed. Hake and Rickett, p. 89): "If I write any more necrological eulogies on deceased poets, I shall be taken for an undertaker's laureate, or the forehorse of a funeral cart hired out to trot in trappings on all such occasions as regularly as Mr Mould and his Merry Men and shall feel like Bosola in the *Duchess of Malfi*".

371. *Beares up in blood*: keeps his courage. It does *not* mean "keeps on in his bloody course of action". *In blood* is a technical hunting-term of a stag in full mettle (as contrasted with "out of blood"). Cf. *Love's Lab. Lost*, iv. 2. 4; 1 *Hen. VI*, iv. 2. 48 ("If we be English deer, be then in blood"); *Coriolanus*, i. 1. 165; *Sejanus*, ii. 2.

372. *Securitie*: confidence that one is secure.

376. *biters*: deceivers.

379–80. *weakest Arme . . . Justice*: from *Arcadia*, iii. (*Wks*. i. 422): "Think not lightly of never so weake an arme, which strikes with the sword of justice"; cf. *Char*. "Commander", 27–8.

v. 3.

Outer stage.

[*Milan*.] This is a good example of the inappropriateness of the geographical pedantries too common in modern editions of Elizabethans. There is here no conceivable reason why the Duchess should be buried at Milan, where none the less the scene is certainly laid in so far as it is laid anywhere definite. But that is the whole point; for an Elizabethan audience the scene here was not some precise spot on the map, but somewhere near both to the Cardinal's dwelling and to the Duchess's grave.

10–3. *I doe love . . . History*. From Montaigne iii. 9: "And yet I cannot so often survay the vast toombe of that Citie (Rome), so great, so populous, and so puissant, but I as often admire and reverence the same. . . . 'for which way soever we walke, we set our foote upon some History'". (A rendering of Cicero's "quacunque enim ingredimur, in aliquam historiam vestigium ponimus".) (C.) There is a not dissimilar passage in Marston, *Sophonisba*, iv. 1. 144 ff.

In a work called *Really and Truly* by "C.F." (Robert Ross) (1915), p. 8, there is the following foot-note which not all readers I hope, will find irrelevant: "In some trenches near Ypres, there was quartered a sulky young Scotchman of my acquaintance. For many weeks he had not exchanged a word with any of his brother officers beyond what the exigencies of the trenches demanded. One early morning moved by the silhouette of the battered city against

the coming dawn, he murmured half aloud to himself Antonio's
lines in the *Duchess of Malfi* (v. iii):

> I do love, etc.

A young Englishman near him immediately took up the quotation
with the end of the speech—

> Churches and cities, which have diseases like to men,
> Must have like death that we have.

They became great friends. A common interest in literature achieved
that which the terrible realities of warfare had failed to bring about".

So romantic a feeling for old ruins strikes us as belonging more
to the age of Scott than of Shakespeare: it is all the more curious to
find the same mood in an almost contemporary French poem,
Saint-Amant's "La Solitude" (*c.* 1619):

> Que j'aime à voir la décadence
> De ces vieux châteaux ruinés,
> Contre qui les ans mutinés
> Ont déployé leur insolence.

Webster need not however fear the comparison; Saint-Amant,
expressing himself at much greater length, fails to keep up this level
and produces far less effect; indeed we may say here of Webster,
as Johnson of Gray in the not dissimilar mood of the *Elegy*,
"Had he written often thus, it had been vain to blame, and useless
to praise him".

21. *Eccho.* An interesting study might be written on Echo-scenes (in
which Echo catches up and twists the ends of a speaker's sentences)
from Euripides to Thomas Hardy. It is a device which has produced
much frigidity of conceit, some humour, and very rarely, as here, a
shimmering, unearthly beauty. The earliest example known to me
occurs in some charming fragments of Euripides' lost *Andromeda*,
where the heroine waits chained and weeping by the sea-cliff for the
coming of dawn and with it the devouring monster of the deep, while
Echo in the caverns of the rocks answers lament for lament. It was
a famous scene, famously parodied by Aristophanes (*Thesmophori-
azusae*, 1056–97). The subsequent popularity of the device may be
seen from the list which follows and does not pretend to be exhaustive:
Callimachus, *Epigr.* 30; Ovid, *Metam.* III, 380–92 (a typical piece
of his charming un-Roman grace—"Dixerat 'ecquis adest?' et 'adest'
responderat Echo"); Martial II. 86. 3: Gauradas (in *Appendix
Planud.* of *Palat. Anthol.* 152); Politian, *Miscell.* XXII; Erasmus,
Colloquia, "Echo"; Gascoigne's Masque at Kenilworth, 1575 (the
Queen was met, coming from hunting, by a wild man "all in ivie",
who held a dialogue with Echo); R. Wilson, *Cobler's Prophesie*,
sig. C 2 (H.D.S.); *Arcadia*, II. (*Wks.* I. 352–3); Lodge, *Wounds of
Civil War*, III; Heywood, *Love's Mistress*, I. 1; Dekker, *Old For-
tunatus*, I. 1; Jonson, *Cynthia's Revels*, I. 1; *Return from Parnassus*,

II. 2; *The Hog hath lost his pearl* (Hazlitt's *Dodsley* (1874), XI. 477); *A.Q.L.* V. I. 391 ff.; Herbert, *Poems*, "Heaven"; Butler, *Hudibras*, I. 3. 189; Poe, "The Raven"; T. Hardy, *Human Shows; Far Phantasies*, p. 201. It may be added that Addison discusses the form in connection with "false wit" in *The Spectator*, No. 59.

Many of these passages are poor enough. The most ingenious and amusing is Erasmus (whose Echo shows, incidentally, a fine disregard of false quantities). A few of the remarks and answers may be quoted in illustration: "Quid superest remedii, ubi quem adstrinxerit iam nodus insolubilis (of marriage)? *Echo.* Bilis!...Quid captant plerique qui ambiunt sacerdotium? *Echo.* Otium!...Praeterea nihil habet sacerdos? *Echo.* κέρδος ....Decem iam annos trivi in Cicerone. *Echo.* Ὄνε....Non me delectant sermones dissyllabi. *Echo.* Abi!"

Disraeli in his *Curiosities of Lit.* (1881 ed. II. 236) quotes a peculiar poem from the end of a comedy by F. Cole acted at Trinity College, Cambridge, in 1641, in which Echo even becomes political—

> "Now, Eccho, on what's religion grounded?"
> "Round-head."
> "Whose its professors most considerable?"
> "Rabble."
> "How do these prove themselves to be godly?"
> "Oddly."

Echo-scenes form an interesting literary by-way, though it has proved a blind alley for most who have followed it. And the present scene is one more example of Webster's power of remoulding the commonplace and making beautiful what most of his contemporaries made banal.

22. *the Eccho hath caught you*: an effective phrase—as if Echo, the voice of Fate, were here Fate itself seizing hold of its victim.

55. *mark'd*: heeded. These three lines, though themselves little heeded by past criticism, are as lovely as any in the play.

62. *I will not henceforth save my selfe by halves*: Antonio's character has strengthened with despair.

66. *his*: the Cardinal's.

69. *How ever*: "however things happen", "in any case"—a common use.

V. 4.

Whole stage.

31. *I would pray now*: this recalls the remorse of the guilty Claudius in *Haml.* III. 3 (cf. too 48–9 below—"Could I take him At his prayers").

45. *blacke deedes...cur'de with death*: again an adaptation of the Senecan:

> Per scelera semper sceleribus tutum est iter.

See on *W.D.* II. I. 315.

48–9. *Could I take him At his prayers*, etc. Doubtless Bosola imagines himself to be meant here by *him*; *i.e.* he mistakes Antonio for some cut-throat who hopes to get a pardon from the Cardinal in return for murdering the inconvenient Bosola. Hence Bosola's instant stab in reply. In the state of nervous tension which he has now reached, it is quite plausible.

52. *suit*: probably "petition"; cf. *to pray* in the previous line. It might however mean "quarrel".

57. *To appeare my selfe*: Sampson and Allen explain this—"to appear in my true light as a most wretched thing". Or does it mean: "Now at last with death the need for hiding and secrecy is over—I can at all events die openly, if I could not live, as Antonio Bologna"?

Was there also running in Webster's mind the famous tag of Seneca's *Thyestes* (401–3), so dear to Elizabethans?—

> Illi mors gravis incubat
> Qui notus nimis omnibus,
> *Ignotus moritur sibi.*

The general sense is different: but Webster's idea of self-realization in death *may* have been partly suggested by this opposed self-ignorance in Seneca.

63. *Starres tennys-balls*. Cf. *Arcadia*, II. (*Wks.* I. 330): "he quickly made his kingdome a Tenniscourt, where his subjects should be the balles"; and, again, *Arcadia*, v. (*Wks.* II. 177): "(mankind) are but like tenisbals, tossed by the racket of the hyer powers" (part of a sentence copied also below in v. 5. 125 ff.). (H.D.S.) The earliest expression of the idea known to me is Plautus, *Captivi*, Prol. 22:

> di nos quasi pilas homines habent.

This is quoted, of the vicissitudes of ambition, by Carleton writing to Sir T. Edmondes, July 17th 1610 (Birch) and was doubtless one of the familiar tags of an educated man of the time. Cf. also Montaigne III. 9.

65 ff. Notice that of the two lovers, the Duchess and Antonio, each dies with the voice of Bosola whispering, like an evil angel turned pitiful at last, tidings of the other's fate. Cf. IV. 2. 377.

73. *in sadnes*: in serious truth, really (with the old sense of "sad" = "earnest"). But it is likely, I think, that *sad* in the previous line should be *glad*. This is slightly supported by *F.M.I.* IV. 2. 353:

> do not entertain't
> With too quick an apprehension of joy,
> For that may hurt thee, I have heard some dye of't.

81. *processe*: story, account. Cf. *Haml.* I. 5. 37: "a forged process of my death".

84. *flie the Courts of Princes*. Cf. Vittoria's last words, *W.D.* v. 6. 261.

88. *I doe not aske thee that*: (sadly ironic)—*aske* = "require", "ask for", not "inquire". "There is no need for reconciliation now."

93. *misprision*: "mistake". There are two distinct words of this form (similarly with the verb "to misprize"): (1) "mistake", from Lat.

minus, prehendere, Fr. *méprendre*, "to get hold of wrongly". (2) "Contempt", from Lat. *minus, pretiare*, Fr. *mépriser*, "to value little".

94 ff. The invincible individualism of the Renaissance. Cf. *W.D.* v. 6. 256 ff.

v. 5.

Inner stage, representing the Cardinal's Study: Malateste and his companions appear on the upper stage at 25 (cf. 31, "goe *downe* to him").

Cardinall (with a Booke): Stoll has pointed out that these appearances book in hand are a common feature of Revenge Tragedy. Cf. Marston, *Antonio's Revenge*, ii. 2; *Second Maiden's Tragedy* (Hazlitt's Dodsley (1874), x. 450); Hieronimo in *Spanish Trag.* after the scene with the Painter.

4. *Lay him by.* A fine touch of intense hopelessness.

5–7. *Fish-ponds ... Rake.* The doomed Pertinax (J. Capitolinus, xiv.) saw "in piscina" a sworded spectre. (Bullen.) This rake is eerier.

27. *My Dukedome, for rescew!* Cf. *Rich. III*, v. 4. 7 (Sampson): "A horse! a horse! my kingdom for a horse!" The resemblance is clearer at 64: "give me a fresh horse".

56–8. *thy Greatnes...drive thee*: from *Arcadia*, ii. (*Wks.* i. 332): "Antiphilus that had no greatnesse but outwarde, that taken away, was readie to fall faster then calamitie could thrust him". (H.D.S.)

66. *I give you the honour of Armes*: "martial salute" (Sampson, Allen). But surely even the Duke is not so mad as to cry "Yield" in one breath, "I salute you" in the next. He means "I will grant you quarter and a fair surrender with the honours of war".

71. *There flies your ransome*: because, being killed, he cannot be held to ransome.

74. *Sorrow...sin.* Cf. *W.D.* v. 4. 18–9.

84. *wet hay...broken-winded.* Cf. G. Markham, *Masterpiece Revived* (1688 ed.), p. 72: "The best diet for a horse in this case (broken-winded) is Grass in Summer, and Hay sprinkled with water in Winter".

86. *vault credit*: "do incredible things" (Sampson, Allen). But surely it means "disregard probability, overleap rational expectation and aspire to ('affect') high pleasures in another world". "High pleasures" hereafter were not a *probable* prospect, under any scheme of Divine Justice, for the soul of Duke Ferdinand.

89. *neere the bottom.* Cf. *W.D.* v. 6. 254.

92. Proverbial (see Tilley, D 323). Cf. the lines attributed to Charles I (Disraeli, *Curiosities of Lit.* (1881 ed.), ii. 334):

> With my own power my majesty they wound;
> In the king's name, the king himself uncrowned;
> So doth the dust destroy the diamond.

94. *soule...teeth*: from Montaigne ii. 35: "the soule must be held fast with one's teeth". (C.)

95. Cf. *W.D.* v. 6. 295.

108. *Neglected*: Bosola's rankling grievance dies only with Bosola himself. It is the first note he strikes, and almost the last.

112–3. *let me Be layd by, and never thought of*: a wish not without historical counterparts at this time. We may recall Marston's chosen epitaph "*Oblivioni sacrum*"; and Lord Chancellor Egerton, three years after this, "gave order in his will to have no solemn funeral, no monument, but to be buried in oblivion, alleging the precedents of Seneca, Warham, Archbishop of Canterbury and Chancellor, and Budeus, the learned Frenchman, who all took the like course". (Chamberlain to Carleton, March 29th 1617.)

116. *thing of blood*. Cf. *Coriol.* II. 2. 114:

> He was a thing of blood, whose every motion
> Was tim'd with dying cries.

118. *In a mist*. Cf. *W.D.* v. 6. 260. Both of Webster's villains die with darkened eyes at last.

125–6. *shadow...live*: from *Arcadia*, v. (*Wks.* II. 177): "In such a shadowe, or rather pit of darkenes, the *wormish* mankinde lives, that neither they knowe how to foresee, nor what to feare: and are but like tenisbals, tossed by the racket of the hyer powers". (H.D.S.)

132. It is worth noting that both Webster's tragedies close with the reconciling figure of a child. This "yong hopefull gentleman", however, was destined to get his author into trouble with neo-classic criticism, as an awful example of the violation of the Unity of Time. Thus C. Gildon in *The Laws of Poetry* (1721) states that an infant grows to manhood in the course of the play: and Malone most unreasonably thought that Ben Jonson was alluding to *The Duchess of Malfi* in the prologue to *Ev. Man in his H.* (printed 1616):

> To make a child new-swaddled to proceed
> Man, and then shoot up in one beard and weed
> Past three score years. (See Malone's note on *Timon*, III. 3.)

There is no reason to imagine Antonio's son as more than a child. The historical Antonio's eldest son must have been about seven or eight when his father was murdered. But Webster seems to forget that the Duchess's heir was her son by her first husband, whom he mentions at III. 3. 82.

146. Cf. the last words of the prose Epilogue to *W.D.*

TEXTUAL NOTES

THE DUCHESS OF MALFI

(These do not deal with trivial misprints or variants. Fuller details in *Wks.* II. 200–10. But the ordinary reader may take it that he is here given everything that matters to him—perhaps more. The most interesting problems are starred.)

The four main Quartos (each printed from its predecessor) are symbolized thus: A = 1623; B = 1640 (the sheets of this were reissued, with fresh title-page, *c.* 1664; see *Wks.* I. 7); C = 1678; D = 1708 (of slight interest). Qq = ABC.

Further, the printer of A, after the light-hearted fashion of his age, went on correcting the book while in the press. Some differences were noted by Dyce. What Webster might have called the "happy and copious industry" of Mr J. R. Brown has collated 18 copies of A; recorded over 40 variants; and shown that the outer forme of signature G was twice corrected—it exists in three different states. (See his articles in *Stud. Bibl.* VI. 116–40, VIII. 113–27.)[1]

All this is interesting and curious; but the practical effect on the text printed in 1927 appears, unless I am deceiving myself, surprisingly slight. A few questionable readings are now confirmed: but no changes seem needed beyond two or three variant spellings such as *doome* for *doombe* and *Bermootha's* for *Bermoothes*.

Mr Brown argues that some of the corrections on the inner forme of sheet H "make it all but certain that it was the author who was helping with the proof-correcting at this stage". But here, I am afraid, I cannot share his view. No doubt some of the changes in III. 4 may seem to suggest the author's intervention—*habit* for *order* (III. 4 S.D.), *Ditty* for *Hymne*, or the marginal addition (III. 4. 11–4), *The Author disclaimes this Ditty to be His*. Yet it remains very odd for the author himself not to notice that after *habit* an essential *of* still remained omitted (to say nothing of other misprints in III. 3–5).

It is harder still to think that Webster's eye fell on the corrections of A as a whole. They are a queer lot. Often the grossest errors are ignored—such as *Danae* turned into a *Dane*, *of fashion* into *off fhashion*; speeches omitted, or given to the wrong speakers; prose printed as verse. Even if mistakes *are* corrected, nonsense is apt to be replaced by other nonsense (*e.g.* the absurd *Sirina* by the still absurder *Siriux*). And yet trivial changes are sometimes made in spelling—such as *taine* for *ta'ne* (III. 2. 131), though *ta'ne* is a spelling as good, and is left untouched elsewhere. In fine, the compositors and press-corrector of A seem compounded of indifference, incompetence, and inconsistency—as if they thought spasms of zeal would make up for constant carelessness.

Clearly Webster was no Alfred de Musset to lie awake all night over a

[1] He also suggests, on the basis of various peculiarities in spelling and punctuation, that the copy for A was a transcript made by Ralph Crane, who was employed by the King's Men about this time. (See F. P. Wilson in *The Library*, VII (1926), 194–215.)

misprinted comma; clearly he is far from the carefulness of Jonson; but if he stood in the printing-house while all this passed under his nose, he was an even greater fool than Shaw and Archer took him for. Of the more striking corrections in III. 4 (*Ditty* for *Hymne*, etc.) I can only suppose either that they were casually sent or brought by the author to the printer, without staying for an answer; or, conceivably, that they had been present in the copy all the time, but were at first ignored by the compositor, as can sometimes happen even in modern proof-correcting.

In the notes that follow, A_a = the first, uncorrected state of A; A_b = its second state; A_c = its third state (in sheet G, outer forme). All copies of A are of course varying combinations of corrected and uncorrected formes, bound up as chance directed. Apart from modernizing long ∫ and the use of *i* and *j*, *u* and *v*, the present text follows the revised version of A, except where it seemed necessary to emend, or to make a few odd spellings intelligible to the ordinary reader.[1] Such changes are marked by square brackets; omissions by ∧.

Similarly with punctuation. The theory of Elizabethan punctuation was in some ways admirable—elocution rather than logic; pauses rather than clauses. But Elizabethan practice remained often careless. My principle here too has been—"A minimum of alteration—but no needless ambiguities to distract from the poetry". Commas (*very* rarely) have been added, dropped, or replaced by a dash (dashes occurring in the original are printed, as usually in the original, twice the length of modern ones); still more rarely, semicolons, colons, or full stops have been changed to three dots. My aim is to give the modern reader something as close as possible (though purged of errors and needless obscurities) to what Webster's first readers had before them.

THE ACTORS' NAMES

C and D give later casts; respectively assigning Ferdinand to Harris and Verbruggen; Antonio to Smith and Booth; the Cardinal to Young and Keen; Bosola to Betterton and Mills; the Duchess to Mrs Betterton and Mrs Porter.

As Forobosco is a mere character of straw, never audible, even if ever visible, it seems possible that Towley's name should be attached to Malateste.

In A the bracket opposite *Pallant* covers *The Doctor, Cariola,* and *Court Officers.* I have changed it. Only a ventriloquist could even attempt to personate four officers in full tattle (III. 2); and the part of Cariola cannot be doubled with any of them, since she appears to be on the stage simultaneously. Pallant (b. 1605) may seem young for the Doctor; but we may recall Jonson's Salathiel Pavy who, at thirteen, acted old men so well that the Fates mistook him for one, and killed him.

I. 1.

Actus Primus, Scena Prima. Italic here in A: subsequent headings roman. Throughout, Qq print at the head of each scene all the characters appearing in it.

[1] Thus *of* [∫] is printed for *of*, where the reader might be momentarily confused; similarly, *to* [o] for *to*, and *the* [ir] for *there*.

8–11. Punctuation (see Commentary) as in A, except that I have added comma after *Sicophants* (as BCD), and dash after *persons*.

32 ff. Here, and throughout the play, A prints prose, as if verse, with capitals at beginning of lines.

*60. *dogges,* ∧ *when* BC Dyce: *dogges, and when* A: *dogges, and horses, when* would be possible (cf. Massinger, *Bashful Lover*, v. 1: "servants, who, grown old, Are turn'd off, like lame hounds and hunting horses"). But technically *rewards* (see Commentary) suit only *hawkes, and dogges*; and A_a slips in another superfluous *and* at III. 2. 273.

83. Here Qq mark "Scena II", with the usual initial list of characters appearing in the course of the scene.

117–8. *How...Gennit?*] Sampson suggests giving to Ferdinand. But that would make Ferdinand, not Castruchio, the butt for the sneer of Silvio, the jeers of Roderigo and Grisolan. And I cannot picture Duke Ferdinand as ridiculous, or tolerating ridicule.

126. *laugh when I laugh*] *not laugh but when I laugh* D: *laugh but when I laugh* Dyce. But change is needless, if one puts the stress on *I*.

*198. *[you]] your* Qq. The emendation *you* suggested by J. C. Maxwell (*N.Q.* CXCIII. 302) seems to me confirmed by Webster's evident source— G. Pettie's translation (1581, 1586) of S. Guazzo's *La Civil Conversatione* (1574): "Next, her talke and discourses are so delightfull, that you wyll only then beginne to bee sory, when shee endeth to speake: and wishe that shee woulde bee no more weary to speake, then you are to heare" (ed. Sir E. Sullivan, 1925, Bk. II. p. 241). See M. L. Anderson, *Webster's Debt to Guazzo*, in *St. Phil.* XXXVI. 192–205.

To read *[you]* seems far simpler than to supply *is* after *pennance*.

200. *able raise* AB: *able to raise* C (perhaps rightly).

223. *entreat for*] ? *entreat for him.*

228–9. *Wee [are] now upon parting* D Dyce Sampson: ABC omit *are*. Sampson suggests, alternatively, changing the colon after *parting* to a comma, so that *Wee* becomes subject of *do us commend*.

232. *[Duch.]* Sampson: *Ferd.* Qq Dyce. But Ferdinand knows already (139) where Silvio is going.

288. *take me to Hell* D: *take me Hell* Qq (an example of their blind carelessness).

312. *Provisor-ship* BC: *Provisosr-ship* A_a: *Provisors-ship* A_b. Seemingly a bungled correction; for the form *Provisor-ship* occurs elsewhere (224, 291).

*340. *You live in a ranke pasture here, i'th Court—*] A has comma after *Court* (which I have changed to a dash); D and Dyce have a semicolon; Sampson a full stop. Possibly, however, one should punctuate: *You live in a ranke pasture; here, i'th Court, There is a kind of honney-dew. . . .* (Or the semicolon could come after *here*, instead of before it.)

353. *E[a]ves*] *Eeves* A_a: *Eves* A_b BCD Dyce. Dyce, since his spelling is modernized, apparently thought of the word as plural of *eve* (evening). But, in spite of the proximity of *night*, the primary sense is "eaves" (of which *eeves* and *eves* are merely variant spellings).

358. *Such weddings,*] The comma might mark a rhetorical pause. But one cannot rely on A's punctuation enough to know.

375. *woemen like*] *woemen, like* A.

412. *[these] triumphs* Dyce Vaughan: *this triumphs* AB: *this triumph* C Sampson.

445. *Win[i]frid* Dyce Vaughan: *Winfrid* Qq Sampson. The Devon saint seems pointless: but the Duchess might swear here, not without some appropriateness, by the Welsh virgin (whose name recurs in a character of *D.L.*). See Commentary.

446-7. Qq end the lines with *you* and *again*: Brereton corrects.

446. *strange* Qq: *stranger* Dyce, Sampson (in note), Vaughan. A needless change: cf. *A.V.* III. 2. 9-10: "'Tis strange that..." followed by the retort: "It were strange indeed, if..."

548. *[de]* Sampson added. Better law, better Latin, better metre. For Webster's legal knowledge see p. 9 note.

II. 1.

1. *taken—for*] The dash represents a comma in A; perhaps accidental, but conceivably an ironic pause.

25. *These...in thy face*] *These in thy face* Qq. A word like *dimples* may have dropped out; or Bosola may simply point.

*32. *[I]] you* Qq edd. But how could the Old Lady call it anything so self-disparaging? And she had asked Bosola what *he* called it. Corruption may have been due to *you call* immediately above. *No, no, but call it* is a conceivable alternative.

32. *[it]* C: AB omit.

37ff. Printed by Qq, like all prose, with initial capitals. With rearrangement, the lines can be tortured into improbable verse. But after *Observe my meditation now* (45-6) it is likely enough that Bosola should change from prose to blank verse; just as Romelio in *D.L.*, after *I have a certaine Meditation* (II. 3. 111) changes from blank verse into octosyllabic couplets.

39. *children['s] ordures*] *children ordures* A: *children's ordure* BC Dyce Sampson. There seems little to choose between *ordure* and *ordures*. The plural, though commoner in older English, is still found in Dryden.

63-5. *Your wife...foote:*] Most editors, except Sampson, print as prose.

89. *o[f f]ashion* BC: *off shashion* A.

107. *goe* A: *to goe* BC.

126. *[Duch.]* D adds. (Another instance of the fecklessness of ABC.)

II. 2

1-3. AB print these three lines as if addressed by Bosola to the Old Lady. But such directness seems out of place—his subsequent remarks to her are teasing innuendoes. Dyce delays her entry till *breeding* (after which he puts a full stop).

3. *breeding—now?*] *breeding, now?* AB: *breeding: now?* C: *breeding. Now?* D Dyce.

11. *woemen?*] The old ? perhaps corresponds here, as often, to our ! (*still* meaning "always").

18. *Dan[ae]s*] *Danes* AB: *Dames* C: *Danae's* D.

37-8, 43-7. Dyce Sampson print as prose: Qq as here.

87-9. *[Enter Car. with a Child.]* supplied by D.

II. 3.

[Enter...lanthorn.] This, and the next stage-direction, are from D.

54. [*Bos.*] Two successive speeches being marked *Ant.*, one by Bosola seems omitted. See Commentary.
61. *wrought* AB: Sampson: *wrote* CD Dyce Vaughan. But the letters seem *wrought* in a handkerchief or the like.
67. [*quit*] C: *quite* AB.
92. ne[*v*]'*r*] *nea'r* A.

II. 4.

15. *my Lord?*] *my Lord!* Dyce. Possible; but the Cardinal seems to answer her question.
35. *me make* A: *make me* BCD Dyce Sampson. A's order is conceivable, for emphasis.

II. 5.

73. *Yes—I*] *Yes, I* A: *Yes, but I* Dyce: *Yes, yet I* Brereton. The last is simplest, and makes good sense (though awkward metre). But no change seems needed if *I* is stressed enough.
74. *rupture*] ? *rapture* Dyce. Needless.
92. *to boile*] *to-boil* Dyce (cf. Chaucer, *Troilus*, III, 348: "to-melt"). Needless. For superfluous *to* cf. *A.V.* II. 3. 93.

III.1

69. Dyce makes Bosola enter here; Sampson, more simply, at 42.
91. *lenative*] *lenitive* Dyce. But see Commentary.
109. *thinke then, pray?*] *thinke then? pray?* A (which is possible, if *pray?* = "pray tell me"; but confusing).

III. 2.

6. *Noblemen* Dyce: *Noble men* Qq: *noble men* Sampson.
20. *I pray thee* ABC Sampson: *I* (= *Ay*), *prithee* D: *Ay, pray thee* Dyce.
32. [*f l*]*light* Dyce: *slight* Qq (conceivably right).
33-4. *Siri*[*n*]*x ... Anaxar*[*e*]*te*] *Sirina ... Anaxorate* A$_a$ *Siriux ... Anaxarate* A$_b$BC. (Typical of the intelligence with which A was corrected—folly replaces folly.)
69-71. [*Enter...unseen.*] D adds.
71. *brothers*] ? *brother* Sampson (because of *His* in 72). Not really necessary; cf. 75.
79-80. *Ferdinand...ponyard* added by A$_b$.
82. *ecclipze* A: *clip* BC (unconvincing; though *clips* (verb) is an old variant of *ecclipse*, and *clip* also = *embrace*).
112. *damp*[*n*]*e*] *dampe* A. *N.E.D.* gives an old variant form *damp*, but no examples after the 14th century.
131. *taine* A$_{bc}$: *ta'ne* A$_a$. Worth note as an example of the pointless capriciousness of A's corrections; *ta'ne* is quite unobjectionable, and is left elsewhere, *e.g.* in IV. 2. 350.
191. *me thinkes unjust*] ? *me thinkes that unjust* Sampson. Metrically easier.

205. *forfeyt*] ? *forfeyted* Sampson.   Metrically easier.
206. [*aside*] Dyce: Sampson omits.   If addressing the Duchess, Bosola refers
to Antonio's supposed fraud: but this seems less likely.
236. *service, you may see:* Qq: *service! You· may see*, Dyce Sampson.   Very
possible: not essential.
239. *As loth* A$_c$BC: *A-loth* A$_{ab}$ Dyce Sampson.
259–60. *those...money* bracketed in A$_{ab}$: A$_c$ corrects.   Cf. on 131 above.
273. *first-borne* A$_c$: *first-borne and* A$_{ab}$.
325. *peace*, AB Sampson.   C has colon; Dyce, full stop.
326. *but:* A Sampson.   No stop in BC Dyce.

<h3 style="text-align:center">III. 3.</h3>

*25. *Painters* A$_c$BC: *Pewterers* A$_{ab}$ edd.   Possibly. *Painters* was misread as
Pewters, then converted to *Pewterers*.   Cf. *Flatters* for *Flatterers* in
I. 1. 162.
50–7, 61–4. Dyce Sampson print as prose: I have changed the Qq lineation
as little as possible.   The metre is rough, but not inconceivably so for
Webster.

<h3 style="text-align:center">III. 4.</h3>

8–9. s.d. *habit* [*of*] *a Souldier* BC: *order a Souldier* A$_a$: *habit a Souldier* A$_b$.
s.d. *Banishment in dumbe-shew*, A$_b$: *Banishment* A$_a$.
s.d. *Ditty* A$_b$: *Hymne* A$_a$.
9. Before this lyric, as title, A$_a$ inserts *The Hymne*.
11. Marginal Note.   Only in A$_b$; omitted by A$_a$BCD.

<h3 style="text-align:center">III. 5.</h3>

s.d. Qq, giving, as usual, at the head of the scene all the characters to appear
in it, include here *Bosola, Souldiers, with Vizards*.   As this last detail is of
some interest, I have added [*with Vizards*] to the s.d. at 110.
31. *Ferdinand...your brother*.   The dots represent a semicolon in A; which
may be genuine, and imply a pause.   Similarly in 69 below.
36–7. s.d. *A Letter*.   This begins 37 in Qq, as if part of the Duchess's
words.   Conceivable, but unlikely; the more so as the two words are slightly
indented from the left margin (forming one line with 37–8).
69. See on 31.
74. *Farewell: Since we must part,*] *farewell, since we must part:* Dyce
Vaughan.   A has no stop after *part*; Sampson, a comma.   The capital
of *Since* strongly suggests that it begins a new sentence (cf. v. 2. 98).
*97. *Heaven*] G. P. V. Akrigg (*N.Q.* CXCV. 231–3), noting the absence of
"God" from *D.M.* (whereas it is common in *W.D.*), and the frequency of
"Heaven", plausibly suggests that the change is due to some tightening of
restrictions on profanity; and that in many places Webster originally
wrote "God", as Donne in the parallel passage to this (see Commentary).
"Heaven" may have been similarly substituted for "God" in I. 1. 549,
II. 5. 84, III. 5. 116, IV. 2. 228; in III. 5. 95 and v. 3. 52 I doubt it.
110. *Enter Bosola with a Guard*.   A$_b$ adds,

112. *Princes*] ? *poises* Daniel (i.e. "weights"). Quite needless; and disproved, I think, by the parallel in W. Alexander, *Alexandraean Tragedy*, 2836–8:

> The wheele of fortune still must slipperie prove,
> And chiefely when it burdend is with kings,
> Whose states as weightiest most must 'make it move.

165–6. *stretched...wretch[e]d* D: *stretched...wretch'd* AB: *stretch'd...wretch'd* C Dyce.

IV. 1.

*10. *foure* Qq Dyce Sampson: *for* Collier Hazlitt Vaughan. A most un-called for emendation; cf. *W.D.* v. 6. 36, *D.L.* II. 2. 5, v. 4. 175, *Hamlet* II. 2. 160, *Lear* I. 2. 175, *W. Tale* v. 2. 155.

17. *she's*] ? *that she's* or *she is* Sampson (for metre).

41. *Whom!*] *Whom?* Qq edd. But clearly an angry exclamation.

**66. s.D. *Antonio and his children.*] ? *Antonio and his [child]* (i.e. the elder son whom he rode off with in III. 5.) The younger boy and the girl are im-prisoned with the Duchess (40); and she dies leaving instructions for their care (IV. 2. 207–9). Why, if she thought them dead? Was she distracted? Or the author? And why should an avaricious Duke go to the cost and trouble of wax corpses for two children who were in a few minutes to be real ones? It would have been so much simpler to strangle them a little sooner.

106. *it[self]*] D: *it* Qq.

108. Dyce Sampson make the Servant enter here; Sampson sends him off at 111. But it seems simpler for him to enter with the those bringing lights at 64, and leave with the others at 133.

IV. 2.

55. *fashion* A Sampson: *fashions* BC Dyce.

*64. [*Enter Madmen.*] First supplied by D (in the form *Enter Madman*), but before 49. An audience however is more likely to listen to their description if not distracted by their actual appearance (cf. 63, *let them loose*).

82. *womens* A: *mens* BC. But cf. II. 2. 9.

112–3. s.D. (*like an old man*) Qq: *like an Old Bell-man* D.

119–22. Possibly verse (with lines rearranged to end *since | insensible | sure | I?*).

179. [*Rings his bell*] D adds.

209–10. [*Cariola...off.*] D adds.

*246–7. [*Re-enter...Cariola.*] *Enter Cariola* D Sampson. Dyce brings in the children too to be strangled. But no need for this extra horror. *Fetch her: Some other strangle the children* suggests that they may well be strangled "off", and their bodies revealed, perhaps by drawing a curtain, at 272.

305. *And that was the mayne cause:* A Sampson: *And what...cause;* B: *And what...cause?* CD Dyce.

305. *Marriage—*] *Marriage,* Qq. (But the comma becomes a little ambiguous.)

321. *sentence* A: *service* BCD.

321. *yours—*] No punctuation in A; a full stop may have dropped out.

403. [*with the body*] D adds,

V. 2.

37. [*Throws...ground.*] D adds.
74. *him*—] *him*, AB (but perhaps a printer's error).
78. [*Throws...him*] D adds.
105–6. [*Exeunt...Bosola.*] D adds.
118. [*I'll*]] *I'll'd, I'ld, I'd* Qq Sampson Dyce.
*145. [*bought*] Dyce: *brought* Qq. I am not sure Dyce is right. Picture-makers might also be picture-dealers, to whom Antonio in need could sell a miniature; nor does it follow that the Duchess's portrait was normally on sale in Milan.
183. *Why, ignorance*] Sampson moves to end 182 (for metre). But the line is not abnormally free, for Webster—"Why, ig|norance in court|ship can|not make *you* | do amisse."
*246. *quit off* AB Sampson: *quit off her* CD: *quit of her* Dyce. *Quit off* can be partly supported by the analogy of "rid off". But the true reading may be *quite off*; cf. phrases like "his fever seemed quite off", or Steele, *Tatler*, 223: "A Youth married under Fourteen Years may be off if he pleases when he comes to that age."
271–3. Qq punctuate: *Very well, why imagine...?*
345. B[ie]re] *Beare* A (old spelling, but now confusing).
370. Pre[ce]dent] *President* A (old spelling, but now confusing).
381. D adds stage direction, *Starts*.

V. 3.

34. *let's* D: *let's us* Qq: *let us* Dyce.
42. *pass[age]s* D Dyce Sampson: *passes* Qq Brereton. But *passages* is easier metrically; and cf. *D.L.* IV. 2. 17–8: "to what a violent issue These passages will come".
69. [*Ant.*] Qq Dyce Sampson omit. But *How ever...*begins a fresh line; and it seems better that stoicism should be expressed by Antonio, than preached at him. Cf. 59–63.

V. 4.

41. *So—it*] Qq have no stop; Dyce semicolon; Sampson colon.
*72. *sad*] ? *glad* Brereton. Very possible; see Commentary.
84. Should perhaps end with *Sonne*.

V. 5.

25–6. [*Enter...above.*] D adds (except for *Grisolan*, supplied by Dyce).
35. *serve;...honour!*] *serve;...honour.*AB: *serve...honour.*C Dyce Sampson (possibly rightly).
*69. *The divell?* Qq D: Dyce Sampson change *?* to *!* It depends whether Ferdinand now imagines himself the devil's brother (cf. v. 4. 25-6), or is simply swearing.
104. [*t*]*his* D Dyce Sampson: *his* Qq.
122. *yeildes* Qq: *yield* Dyce (needless).

APPENDIX I

WEBSTER'S BORROWINGS

Un juge sourcilleux, épiant mes ouvrages,
Tout à coup, à grands cris, dénonce vingt passages
Traduits de tel auteur qu'il nomme; et, les trouvant,
Il admire et se plaît de se voir si savant.
Que ne vient-il vers moi? Je lui ferai connaître
Mille de mes larcins qu'il ignore peut-être.

ANDRÉ CHÉNIER

"At morn he was born," says the Homeric Hymn, of Hermes, "that noon he harped, that eve he stole the archer Apollo's kine." To combine music and theft has been the privilege of poets also. In literature, as in the days of Homer or Elizabeth, freebooting has long been respectable, and piracy too can attain the heroic.

And why not? Really original minds do not bother about originality; it is theirs because they are they. It is the pretentious and the decadent, rather, who grow touchy and tetchy on the subject; and, straining to cut a figure that shall at all costs be new, achieve zero.

Virgil stole, Horace stole, Ronsard stole (though they stole mainly from foreigners); Molière "prenait son bien où il le trouvait"; Goldsmith borrowed as freely from books as from friends; Sterne, while satirizing the shamelessness of plagiarists, plagiarized shamelessly himself. But few writers have found it better to "rob and pill" than Webster. He turns out a complete Autolycus. Montaigne,[1] Shakespeare, Sidney,[2] Donne, Chapman,[3] Jonson, Dekker, Marston, the Bible, William

---

[1] Cf. Jonson, *Volpone*, III. 4. 87–90 (of Guarini's *Pastor Fido*):

All our *English* writers,
I meane such, as are happy in th' *Italian*,
Will deigne to steale out of this author, mainely;
Almost as much as from MONTAGNIE.

[2] Cf. J. Stephens, "the common-helping *Arcadia*"; Shirley, *Love in a Maze*, I. 2: "The midwife wrapt my head up in a sheet of Sir Philip Sidney: that inspired me."

[3] It is in *D.M.* that Chapman's influence becomes noticeable. But Dr G. K. Hunter has pointed out to me two passages in *W.D.* also, where Webster *may* have borrowed. Cf. *W.D.* IV. 3. 152 with Chapman, *Byron's Tragedy*, I. 3: "you were our golden plummet To sound this gulf of all ingratitude"; and *W.D.* v. 2. 25-6 with *Byron's Conspiracy*, III. 3:

And being great, like trees that broadest sprout,
Their own top-heavy state grubs up their root.

Alexander, Pierre Matthieu, Stefano Guazzo—year after year, research has detected more and more borrowed feathers in his plumage; till one begins to wonder if he will not be left, at last, bald as a coot.

Take, for example, Act v of *The White Devil*. One can almost see Webster's commonplace-book[1] fluttering at his elbow. In this single Act not only does his mad Cornelia echo Shakespeare's mad Ophelia;[2] not only are there borrowings from Montaigne and (probably) Sidney.[3] In addition, the sinister Latin gabbled by the disguised friars to the dying Brachiano comes *verbatim* from Erasmus' *Colloquia*.[4] Then there are a dozen parallels from Pettie's Guazzo (1581-6), a dozen more from the *Monarchicke Tragedies* (1607) of William Alexander.[5]

In *The Duchess of Malfi* Webster further extends his depredations to Sidney's *Arcadia*,[6] to E. Grimeston's translation (1612) of P. Matthieu's *Histoire de la Mort deplorable de Henry IV*,[7] and to Sir Thomas Elyot's *Image of Governance*.[8]

[1] Cf. Jonson's *Discoveries*; and Fuller: "I know some have a common-place against Common-place-books, and yet perchance will privately make use of what publickly they declaim against." (Bacon kept four different kinds of them!)

[2] See on v. 4. 60 ff.

[3] See Commentary, and C. Crawford, *Collectanea*, 1906-7 (I. "Webster and Sidney"; II. "Webster, Marston, Montaigne, Donne, etc.").

[4] "Funus" ("The Death-bed")—a violent satire on Friars. See A. W. Reed, *T.L.S.* 14/6/47, and Commentary. Webster makes the friars' speeches more dramatic by splitting them up; and omits two words, "quod diploma", perhaps as puzzling for his audience. In view of his own Echo-scene in *D.M.* v. 3, it is of some interest that in the *Colloquies* "The Death-bed" is followed by a dialogue with Echo.

[5] See *W.D.* Appendix I; M. L. Anderson, *St. Phil.* XXXVI. 192–205; R. W. Dent, *MLN.* LXV. 73–82. Guazzo (1530–93) is the source also of *D.M.* I. 1. 196–8; and Alexander, of a dozen passages in that play. (Sir William Alexander (1567?–1640), Earl of Stirling, Viscount Canada, favourite of James I and attached in turn to Prince Henry and Prince Charles, received in 1621 a grant of Nova Scotia, which he vainly tried to colonize. He published in 1607 four "monarchicke" tragedies, classically Senecan and interminably tedious. See *Poetical Works*, ed. Kastner and Charlton, 1921.)

Dr. G. K. Hunter points out to me that, besides the parallels noted by Dent, *D.M.* v. 2. 121–2 closely follows Alexander, *Julius Caesar*, 1803–4:

> Who muse of many things, resolve of none,
> And (thinking of the end) cannot begin.

[6] See Commentary and C. Crawford, *Collectanea*, I (1906).

[7] See R. W. Dent, in *HLQ.* XVII. 75–82. From Grimeston's P. Matthieu come:— the tale of Love, Death, and Reputation (III. 2. 145–56); III. 2. 278–80 (princes and flatterers); III. 3. 50–2 (pedants discussing the knots in Hercules' club, or the hue of Achilles' beard); III. 5. 17–24 (the Duchess's dream of pearls, betokening tears).

The parallel in Grimeston (p. 53) to the last of these tells a dream of

Such a catalogue of debts is at first rather disconcerting; especially as some of these passages are among Webster's most memorable. But one must look closer. There is borrowing and borrowing.

Were one to compose an "Art of Plagiarism", there would be certain basic principles. First of all, the plagiarist should have a forcible personality, so that the stamp and colour even of what he takes from others somehow become his own. Further, one may steal either work that is major, or work that is minor. And one may either leave what one steals little changed, or remould it drastically.

Clearly, though fine work is more tempting, it is more prudent to steal what is imperfect. Taking passages from Homer, said Virgil, was like trying to wrest the club from Hercules.

Still it can be done. Virgil did it. It was rash of Dryden to take the theme of Shakespeare's *Antony and Cleopatra*; and yet the product was Dryden's best play. It was rash of Webster to borrow from the mad Ophelia for his mad Cornelia; and yet I do not feel the result a failure.

In such cases, however, it is necessary to remould a good deal. *All for Love* is very different, on the whole, from *Antony and Cleopatra*; and when Dryden sails too close to Shakespeare's vision of Cleopatra in her barge, Dryden, I feel, is sunk by the inevitable comparison. And though Webster's mad Cornelia is moving, still Ophelia's ghost hovers a little disturbingly in the background. Indeed, I am not wholly happy when Shakespeare himself draws his Helen too clearly from Marlowe's—

> why, she is a pearl
> Whose price hath launch'd above a thousand ships,
> And turn'd crown'd kings to merchants.

An imitative passage should seem either sufficiently different[1] from its original, or sufficiently superior. For if it is similar without seeming distinctly better, it is likely to seem distinctly worse.

Henri IV's Queen before his murder; it is a little curious that Grimeston's next page (p. 54) recalls *W.D.* v.3.32-3, ("the dull Owle Beates not against thy casement")—"the King and Queene said that their sleepes had beene interrup[t]led by a Scrike owle, a night bird which betokens funerals, which had made a croking all night at their Chamber window". A borrowing from Grimeston (1612) would help date *The White Devil*; but ominous owls are common, after all, and this seems likelier to be coincidence.

[8] See J. R. Brown, in *Phil. Quart.* XXXI. 360–2. Elyot is the source for *D.M.* I. I. 6–16 (a good prince's court like a pure spring for his country); I. I. 456–61 (little son riding a cockhorse).

[1] Hence the advantage of borrowing, as Virgil or Ronsard did, from writers in a different language; or, for a poet, of borrowing, as Webster usually does, from prose. (True, he borrows heavily from the verse of William Alexander; but it might be answered that Alexander's verse is prosier than prose itself.)

Hence it remains safer to steal work that is minor. Here too one may change either little or much. If one changes little, the motive may be mere convenience—as when Shakespeare is content, with lordly indolence, to turn a bald passage of Holinshed's prose, about Hugh Capet, into three bald verses of his own (*Henry V*, 1. 2. 66–8). Or one may hope that the bare stone taken from an older edifice may gain by being slightly reshaped and better placed; as when Webster takes Alexander's "As dogges that once get bloud, would always kill" (*Alexandraean Tragedy*, 2184) and trusts to the click of his couplet to liven it—

> I know that thou art fashion'd for all ill,
> Like dogges, that once get bloud, they'l ever kill.
> > (*W.D.* IV. 3. 105–6.)

Similarly, the praise of Alexander's Olympias for her son, Alexander the Great—

> Staine of times past, and light of times to come,

is used by Webster's Antonio, hardly changed, as a bouquet for his Duchess—

> All her particular worth growes to this somme:
> She staines the time past: lights the time to come.[1]

Even at one of the most passionate crises of *The Duchess* Webster remains content merely to metricize Sidney's prose:

O virtue, where dost thou hide thyself? What hideous thing is this which doth eclipse thee? Or is it true that thou wert never but a vain name, and no essential thing?...

O imperfect proportion of reason, which can too much foresee, and too little prevent!...In shame there is no comfort but to be beyond all bounds of shame.

> Virtue, where art thou hid? What hideous thing
> Is it, that doth eclipse thee?...
> Or is it true, thou art but a bare name,
> And no essential thing?...
> O most imperfect light of human reason,
> That mak'st us so unhappy to foresee
> What we can least prevent!
> ...there's in shame no comfort
> But to be past all bounds, and sense of shame.[2]

---

[1] *Alexandraean Tragedy*, 1319; *D.M.* I. I. 213–4.
[2] *Arcadia* II; *D.M.* III. 2. 81–94. (Spelling modernized in both, to bring out the essential resemblances.)

The only justification for such audacious pilfering is that to-day Webster's verse is still alive, and Sidney's prose (unlike his sometimes admirable poetry) is not.

Montaigne's prose, unlike Sidney's, is also very much alive. But here, by totally changing, not necessarily the language, but the application, the intention, the tone, Webster can at moments become brilliantly successful in making old things new. For example, Montaigne (II. 13) had given an instance of the illusions imposed by our senses—"As they who travell by sea, to whom mountaines, fields, townes, heaven and earth, seeme to goe the same motion, and keepe the same course they doe." This, by an astonishing twist, Webster transforms from science to art, from a philosophic observation to a passionate symbol of ecstasy (*W.D.* I. 2. 50–2). "So perfect shall be thy happinesse," murmurs the seductive Flamineo, "that as men at Sea thinke land and trees and shippes go that way they go, so both heaven and earth shall seeme to go your voyage." This seems to me the true art of Midas, of turning lead to gold.

But it is above all by his gift for style—by his eye for some essential word, by his ear for some haunting rhythm, by terse compression or imaginative amplication, by a sense of reality that turns abstract to concrete—that Webster makes what he takes, his own.

Where Montaigne had written (II. 12), "The opinion of wisdom is the plague of man", Bosola makes that plague far more pestilential (*D.M.* II. 1. 81–2)—"O Sir, the opinion of wisedome is a *foule tettor, that runs all over a mans body.*" Where Montaigne, paraphrasing Cicero (III. 9), had spoken of "wondrous-strange ruines"—"which way soever we walke, we set our foote upon some History", it is Webster that lights up those grey stones with a poet's vision (*D.M.* v. 3. 10–2)—

> I doe love these auncient ruynes:
> We never tread upon them, but we set
> Our foote upon some reverend History.

Where Grimeston's Matthieu mocks at pedants who "spend whole nights to finde how many knots were in *Hercules* club, and of what coulor *Achilles* beard was" (p. 102), Webster, while content merely to metricize this (*D.M.* III. 3. 50-2), immediately adds further absurdities, still more fantastic, that seem his own—

> Or whether *Hector* were not troubled with the tooth-ach—
> He hath studdied himselfe halfe blear-ei'd, to know
> The true semitry of *Caesars* nose by a shooing-horne[1].

Where William Alexander bumbles sententiously along (*Alexandraean Tragedy*, 2357–62)—

---

[1] One trusts that these too will not turn out to have been looted from somewhere else.

O never were my thoughts enlarg'd till now
To marke my selfe, and quintessence my minde:[1]
For, long (a prey to pride)[2] I know not how,[2]
A mist of fancies[3] made my judgement blinde.
As those who dreame sweet dreames, awakt, at last,[2]
Do finde their errour when their eyes finde light"[1]—

Webster compresses it all into an angry epitome of his tragic sense of life
(*D.M.* IV. 2. 349–51)—

I stand like one
That long hath ta'ne a sweet, and golden dreame.
I am angry with my selfe, now that I wake.

In short, Webster's retouchings of what he took might provide texts
for a whole lecture on style—brevity, clarity, concreteness, harmony, the
vivid epithet, the poetic imagination.

Further parallels will be found, superabundantly, in the Commentary,
and in the articles cited.[4] Such echoes are curious; but what is merely
curious soon bores. The real interest lies in the paradox of Webster's
art. Here is a writer like Sterne in this respect (though otherwise
so unlike)—that, though many may question his final rank, few or
none would deny him a curious originality. And yet, like Sterne,
Webster combines this curious originality with unblushing plagiarism.
Whatever the squirrel eats, becomes squirrel; whatever the raven eats,
becomes raven. A truism: yet a constant miracle. By borrowing, which
impoverishes others, Webster was enriched. By a commonplace book
he grew extraordinary. He soared to the heights on plumes often not
his own.

[1] Preciosity.   [2] Padding.
[3] Very Websterian; but even this, elsewhere, Webster makes more pungent
—"mist of error"—or (tersely more sinister)—"in a mist". One wonders
if the repeated denunciations of court-life in *W.D.* and *D.M.* also owe something
to Alexander, who filled his pages with attacks on courts and worldly ambi-
tions, and yet spent his long life pursuing them.
[4] See also Appendices I and III to *W.D.*

APPENDIX II

Another interesting batch of borrowings in this play has recently been pointed out by R. W. Dent (*MLN.* LXX. 568–70)—this time from Whetstone's *Heptameron of Civill Discourses* (1582, 1593—see footnote to p. 25 above). In the following summary Whetstone's versions are bracketed.

D.M. I. I. 57–8: "what creature ever fed worse, then hoping *Tantalus?*" (Sig. I2v: "no man dyneth worse, then hoping *Tantalus*"); I. I. 328–9: "Their livers are more spotted Then *Labans* sheepe." (C3v: "a company as spotted as Labans Sheepe."); IV. I. 91–4:

> Leave this vaine sorrow;
> Things being at the worst, begin to mend: the Bee
> When he hath shot his sting into your hand
> May then play with your eye-lyd.

(U3: "let this comfort you: that thinges when they are at the worst, begin againe to amend. . . . The Bee, when he hath lefte his stinge in your hand without dainger may playe with your eye lidde."); v. 5. 57–7: "*Caesars* Fortune was harder then *Pompeys: Caesar* died in the armes of prosperity, *Pompey* at the feete of disgrace:" (H2: "What difference was there betwene the Fortunes of *Cesar* and *Pompey* . . . saue that I hould *Cesars* to be the harder: for that he was murthered in the Armes of Prosperytie, and Pompey, at the feete of Disgrace.")

But the most unblushing plagiarism is the nine-line passage on marriage in III. 2. 31–9. Compare Whetstone (C4): "And•where *Ismarito*, attributes suche Glorie unto a *Single lyfe*, because that *Daphne* was metamorphosed into a *Bay* Tree, whose Branches are alwayes greene: In my op[i]nion, his reason is fayre lyke the *Bay* Tree; for the *Bay* Tree is barren of pleasant fruict, & his plesing words of weighty matter.

"Furthermore, what remembrance is theare of faire *Sirinx* coynesse, refusing to be God *Pans* wife? other then that she was metamorphosed into a fewe unprofitable Reedes: Or of *Anaxaretes* chaste crueltie towardes *Iphis*, o[th]er then that she remaineth an Image of Stone in *Samarin*. . . .

"But in the behalf of *Mariage*, thousands haue ben changed into *Olyue, Pomegranate, Mulberie*, and other fruictfull trees, sweete flowers, Starres, and precious Stones. . . ."

It will be noted that Webster has a way of sometimes borrowing in clusters—here, for example, from Whetstone; in *W.D.* (see Appendix III to that play), from Nicolas de Montreux. One imagines him as keeping a commonplace-book also. But cases like this suggest that sometimes he would freely plunder some work recently read; and then dismiss it from his mind again.